Praise for *A Bend in the Nile*

This is an extremely absorbing and well-written book. McIvor imbues each page with his humble curiosity about a continent which has since become his home. *A Bend in the Nile* is more than just a travelogue: it's a coming of age story of an innocent Scottish boy who embarks on a journey to become a sensitive and thoughtful young man.

Janet Van Eeden, *Litnet*

Currently country director for Save the Children in Mozambique, it was his three-year stint as a teacher in Sudan that formed the man he was to become – as he fell in love with a local girl, converted to Islam but, ultimately, decided not to marry. In *A Bend In The Nile*, Chris is a naive, intelligent and curious young man who immerses himself in the local community.

Annie Brown, *Daily Record*

The new book (*In the Old Chief's Country*) will also look at the ancient city of Great Zimbabwe which dates from around the 11th century, land issues, wildlife and tourism, expatriates who worked in the country and the individual characters McIvor met during his time there. He sees no reason why Zimbabwe cannot become a vibrant country again.

Gordon Calder, *Northern Times*

D1421854

ALSO BY CHRIS MCIVOR

MEMOIR
A Bend in the Nile

BOOKS
The Earth in our Hands
We Have Something to Say
Children's Feedback Committees in Zimbabwe – An Experiment in
Humanitarian Accountability
Zimbabwe – The Struggle for Health
The Impact of Tourism and National Parks on Local Communities in
Zimbabwe

AS EDITOR OR CO-EDITOR

OTHER NON FICTION
In Our Own Words – Voices of Disabled People in Morocco
Do Not Look Down On Us – The situation of children in squatter
communities in Zimbabwe
The Paradise Project – Children's Perceptions of Tourism in the Caribbean
A Bridge across the Zambezi – Child Exploitation in Mozambique
Our Broken Dreams – Voices of Migrant Children in Southern Africa
Better Choices for Children – Community grants in Mozambique
Speaking Out – Voices of Child Parliamentarians in Mozambique
Denied Our Rights – Children, Women and Disinheritance in Mozambique

MAGAZINE
Editor of Third World Now
Zimbabwe correspondent for New African, Africa Now and African Events

AS CONTRIBUTOR
Children in Our Midst – The voices of children from commercial farms
We Learn With Hope – Issues around education in Zimbabwe's commercial
farming communities
Getting Started – A communications guide for NGO workers
Child Rights In Zimbabwe – A text for schools on children's views
of human rights
Earning a Life- Chapter on Informal Mineworkers in Zimbabwe
Promoting Humanitarian Principles in a Situation of Political Complexity
Neutrality in Emergency Operations and Accountability to Children in
Humanitarian Operations
Social Change and Conservation – Chapter on Tourism in Zimbabwe
Letters from Zimbabwe – Quarterly Contribution to Sandstone Press
Culture and Landscape in Scotland – Published paper and presentation to the
Neil Gunn Annual Symposium

CHRIS McIVOR

Chris McIvor OBE has worked for over thirty years in emergency response and development in countries as diverse as Sudan, Morocco, Algeria, Cuba, Haiti, Jamaica, Zimbabwe and Mozambique. He is currently Deputy Regional Director for the charity *Save the Children* UK in Southern Africa.

He has published many articles about development issues in poorer countries, and was a frequent correspondent for the Irish Times between 1983 and 1986, and was Zimbabwe correspondent for New Africa and Africa Now magazines between 1986 and 1993. He is the author of several books on the environment, land reform in Zimbabwe, disabled peoples' rights, unaccompanied child migration as well as the principles and practice of community involvement in development programmes.

Chris McIvor has published short stories in a variety of journals across the world. Much of his writing reflects his experience in Africa as well as his home background in the far north of Scotland, where his parents still live. In 2005 he was awarded an OBE for his services on behalf of *Save the Children* in Zimbabwe.

The first book in his series of African memoirs, *A Bend in the Nile*, was published by Sandstone Press in 2008.

IN THE OLD CHIEF'S COUNTRY

My Life in Zimbabwe and Other Places

CHRIS McIVOR

SANDSTONEPRESS
HIGHLAND | SCOTLAND

First published in Great Britain in 2012 by
Sandstone Press Ltd,
PO Box 5725,
One High Street,
Dingwall,
Ross-shire,
IV15 9WJ,
Scotland.

www.sandstonepress.com

Editor: Robert Davidson

The publisher acknowledges subsidy from
Creative Scotland towards publication of this volume.

ISBN: 978-1-905207-91-6
ISBN (e): 978-1-905207-93-0

Cover images by Margaret Waller www.margaretwaller.com.au
Cover design by River Design, Edinburgh.

Typeset in Linotype Sabon by Iolaire Typesetting, Newtonmore
Printed and bound by TOTEM, Poland

For My Sons, Mhiko and Darren

Contents

Acknowledgements

This book follows on from my first African memoir, A Bend in the Nile. It was compiled from articles, letters, notes and memories of my first seven years in southern Africa during the mid 1980s and early 1990s, when I was employed as the country director of a British charity in Zimbabwe. My Zimbabwe friends and colleagues, the expatriate volunteers I had the privilege to work with, the people I met who offered their time and wisdom are too numerous to mention. Sekuru Francis and Kwadzi Nyanungo, who influenced my life in ways I would never have imagined when I first came to the country, deserve a special mention.

I would also like to thank Bob Davidson from Sandstone Press for his constant support and encouragement. This book also owes a debt to my twin sister, Gisela McIvor, whose editorial assistance prompted to be more concise and clear whenever I felt tempted to ramble.

I would also like to acknowledge the Irish Times, New African, Africa Now, Africa Events, Development and Change, Earthscan Publications and my own local newspaper in the north of Scotland, the Caithness Courier, for having published the articles I wrote during my time in southern Africa. I would like to thank the Catholic Institute for International Relations for having employed me for seven years, and for publishing my very first book on the situation of commercial farm workers in Zimbabwe.

After all, it can be said of all white dominated Africa that it was and indeed still is – the Old Chief's Country. So all the stories I write of a certain kind, I think of as belonging under that heading: tales about white people, sometimes about black people, living in a landscape that not so very long ago was settled by black tribes, living in complex societies that the white people are only just beginning to study, let alone understand. Truly to understand, we have to lose the arrogance that is the white man's burden, to stop feeling superior and this is only just beginning to happen now.

Doris Lessing, January 1972,
Preface to the 1973 Collection,
'This Was the Old Chief's Country',
Flamingo Books.

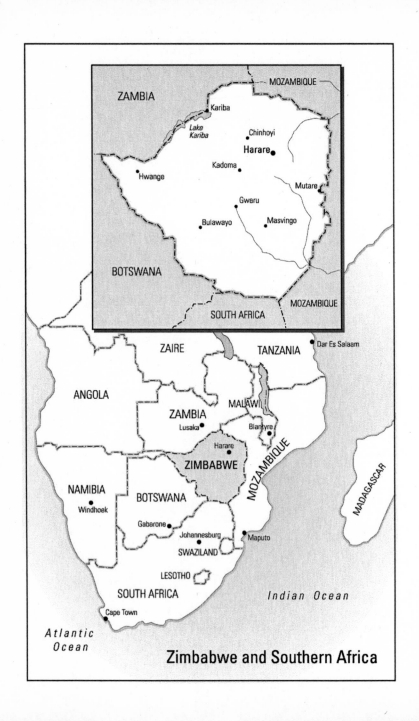

Zimbabwe and Southern Africa

1

Homecoming

Somewhere over the Central African Republic we were wakened by a vigorous thumping of the aeroplane.

'Please fasten your seat-belts,' the steward announced. 'We are passing an area of turbulence.'

Through the windows of the 737 I could see large mushroom-like clouds, heavy with rain and frequent flashes of lightning. We would be in Zimbabwe in a few hours and this weather would accompany us all the way to Harare.

'Don't worry, the pilots are white,' a passenger beside me said, a thick-set individual called Jerry. He had spent much of the flight complaining about the incompetence of black Zimbabweans and remarking how much better things had been when his country was Rhodesia. 'Why on earth are you trading your comfortable life in Europe to help a few Africans?' he had asked me.

I had tried to ignore him as best I could by pretending to sleep, but every time I opened my eyes he was ready to offer me his advice on 'how best to deal with the natives'. I did not tell him I had worked in Africa before, that this journey for me was something of a homecoming. To his observation that I seemed 'naïve and innocent' I knew he would then have added the word 'foolish'.

Boarding the British Airways flight from London to Harare there was little to remind me of my previous journeys to the continent. The vast majority of the passengers were white for a start, although to my relief not all of them turned out to be like Jerry. During one of his excursions to find more alcohol, another passenger to my left turned towards me and told me to ignore him.

Rob was a farmer north of Harare near a place called Chinhoyi and had lived in Zimbabwe all his life. Having spent several weeks in England visiting some relatives, he was keen to get home.

'Some of us have managed to move on,' he said, 'while others like Jerry remain stuck in the past. It's a fantastic country with fantastic people. Don't listen to what he tells you.'

As we bumped our way southwards towards Harare my thoughts constantly returned to my previous arrivals in Sudan and Algeria. I was trying to find something familiar but as with the racial composition of the passengers all I could see was difference. There had never been anything but clear blue sky and a dry, parched landscape below us whenever I had arrived in either country. The communities we flew over would have prayed for just an hour of the rain that was falling steadily; rain which had flooded people from their homes in Zimbabwe only a few weeks ago.

Some time later, when a break in the clouds allowed a glimpse of the terrain we were passing over, I was struck by its rich green colour and the numerous rivers and streams that seemed to cut across it. There was a lake as well, a long ribbon of water that lost itself beyond our horizon.

We were flying over Lake Kariba, somewhere between Zambia and western Zimbabwe, Rob said. When I expressed my surprise that a continent known for its frequent droughts could look so fertile, he told me not to jump to quick conclusions. 'Fly over this same landscape in six months and it will look very different. Don't be fooled by all this water. We have drought here too, you know.'

In Sudan, flights had never turned up on time. The

2

airports that serviced the towns I occasionally flew into had been little more than exotic bus terminals, but with planes rather than vehicles arriving and departing. No one respected the signs that read 'Passengers Only.' Taxi drivers, dealers in foreign currency, tour operators and beggars clamored for your attention as soon as you arrived. Chaotic, confusing and colorful it was as if the country wanted to announce itself the moment you touched down.

Pointed towards the arrivals lounge by a surly attendant, I fully expected Harare airport to be the same. But it seemed that I would have to wait. There were orderly queues. Smart officials dressed in neat uniforms inspected passports, checked for visas and then directed passengers to the 'Baggage Reclaim,' much as they would have in a London airport.

'Why are you in Zimbabwe sir?' someone asked in perfect English.

'To work.'

'For whom?'

'A charity. I'm here for three years to work with the Catholic Institute for International Relations.'

'What is your address in Harare?'

'I'm not sure. Someone will pick me up at the airport.'

'We need to have an address,' the official persisted, pointing to the form he was filling out. 'Who knows when we might need to find you.'

I was taken aback. In Khartoum airport I had only once been asked for my address by an immigration officer and it turned out that he had wanted it so he could visit me in Scotland. I rummaged in my bag for the letter of appointment I had received from my new organisation, the one that had the address of the office in Harare and a telephone number for emergencies. 'Will this do?'

'That's fine. Have a good day, sir . . . Next please.'

A few minutes later, with my suitcase in tow, I entered the main concourse. No one rushed forward to offer me a taxi or steer me towards the best hotel in town. No dealer sidled up to sell Zimbabwe dollars at a favorable rate. Instead there were signs pointing to several banks offering foreign currency. I could see a taxi rank outside with yellow cabs in neat rows. At a hotel information desk a smiling young woman was handing out brochures offering a service for tourists who had not bothered to book their accommodation in advance.

With all these white faces around me, with a large mural on the wall advertising Johnnie Walker whisky, with signs in English rather than Arabic, I wondered if I had stepped off the wrong flight and ended up in the wrong place. When a loudspeaker announced in a clear voice, 'Would Mr. Christopher McIvor please report to the airport information desk,' my jaw dropped even further.

This was too much like home. This was too much like what I had decided to exchange for something more exotic and different. To arrive on time at an African airport, to pass through immigration and collect your baggage in fifteen minutes, to have your name announced over a loudspeaker was not part of the novelty I was looking for. Had I made a mistake? Had Zimbabwe been a wrong choice? Having decided to come back to the continent that had already played such an important part in my life perhaps I should have returned to the places I was familiar with.

My route from teacher to aid worker had been a circuitous one. Two years previously I was in the desert region of Algeria, in a community called El Golea. School had finished and I had decided to explore the far south of the country and to cross over into neighbouring Niger.

Part of my desire to travel was to clear my head and decide on my future. My teaching experience that past year had not been positive. The boys were surly. The girls were uncommunicative. On the rare occasion when I managed to prompt my students to have a discussion, several of them told me that learning English was a waste of time. French and Arabic were good enough. The books I taught, pre-scribed material from the Algerian Ministry of Education, were boring. 'Why,' asked one pupil, 'do we need to learn something that is not useful for us beyond the walls of this classroom and the exams at the end of the year?'

I had found it difficult not to nod my head in agreement. In this remote and isolated desert community, English was an irrelevance. The children needed practical subjects rather than grounding in grammar. 'You are wasting your time trying to convince them' I said to myself, even as I voiced my arguments to get my students more enthused.

But despite the dilemmas that teaching English had evoked, I was aware too that it had offered me an entry into places I was curious to learn about. The indifference of many of my students notwithstanding, teaching was still highly regarded within the community and had earned me considerable respect. In return for educating their children, people had opened up, shared part of their lives and allowed me an interaction with their culture that would have been impossible if I was just passing through.

They were keen to assist me too in whatever way they could. When I had told some of my students in El Golea that I was interested in travelling around the Sahara for a few months, I was visited a few days later by the father of one of the boys I had spoken to.

Abdel Razzaq was one of the richest merchants in town but from his appearance you would never have known it. Like everywhere else, El Golea had its hierarchy of wealth and privilege but this was countered by a widespread aversion to any ostentatious display of economic status.

'Money and power are gifts from Allah,' a teaching colleague once told me, 'and no one in this town will tempt fate by showing off in front of others.' So Abdel Razzaq, who controlled the lucrative export of dates from El Golea, trotted around town on a tired, old donkey, and wore the same djellabiya, headscarf and sandals as everyone else.

I had only met him on one previous occasion and wondered why he was now knocking at my door. Had his son complained about my teaching? It turned out that he was here to help me. He owned several lorries that regularly plied the desert routes between Algeria and the countries I was keen to visit. 'These places are not safe on your own,' he told me. 'You will travel with my eldest son, Khalid, who will look after you.'

For several days we travelled south. The first part of the journey had been on tarred road but this changed soon enough into ploughed tracks thought the desert. Once again I was struck by the ability of the driver to negotiate a terrain that seemed to have no defining features. A small hill, an outcrop of rock, a particular formation in the sand that would never have caught my attention was enough to give him a fix on our position and the best route ahead.

Along the way we had seen the skeletons of several abandoned vehicles. These were cars driven by European tourists, mostly from France, who, thinking that the Sahara was a thin ribbon of sand much like their beaches back home, had decided to drive across it. Ill-prepared, ill-equipped and ill-advised many of them never made it. The previous year Khalid had heard of ten tourists who had perished.

One evening, south of Algeria's last town before the border with Niger, we had seen some lights in the distance.

They were flickering on and off in a frantic pattern and Khalid signaled our driver to investigate. An hour later we came across a car with two frightened passengers inside: a French couple who had lost their way. Rather than explore another direction which might take them even further from the principal route, they had done the sensible thing and stopped where they were. Then they had waited for evening to see if their flashing lights would attract attention.

I asked them later how they had found themselves in the middle of the largest desert in Africa, without a guide and without directions. Even the nomads who lived here took precautions. The woman shrugged her shoulders. They had heard that there was a lucrative market for imported cars south of the Sahara and so had decided to have a holiday and make a profit at the same time. They had thought that the desert would be signposted too, with identifiable roads, villages to stop off at and people on the way they could ask for directions.

They asked Khalid if they could follow behind us to Nigeria where we were headed. He refused, even when they offered him money. 'I don't want to be responsible for you,' he said, irritated that they had treated his environment in such a cavalier and disrespectful fashion. He would show them the way to the border. Then they were on their own.

I had no visa for Niger having been informed by my friends in El Golea that I would not need one. 'Don't worry,' Khalid said, when I expressed my concern that I might be turned back by the authorities. 'I know these people.'

A sack of dates was offloaded at a complex of buildings that marked the border between the two countries. 'Part of the usual bribe,' Khalid explained as we drove off, waved through by an official who never bothered to check our papers.

At a nearby village where we stopped to buy some fuel, I witnessed a scene that brought me back to my time in

Sudan. Outside the local police station a group of men had been tied together. Dressed in their identifiable blue gowns and purple headscarves, they were Tuareg, the principal group of nomads who occupied a large swathe of territory in this part of the Sahara. Made to sit in the hot sun, a guard with a rifle spat contemptuously in their direction.

Khalid told me that relations between nomads and settled peoples had always been difficult. For centuries the Tuareg had raided the communities further south in search of gold and slaves. Many people could still recall that time, directly if they were old enough to have experienced these raids or indirectly in the songs and stories related by their grand-parents of that period in their history.

When France had withdrawn from its colonies in this part of Africa, power had generally been handed over to the people in towns and cities, rather than the clans and tribes that the French had never been able to subdue. The former had taken their revenge for past injustices, including the imposition of restrictions on the movement of nomads across their territories.

Deprived of water and pasture for their animals, the nomads became desperate. Conflicts had erupted that had led to bloodshed. Some years previously Mali had fought a full scale war with Tuareg insurgents in the north of the country. Niger had also experienced conflict. 'Don't worry,' Khalid said when I looked alarmed. 'The clan I come from and the Tuareg are related. Generally they let us pass without any problems.'

It wasn't the Tuareg we had problems with but an officious policeman in a large town called Agadez some-where in the centre of the country. With no permission to be there he told me to follow him to the station. 'I don't know the people here,' Khalid whispered as we walked behind him. 'That's not good.'

8

'Why are you here?' I was asked a few hours later by a gentleman who introduced himself as the district commissioner of police.

'I'm on my way to Nigeria,' I replied. 'We're passing through, that's all.'

'Do you know that parts of our country are not safe?'

'No, I was not aware of that. But the people I'm travelling with come here all the time. I'm sure I'm safe with them.'

'But imagine if you are shot? What do you think your embassy would say? They would point to us and claim we were negligent. I see that you don't have a visa,' he continued.

'There was no place in southern Algeria where I could get one.'

'So why didn't you go to Algiers? We have an embassy there.'

'I thought I could get a visa at the border.'

'How did you get through the border without the necessary documents?'

I shrugged my shoulders and said nothing, not wanting to get Khalid's contacts in trouble. From the way he spoke I knew the commissioner would not budge. Even when Khalid tried to intervene he was cut short and admonished for having transported someone into the country without the necessary papers. He should be careful he did not land in trouble too.

'You can't go any further until I sort this out,' the official concluded. He would contact his superiors in the capital, Niamey, and find out whether they would permit my onward travel. If they refused I would have to return the way I had come.

'How long will that take?' I asked.

'A few days. A few weeks. A month. Who knows,' he said and dismissed us with a wave of his hand. He refused to give me back my passport. That way he knew I would not leave without his permission.

I declined Khalid's offer to stay with me until the matter was resolved. It might take a long time to come to a conclusion and meanwhile he had a schedule to keep to. But as the truck drove off a short while later, part of me was worried too. Apart from my departing friends, no one knew I was here. I had no place to stay. Above all, what would I do for several weeks in a dusty, isolated town in the middle of the Sahara? I had little idea that the answer to that question would help point me to my future, the path I would follow that would take me to Zimbabwe a few years later.

In a café near the dilapidated hotel I booked into, I bumped into Charles, a French aid worker employed by an international charity. He was supervising a program in a settlement on the edge of town, which hosted refugees who had fled drought and conflict in various parts of the country. 'If you're stuck here for a few weeks why don't you come and help out?'

With time on my hands and my movements restricted I had nothing better to do. But part of me was skeptical. My experience of aid and its practitioners in Sudan had left me cautious.

I had seen projects that were impractical and poorly designed. There was the irrigation scheme in the middle of the desert that had been abandoned because there was no water. I had met aid workers like John in Khartoum, who were dismissive of local culture and displayed no interest in learning about it. Driving through Chad I had accompanied a United Nations food convoy that had been diverted from its intended recipients to benefit corrupt officials. Would the project in Agadez be any different? In the end I decided there was only one way to find out.

The first thing I noticed about Charles and several of the colleagues who worked with him, was the way they treated the people they were helping. There was none of the holier-than-thou, superior and patronising behavior I had seen before. They did everything they could to ensure that their beneficiaries were not made to feel helpless and dependent.

Although the camp administration was nominally in the hands of the Government authorities, Charles and his team had prompted the refugees to come up with their own management committee. This had transformed a passive population into a more proactive community. They helped construct their own shelters, dig their own wells and produce whatever food they could.

'Sometimes the people who dispense charity end up undermining the willingness of people to help themselves,' he said, after he had shown me some of the schemes the community had come up with. 'Maybe they don't do this deliberately or with bad intentions, but that's what happens if aid is delivered in the wrong way.'

As for the schools that had been established, I was impressed by their practical orientation and the enthusiasm with which the pupils inside them seemed to be learning. Why could the education system back in Algeria not have incorporated some of these features? While the curriculum included basic reading, writing and mathematics, there was a stronger focus on skills that were of relevance to the conditions the children had to face in their daily lives.

They could identify cholera, malaria and other diseases and knew how to prevent them. They could plant and look after vegetables so as to improve their nutrition. They also learned how to manage their goats. The impact of these animals on the fragile soils around Agadez and other Saharan towns had been disastrous, claimed Charles, since

11

they ate everything. Deprived of vegetation the soil simply blew away, leaving nothing but sand in its place.

'Nomadic livelihoods might have been perfectly adapted to the desert, but when these people were forced to move to towns and cities no one realised they needed to learn new skills and new ways of looking after their animals. But if someone had insisted that you become a nomad, the first thing you would have been offered would be lessons on what to do.'

I spent three weeks helping out, and would have been happy to spend more. In particular, I learned to appreciate what Charles had been preaching since the first evening I met him. To help others you first had to listen, a skill I had never realised was necessary for aid work. Everyone in his organisation had to learn the local language. How else would they be able to communicate with the people whose lives they needed to understand? The focus on how best to interact with the community was as important as any of the skills in health, water, sanitation and education that Charles and members of his team also brought with them. In the time I was there I could see how much this was appreciated by the refugees they were helping.

Meanwhile, I had been instructed to report to the police station every day. This had become a pointless routine, since the only communication I received was that there had been no progress. But finally one day, in the office of the person who had originally prevented me from travelling onwards to Nigeria, I was told that my request for a visa had been refused. No reason was given. I would have to pack my bags and return to Algeria.

'There's a bus leaving in a few hours,' the commissioner of police replied when I asked him how I would get home. 'Make sure you're on it. I've told our authorities at the border to expect you.'

12

As we drove northwards later that afternoon I felt disappointed that I had only penetrated a short distance along the route I had originally planned. The rest of Niger and Nigeria would have to wait for another time. But I did not feel that my journey had been wasted. These few weeks had indeed helped to clear my head and point me in the new direction I was looking for.

As I had shaken hands with Charles to say goodbye he had remarked that I should consider pursuing the kind of work he himself was involved in. My four years as a teacher in Sudan and Algeria, my frequent travels around the continent, and my recent time with him and his team should help me find a job. Aid work was one way I could marry my curiosity about people in far off places, with a desire to contribute something useful in return. By the time I found myself back in Ireland a few months later, I had written to several charities, asking them to consider me for a post in Africa.

'It's not that your time in these countries was irrelevant, but you're not quite what we're looking for,' the programme officer of an international charity told me, at an interview in London a few months after my return.

This was the fourth one I had attended. 'But what kind of person do you need?' I pressed her. 'I thought my practical experience as a teacher in these countries would be sufficient, and the fact that I worked in remote villages in Africa for the past four years.'

'But you have very little familiarity with development theory,' she replied. 'Your answers to those questions were vague. Nearly everyone that works in aid today has a qualification. Contact us again once you have completed some studies.'

There were other teaching posts in Africa I could have applied for. They were frequently advertised in the newspapers I read. But my memories of that last frustrating year in El Golea Secondary School, trying to motivate disinterested children, prevented me from returning to a profession I had decided to abandon.

At the same time, having been rejected by several aid agencies, I became more determined to penetrate a world that seemed even more worthy and desirable because I had been refused entry. Though part of me wondered at the relevance of learning 'development theory' and the jargon that seemed to go with it, I decided to take the advice of my interviewers and register for a course. It would mean that I would not return to Africa as soon as I had wanted, but I consoled myself that when I finally did it would be in a line of work that did not raise the kind of questions I had asked myself as a teacher.

'But what about your personal life?'

Peter was someone I had known for a number of years, my philosophy tutor at a college in Dublin. My decision to abandon the thesis I had been writing and teach for four years in North Africa, had not been a wise one, he had said. He claimed that I was suffering from some morbid fascination. Convinced that my determination to return was even more foolish, he regularly offered me advice whenever I met him, usually in his favorite pub where he claimed to have delivered his best lectures.

'What do you mean?' I asked.

'Think about it. Who will want to have a relationship with someone who is likely to disappear any moment to a remote part of Africa? What about your girlfriend? What does she think of it all?'

I shrugged my shoulders and avoided the question. Gabriela had a good career as a translator in Ireland. She had made it clear on a number of occasions that sitting in a hut in the middle of the African savannah, while I explored the surrounding communities, was not her idea of the future she wanted.

The issue Peter was raising was one I had thought about before. I was almost thirty years old. Most of my friends were in 'stable' relationships. They had houses and cars and careers. 'When are you going to settle down like them?' my mother would ask me whenever I phoned her. 'It's time to get serious about your future.'

Had I chosen a lifestyle that would come back to haunt me later, I sometimes asked myself. No matter how welcome I had felt in Sudan and Algeria, I was not part of these societies. But having been exposed to them in the way I had been, I didn't feel at home in my own either. My experiences had made me different and maybe that would only get more pronounced the more I travelled, the longer I refused to take my mother's advice to 'settle down.' From the outside at least, my friends seemed happy to have their lives mapped out for them, and part of me envied them their equanimity, their seeming contentment with the choices they had made.

Friend though he was, my conversations with Peter were often uncomfortable, precisely because he was able to articulate many of my fears. 'Part of the problem with people like you, who have lived in strange places, is that you don't fit in when you return. Sometimes you make us feel that our lifestyles and values are questionable. As a philosopher I can appreciate being challenged, but it doesn't make it easy to be in your company. Be careful, Chris. You need to watch that you don't end up like those nomads you keep on talking about, with no place you can ever call home.'

A year later, in the same pub, our conversation about my future continued where it had left off. I had finished my studies and had the piece of paper that I was convinced would open doors for me. Desiring a commitment I could not give her, Gabriela had left me and embarked on a more secure relationship with someone else. Meanwhile a job had come up in Zimbabwe as the country representative of an international charity. I had sent in my application and was scheduled for an interview the following week.

'So you still haven't got rid of your itch,' Peter said, the word he used whenever we talked about my wanting to return to Africa.

'No,' I replied, 'and I suspect it won't go away until I get back there.'

'My fear is that it will never disappear. You'll end up like the drunks in this pub, who realise they have a problem but can't do anything about it. After Zimbabwe, if that's where you end up, it'll be another out-of-the-way place. But since you've made up your mind,' he added, raising his glass, 'I can only hope that you find what you're looking for.'

One week later I was sitting in an office in London being interviewed by a former priest, who told me that the overseas programme of the Catholic Institute for International Relations was entirely secular. 'Whatever your religious persuasion, believer or atheist, will not affect our willingness to offer you the job. What we are interested in is whether you have the right aptitude.'

Remembering the course I had just completed, I had beefed up on topics such as sustainable development, gender equity, log frames and the project cycle. But the panel ignored these issues completely. What they wanted to know was how I would manage people. 'We have thirty often stressed and frustrated professionals working in Zimbabwe who have only one person they can vent their anger on. How will you handle that kind of pressure?'

I told them about my experiences in Sudan and Algeria, where I had had to deal with classes of sixty children many of whom didn't want to be there. They were bored, frustrated and sometimes antagonistic too, but I had kept them in order and managed to get a fair number of them through their final exams. 'I believe I'm up to it.'

My interviewers seemed to think so too. In a telephone call a few days later I was offered the job. 'The other candidates seemed too theoretical, and didn't have your practical experience,' the personnel officer replied when I asked her what had prompted their decision. I wondered then if I had wasted my time over the past year learning concepts and theories that had counted for so little in their final assessment.

'When can you go?' she continued. 'We need someone out there to replace our current director as soon as possible.'

I had little personal business to sort out: no house or flat to put on the market, no relationships to abandon. A trip of a few days to Scotland would be enough to say goodbye to my family. My personal belongings would fit into a couple of suitcases I could leave with friends. 'I'm happy to travel next week, if that's okay with you,' I replied. Six days later I was back in Africa.

2

First Days

Khartoum had been chaotic, dusty and noisy. Its streets teemed with thousands of people who seemed happy to live out a large part of their lives in public. We all complained about the lack of privacy, about the open sewers and pungent smells, about the pushing and shoving that turned an excursion into an ordeal, but at the same time it was new, different and exciting. The very disorder of Khartoum constituted its charm.

My arrival at the airport had already alerted me to the fact that Harare would be different. Cleaner, more organised and more sedate, the road into the city passed through suburbs whose names would have been more appropriate in England: Hatcliffe, Waterfalls, Avondale, Mabelreign. The signposted streets ran in neat lines that intersected in junctions where policemen and lights regulated the traffic. The one set of traffic lights I could remember in Khartoum was permanently green, making a bad driving situation even worse.

I noticed too the contrast in noise. 'Don't people use their horns here?' I asked Farai, the driver of the taxi who had been sent to pick me up.

'In an emergency, to avoid having an accident,' he responded sensibly. 'Isn't that how you drive in England too?'

It was the African faces in the centre of town that reminded me of where I was. What struck me, however, was that everyone seemed to have a purpose. No one was hanging around, chatting with friends or watching what was going on. At 8:30 in the morning people were going about their business much as they would in any European city. Even the few coffee shops we passed had their shutters down. In Sudan and Algeria early morning and early evening would have been their busiest time of the day. 'Why rush to work when you can have a coffee with your friends before you start?' a Sudanese colleague had once informed me when I asked him why he was always late for school.

'Someone is playing a joke on me,' I said to myself when the driver announced that we had arrived in the neighborhood where I would be staying. We had turned into a road called Thurso Drive. Thurso was one of the only two towns in Caithness, the county I came from in the far north of Scotland. I would never have expected to have seen that name in my new neighbourhood. Finding it here, in the middle of southern Africa, only added to my feeling that, when I had stepped off the plane that morning, I had arrived back where I had started.

Outside the gates of a house, Farai sounded his horn. The other houses we had passed were just like it, surrounded by walls with bits of glass on top of them like teeth. There were signs on many of the gates too, with the picture of an angry dog and the words 'Chenjerai Imbwa' printed beneath it. I learned my first words of Shona that morning, though 'Beware of the Dog' hardly seemed the most appropriate introduction to the local language.

The gate was opened a few minutes later by a small, wiry gentleman who waved his hand and grinned as if he knew me. It was his firm handshake followed by a tight hug that reminded me of the hospitality that had been such a prominent feature of my experience in other parts of Africa.

This was Sekuru Francis, the caretaker of my new residence, and on behalf of his family, his clan and the entire people of Zimbabwe I was welcome in his country.

'Don't mind the dog,' he added, indicating an animal that did not seem to share in the general enthusiasm about my arrival. As soon as I entered it set up a noisy racket and took a nip at my ankles.

I was worried that my bags would be too heavy for Sekuru to carry. I guessed that he must be in his sixties, judging by his wizened face and sparse grey hair, but tossing my suitcase on his shoulder and tucking my other bag under his arm he brushed aside my offers to help him, claiming that this was his responsibility. 'What will people think of me if I let you carry your own bags?'

Once inside, he pointed to a chair where I was to sit, and began to fuss around a stove. 'I know that people from England need a cup of tea whenever they have completed a long journey.'

'Actually I'm not from England. I'm from a place called Scotland,' I remarked, wondering if that distinction would make any sense to him.

My announcement prompted an immediate reaction. Abandoning his tea-making he began to dance around the room, contorting his body into strange shapes and throwing fake punches in my direction. He kept up this routine for an impressive five minutes. I wondered if this was some kind of welcoming ceremony practiced by the people of Zimbabwe whenever a stranger appeared among them.

When he finally stopped to catch his breath he turned towards me, clearly anticipating a reaction. I did not want to cause offence by appearing unappreciative, so managed a smile and some applause. Sekuru was not fooled. 'You've no idea who that was,' he said, 'do you?'

I shrugged my shoulders apologetically. 'Sorry. Was I supposed to?'

'It was Ken Buchanan, a boxer from Scotland. He fought Langton Schoolboy for the Commonwealth Title. I'm afraid your countryman lost, knocked out in the fifth round. Don't worry. He put up a good fight.'

For the next few hours Sekuru Francis told me something of his personal history, thankfully providing regular cups of tea so I could keep awake. He had spent many years in the mines of South Africa and seemed surprised that I had never been to Johannesburg, which according to him was the biggest city in the world.

Many people from Zimbabwe had worked there too, part of a history of migrant labour that had existed for generations. Once a year Sekuru would return home to see his wife and children. 'Because these were bad places,' he replied when I asked him why he had not taken them with him.

Working underground, he said, had been dangerous in those days. Many miners died or were left disabled after an accident. There was no compensation if they were hurt. Confined to cramped, isolated and unsanitary compounds their only recreation was drinking beer, gambling and fighting. 'These were not places to bring up children. That's why we left our families back home.'

When he told me that most of the miners, himself included, had had unofficial wives in South Africa too he must have assumed I would be shocked since he went on to insist that his first wife had never objected. 'What were we supposed to do for the eleven months of the year when we weren't at home? So long as we sent money and made sure our children were looked after, they understood.'

Sekuru had finally come home when his lungs had given up. A doctor had told him that any more time underground and he might die within a matter of months. He had found a job as a gardener in Harare, had acquired a reputation for being honest and reliable and had ended up with the organisation I now worked for.

For the last three years he had been the caretaker of the house where the current country director stayed, and which would become my home too. It seemed that 'caretaking' involved considerably more than watering the flowers, feeding the dog and ensuring that the gates were locked at night. If Sekuru were to be believed he had become something of a personal confidant, regularly consulted on a variety of important issues before any decisions were made.

'Do you see this nose?' he asked, pointing to the some-what large protuberance on the front of his face.

'Yes I do,' I replied, wondering if it merited a more appreciative reaction.

'Well, this nose can smell a thief a mile away,' he said, with such obvious pride and conviction that I was forced to shake my head in admiration.

According to Sekuru, Zimbabwe had its fair share of swindlers, cheats and conmen who would try to take advantage of a foreigner in their country. His nose was now at my disposal. Any time I had doubts about anyone, I should simply introduce them to him and he would be able to tell me if they were to be trusted. I forced myself not to laugh, since he looked so serious but, as Sekuru continued to offer me advice about living in his country, I couldn't put the image out of my head of him sniffing at my visitors before they were allowed to see me.

One week after my arrival I was back at Harare airport, not to bid farewell to the country but to the outgoing director I was replacing. She was returning to Jamaica for a well-deserved rest. Sekuru Francis was in tears because his adopted daughter was leaving, although the fact that he had now acquired a new son seemed to compensate for his loss.

Part of me felt tearful too. Gerlin had been informative and sympathetic, fielding my naïve questions with considerable patience. 'Don't worry,' she had said when I apologised for asking about things that must have seemed obvious. 'When I first came here I asked the same questions.'

Because she was black I had assumed that her process of assimilation would have been a speedy one, but she informed me that her upbringing in Jamaica and the work she had done in other parts of Africa had not made Zimbabwe any easier to penetrate. One of the first things we had talked about was my initial impressions of the city. I told her about my taxi ride that first morning and the sharp contrast it had offered with my prior experiences in Africa.

'Don't expect Zimbabwe to reveal itself in the first few months of your arrival,' she had said. 'This is a country that requires patience.'

One day she had taken me on a tour of Harare, after I expressed an interest to see something different from the smart city centre and the westernised suburbs. Formerly called Salisbury, Harare was a relatively recent metropolis. One hundred years previously it had comprised nothing more than a few houses and administrative buildings to oversee the mining and agricultural interests of the country's recent British colonisers. She explained that much of its subsequent construction had been along racial lines. A policy of segregation had created European, Asian, Colored and African enclaves and few people had ever moved between them.

Almost six years after independence, I was struck by the fact that these divisions still seemed to operate. In the suburb of Greendale, where Gerlin lived, I had hardly seen an African family. In Belvedere I could see nothing but Asian faces, with shops, stores and restaurants that could have been anywhere in India or Pakistan. 'This is a Colored area,' Gerlin said as we entered Hatfield. People of mixed race, she added, had never really been accepted by either whites or blacks and felt more comfortable in their own locations.

Change of a sort was taking place. Rich and poor were becoming as strictly segregated as blacks and whites had been before. According to Gerlin, income was slowly replacing race as a determinant of where you lived.

The so called 'low density suburbs' where we resided, were characterised by large houses with spacious gardens, high walls, occasional swimming pools and signs with angry dogs on them. 'I only caught sight of my nearest neighbors several months after I moved in. I invited them over for tea. Four years later, I'm still waiting for them to come round.'

The 'high density' suburbs were where most Africans lived, and it was quite possible to drive through the major arteries of the city without bumping into them at all. Sometimes you could spot them behind a line of trees or some hills. Often located on the outskirts of the city, they were originally created as dormitory towns to house Harare's increasing army of industrial and domestic workers. Warren Park and Dzivarasekwa looked like military encampments and although the standard of housing was considerably higher than what I remembered from the shanty towns of Nairobi and Khartoum, there was something cold and impersonal in the planned and deliberate way they had been constructed.

'It's not safe to get out here,' Sekuru said when we pulled up at Mbare market, where Gerlin claimed we could find a more vibrant, colorful and African part of the city. Sekuru had decided to come with us not just to offer his insights, but to 'protect' us too.

'He's exaggerating,' Gerlin countered, claiming that it was a friendly enough place during the day but that at night when the beer halls began to fill up one had to be more careful. This was where she came not just to buy fruit and vegetables, but to occasionally hang out, when she wanted to remind herself that there was an alternative in Harare to the sanitised shopping malls of Strathaven and Greendale.

With Sekuru in attendance I wandered around for an hour, enjoying the experience of something familiar. In Sudan, markets formed the hub of the community's social life, a place where you went not just to conduct business but to meet and interact with others. Mbare market seemed the same. It might well be that the produce on sale was cheaper than in other parts of the city, but I reckoned that an excuse for social interaction was another reason people were there.

On the way to Mbare we had passed a large Woolworth's store, a Spar grocery and a Wimpy restaurant on the same street. 'Harare isn't that much different from London,' I had remarked, pointing out that if it weren't for the colour of the shoppers and the hot weather this could have been somewhere back home. At a section of the market which sold traditional crafts and various medicinal products, I realised that my impression of a westernised, un-African and characterless city was superficial.

There was the same bewildering variety of exotic looking powders and herbs, charms and fetishes for sale that I had seen in other places on the continent. It was strange to find them here beside Toyota spares and Land Rover parts but the fact that this seemed one of the busiest sections of Mbare told a story too. As I walked around, I remembered Gerlin's advice not to rush to quick judgments. If I were to remain open to the experience that Zimbabwe had to offer, I would also have to stop comparing it to the other places I had been.

Back in the office, Gerlin told me something of the history of our organisation and our current priorities. Prior to 1980, we had been part of an international solidarity movement calling for an end to the war in Rhodesia and a transition to African rule. Once that had taken place, the new Government had asked for further assistance, requesting the deployment of professionals such as doctors, nurses, agricultural advisers, engineers and teachers.

Gerlin pointed to a map on the wall. It had twenty-four colored pins dotted around it. These were where our workers were located and I could see that they were scattered over the length and breadth of the country. 'I hope you like travelling,' she said, adding that much of my time would be spent outside Harare visiting our volunteers or assessing new posts that the Government wanted us to fill.

'There is one thing that this map will not show you,' she continued. 'Most of our workers are located in the poorest parts of Zimbabwe, the places that were generally neglected by the whites when they controlled this country.'

According to Gerlin the same pattern of racial privilege and exclusion that had originally informed the construction of Harare, characterised rural areas as well. Commercial agriculture was comprised of large estates owned by European farmers. The less fertile communal lands were where Africans lived. These areas had been deprived of services and had few schools, clinics and roads to meet the needs of their overcrowded populations. That history of deprivation was slowly being addressed, not just by the new Government but by organisations like our own. She hoped that under my management our programme would continue to prioritise its assistance to such locations.

'Before 1980 the European population had one doctor for

every thousand people. Communal areas had one doctor for every one hundred thousand people. I was shocked when I first came here to find out that Rhodesians lived twenty years longer on average than their African counterparts. Whenever I get complacent I remind myself of that statistic.'

On that first evening when Gerlin had come home, she had shown me the vehicle I would be driving, the one that would have to transport me to the far corners of the country to see the people I would be supervising. In general I was unfamiliar with cars, having only recently acquired my licence as part of my preparations to become more competitive in the job market. But I was knowledgeable enough to realise that what I was looking at was a patched-up wreck, that the black smoke that billowed from the exhaust indicated an engine with serious health problems.

'I'm not going to pretend it's anything different from what you can clearly see,' Gerlin had said. 'I've lost count of the number of times it has broken down and I've had to wait hours, sometimes days, for a mechanic to come and fix it. This is one of the headaches I will be pleased to leave behind.'

I found out later that it chugged along at a maximum of only forty miles an hour. This meant that a trip to the city of Bulawayo in the south of the country would take most of the day, when a bus that left Harare at the same time would have arrived several hours earlier.

She had two bits of advice to offer. 'Take public transport whenever you need to. That way you will be less likely to miss your appointments.'

Her other recommendation was more controversial. 'One thing I should have done when I first came here was to have had an accident; not serious enough to injure myself or anyone else, but sufficient to make sure this vehicle could never be used again. That way the organisation would have been forced to replace it. It's an option you might want to seriously consider.'

On the last evening before Gerlin left, she asked me if I wanted to retain Sekuru Francis as my household manager. She disliked the terms 'servant' or 'domestic' because of the images they conjured up and because she felt that they mischaracterised the nature of the cordial relationship she had developed with him.

I confessed this was something that troubled me. In Sudan I had had no one 'to look after me.' Wasn't there something exploitative in employing someone to do your washing, cleaning and housework?

Gerlin said that I was under no pressure to accept Sekuru, or anyone else for that matter. No commitments had been made but, before I took a final decision, there were a few things I should keep in mind.

'Whatever house you find in the low density suburbs will have a garden. Are you prepared to spend hours every week cutting the grass, watering the flowers and pulling weeds, especially when work will consume most of your time?' I shook my head. 'Another thing you should remember is that when you travel you should have someone to look after your house. Harare has its robberies like any other city and an empty property is an easy target.'

There was the question of Sekuru himself. 'Why not ask him how he feels about this line of work? It brings him a wage. He can help his son through college. In my view the only thing that might ever be called exploitative in your relationship is how you end up treating him.'

I appreciated Gerlin's bluntness and the fact that she spoke her mind. At the end of our week together, and probably fed up with my constant comparisons between life in Zimbabwe and Sudan, she had another observation to offer.

'If you wanted to repeat your experience as a rural teacher living the same kind of lifestyle as the local population then you've ended up in the wrong job. As head of an agency you acquire certain responsibilities and status. This will distance you from others. When you visit a community in a poor part of the country the people there won't see you as someone suffering in solidarity with them, but as someone with something to offer.'

She went on to say that having a nice house, a big garden, my own transport and 'someone to look after you' did not mean I had to be seduced by these things. 'I've seen that some of my colleagues in the aid world only interact with people like themselves. They don't bother to learn the local language. They don't seem curious about the population around them. They have a comfortable circle of friends and acquaintances that they never break out of, but it doesn't have to be like that. Accept the fact that you have certain privileges, but don't let them define how you behave in this country and how you are with ordinary people.'

At the airport when Gerlin finally handed me the keys of the Land Rover, I had mixed feelings about her departure. Although we had discussed many topics, I felt I had more questions to ask her. But part of me felt relieved too. I could now get on with the challenges of the job in front of me and truth to tell I had become fed up over the last week with hearing from everyone we visited what a wonderful director Gerlin had been, how 'irreplaceable' she was.

'Don't get upset,' she had said, when we had exited such a meeting. 'When I first came here everyone said the same wonderful things about my predecessor too. It made me feel that there was no way I could ever live up to his reputation. You'll make your own mark soon enough.'

Heeding her advice about being proactive and curious, I asked Sekuru a few evenings later if he could point me towards some local entertainment. 'There's nothing around here that's suitable,' he had shrugged, adding that after it got dark at around 6 most people locked their gates and their doors, had supper and then went to bed.

'What about this?' I asked him the next day, pointing to an advert I had seen in the national newspaper, announcing an evening of 'inspired and exciting entertainment.' Some musicians had travelled from the United States to perform in Zimbabwe. It would be a concert, so it was claimed, that would be talked about in Harare for years to come.

Satisfied that the venue was reputable enough, Sekuru said I should go. But in the fatherly tone he had now adopted, he suggested that I come home as soon as it had finished. 'You haven't been long enough in Harare to know what to avoid.'

The concert hall was not difficult to find. Several blocks away, the traffic had backed up and a young man, dressed in a luminous jacket to avoid being run over, pointed to where I could park. I had expected a small crowd but it seemed that the rest of Harare was as desperate as I to find something to do. The venue was packed and I had trouble finding a seat.

The atmosphere was certainly friendly. My neighbor to the right said hello and shook my hand. Hearing a foreign accent he asked me where I came from and when I told him, he introduced me to his family and added that I was welcome in his country. An African lady to the left, hearing our conversation, joined in and gave me a friendly hug as well. In fact everyone seemed well disposed. All around me I could see handshakes, hugs and kisses. I decided that my initial impression of Harare as a cold, impersonal city had been wrong.

'There's nothing like an evening of good music to bring people together,' I thought, as the lights dimmed and a small orchestra began to tune their instruments in front of us.

When the lights came on again a young, enthusiastic American lady, our compeer for the evening, said how delighted she was to be in Zimbabwe. To appreciative applause and loud cheers she said that this was a country whose people had a reputation of being god-fearing, decent Christians. She then asked all of us to turn to our neighbors and embrace them. There were more hugs, handshakes and greetings. 'Let's pray before we start,' she said. As I bowed my head to stare at my shoes, I assumed that this was all part of the preamble before the entertainment began.

Five minutes later, I raised my head. All around me people still had their eyes closed. They had clearly taken her invitation to pray more seriously than I had. For the first time that evening, I wondered if I had had misinterpreted what I had read but, repeating to myself the words I had seen in the newspaper that morning; 'riveting music,' 'inspired entertainment,' 'wonderful singing,' I reassured myself that the artists were just building up an atmosphere. It was like this at home too. Musicians always made you wait before they began, so you would be all the more appreciative when they eventually started.

A short while later, I knew I had made a mistake. The music was more of a collective sing-song than a series of inspired performances. Various 'artists' would appear on stage, recite a few lines and wave their microphones towards us so that we could sing along too. My neighbour pushed a piece of paper in front of me. It was the words of a hymn and under his expectant gaze I had to join in, hoping that my lack of conviction would remain unnoticed amid the enthusiastic contributions of the people around me.

'How can I get out of here?' was what I was thinking as I

praised the lord with several thousand other people, promising myself at the same time that I would never take an advert in the national newspaper seriously again.

An hour later the American lady signaled us to stop. 'Now the moment you've all been waiting for,' she said, as the people around me clapped in anticipation. 'It's time to confess our sins.'

As I dropped my eyes to the floor for the second time, I wondered how long a collective confession would take. I imagined a few moments of people praying, asking for forgiveness, and then an announcement that we could all go home, but the evening was about to take another turn.

'Would all those who have coveted their neighbor's possessions please come forward to the stage,' the woman announced. Several hundred people stood up and shuffled through the aisles to where she was standing.

'Would all those who have spread rumor and falsehood come forward too.' About a quarter of the audience stood up and made their way to the front. I noticed with alarm that the crowd around me was rapidly shrinking. Even my neighbours had deserted me. At this rate I would soon be on my own, facing several thousand people who would no doubt be thinking that there was nothing worse than the sin of pride, the inability of someone to acknowledge their failings.

In the end I joined the adulterers, having decided to avoid the embarrassment of being the only person left sitting. There were more hugs and embraces when I reached the stage. Many of my fellow sinners were in tears. One of them asked me how I felt, having now unburdened myself of the guilt I must have been carrying around with me for years.

'Relieved,' I replied, thinking only of escape. As the people on stage continued to mill around and congratulate each other on their collective repentance, I took advantage of the confusion to slip away.

At home Sekuru looked surprised I had come back so early. 'I thought a concert would have lasted longer,' he said. 'Did you have a good time?'

'It wasn't a concert at all' I replied, with considerable irritation.

Describing to his amusement the evening I had had to endure, I told him I would never believe another word of what the Herald printed. 'I was a victim of deception. Someone in that newspaper should be punished for lying.'

3

On the Road

'Fortunate' was the name of our administrator and secretary, who had been with the organisation for the last few years. Gerlin thought highly of her and told me that the office was in safe hands whenever I had to travel.

Young and pretty, I found it difficult to imagine her in the role of ex-combatant, but she had been in the war after abandoning secondary school when she was only seventeen. As she typed away at the letters I would occasionally dictate to her, I wondered at the contrast between what she was doing now and what she must have experienced only a few years before.

Pointing out that she was under no obligation to answer my question, I asked her one day how she had acquired her name. She laughed. There was nothing secretive about it.

Zimbabweans often named their children after special events. She had cousins called Jubilee and Independence. Names were also derived from the feelings generated among the family on the birth of a child. 'My parents tried unsuccessfully to have children for several years before I was born. That's why when I finally came along they decided to call me Fortunate. I even have a relative called Mistake.'

Later she told me that she had also had a 'nom de guerre,' a name she was given as soon as she crossed the border into Mozambique to join the armed struggle. She went on to say that none of the people she had fought alongside had ever shared their true identity with anyone else. They had been sworn to secrecy.

'That way, if any of us were caught and tortured, we could not reveal the true names of our comrades. Their families would have been persecuted if we disclosed who they were.'

The titles they were given were also meant to portray the characteristics they were expected to display, such as Comrade Fearless and Comrade Terror who were members of her unit. 'After a while that was how we began to think of ourselves too, as if these new names defined us. But there was never a moment when we didn't dream of the war being over, when we could return to our old names again.'

One day in the office, only a week after Gerlin had left, Fortunate told me that she had received a telephone call from the Ministry of Education. They wanted us to place a teacher in Nyaminyami and had suggested I visit the area to make an assessment.

'Where is it?' I asked.

On the large map on my wall she pointed to a part of the country that couldn't have been further from Harare. It was barely on the map at all and seemed to merge into Zambia, which indeed it bordered. It was on the edge of Lake Kariba too, the long strip of water I had flown over when first entering Zimbabwe. 'The only thing I can tell you,' Fortunate replied, when I asked her if she knew the area, 'is that it is poor and remote and full of wild animals.'

Sekuru was not happy when I told him that evening that I was contemplating a trip to Nyaminyami. He repeated Fortunate's observation about wild animals, told me that I would return with malaria and warned me about a nasty insect that transmitted a disease that made you fall asleep. A guidebook that Gerlin had left confirmed that the low lying parts of the Zambezi Valley hosted the tsetse fly, which was responsible for killing thousands of cattle every year and infecting humans with sleeping sickness.

The other information that the guidebook imparted was that the indigenous population of that area were neither Shona nor Ndebele, the two principle ethnic groups of Zimbabwe. Most of them were Tonga, a separate people with their own culture, religious beliefs and language. They had lived along the Zambezi River for centuries, until they were forced from their homes when Kariba dam was constructed in the mid-1950s.

One of the biggest dams on the continent, Kariba had been built to supply the rest of the country with cheap electricity. But the Tonga had been sacrificed for the greater good. The districts of Binga and Nyaminyami, to which they were relocated, were reputed to have the poorest soils in the country, the lowest rainfall and the highest proliferation of wildlife.

'While the Tonga are a polite, courteous and friendly people,' the guidebook concluded, 'it would be best to avoid the subject of their eviction. Talk about something else. Memories of the worst period in their history are much too recent to be comfortable.'

'I don't think you should travel on your own,' Fortunate advised, when I told her the next day to confirm my visit to Nyaminyami with the Ministry of Education. 'Imagine if the vehicle breaks down in an area that's full of elephant and buffalo. Remember, you've only been a short while in Zimbabwe. You hardly know your way around.'

Who would go with me? There was no one in the office I could travel with. Only two weeks in country and I had no friends or acquaintances to accompany me either.

'What about Dave, one of our volunteers?' Fortunate suggested. 'He works in the neighboring district to where you're going. He's in town at the moment. I'm sure he'd agree if you asked him.'

Dave was a bluff, humorous and portly Yorkshireman, who had been working in Zimbabwe for the past few years as a teacher in a remote rural location. His story echoed something of my own when I had first gone to Sudan. Originally intending to only stay a year he had extended for three, reluctant to return to a job in Leeds where he had taught pupils who showed little interest in learning. Despite the remonstrations of his family, and friends and colleagues at work who said he was wasting his time, he had ignored their pleas to come home.

'Kids in England are much too spoiled. Because they have everything, they don't appreciate how privileged they are. Here it's different. My pupils are keen to learn. For God's sake, they even ask me for extra lessons. I'm happy teaching in Zimbabwe, so why would I want to go home? I'm happy to stay as long as I feel useful.'

He was up for visiting Nyaminyami with me but would have to get permission. That meant a telephone call to someone in the district education office in his nearest town.

'No problem, 'he said the next morning, sounding bright and cheery. 'They've given me a week. When do we travel?'

We left the next day. My objections were a lost cause to persuade Sekuru that we did not need the extra water, fuel, blankets, mattresses, candles and paraffin lamps he packed in the back of the Land Rover. 'When I travelled before, anything that couldn't fit into a small bag never went with me,' I complained. All this preparation worried me. It was as if we were tempting fate by trying to anticipate every eventuality.

Sudan had boasted nothing more than two or three highways in the entire country. The rest were tracks through the desert with occasional bits of tarmac thrown in to remind you what the real thing should look like. I had known that Zimbabwe would be more developed but nothing had prepared me for the long, straight road out of Harare, the absence of potholes and the signposts telling you how far you still had to go to the nearest town.

According to Dave there were two reasons why the transport system was in such good shape. 'Most of the fighting during the war took place on the periphery of the country, near the borders with Mozambique and Zambia. The army needed to move around quickly. It's partly because of its military past that Zimbabwe has such a developed infrastructure.'

The other reason was economic. Much of the country's wealth derived from its exports of tobacco, wheat, maize and cotton to other countries. To support its agricultural industry a network of roads and railways had been constructed to link centers of production with national and regional markets.

'One thing you'll notice,' Dave continued, 'is that this transport network predominantly serves the commercial farming areas of the country. Once you get to the communal areas, the railways disappear and the roads get shoddy. You'll see what I mean when we turn off to Hurungwe. There you'll find the potholes you're familiar with. By the time we get to Nyaminyami there'll be no road worth speaking of, just a simple track through the bush.'

He was right. Shortly after we took a turn off from the small town of Karoi the road transformed into a thin ribbon of tarmac that could barely accommodate a single vehicle. 'I need to warn you about something,' Dave said, as we crawled along at a sedate twenty miles an hour. 'There are two things you should avoid on roads like this one: buses and Crocodiles.'

It turned out that a Crocodile was not a species of alligator that inhabited Zimbabwe's lakes and rivers. It was the name given to a type of army vehicle that had just as fearsome a reputation. Built during the war it was shaped like a hexagon so that it could deflect the blast of a land-mine. Because of the limited view the driver had through a narrow triangular window, their accident rate was prolific. Each week there was another incident reported in the newspapers. Dave told me that a few days previously, one had collided with a bus, killing all the passengers on the side it had sliced through 'like a knife cutting butter.'

The change of road mirrored a change of landscape. While no sign had announced our transition from a commercial farming area to the communal lands Dave had earlier talked about, the contrast was stark and obvious. As we entered Hurungwe the vast hectares of irrigated wheat, tobacco and maize we had passed transformed into dry, dusty fields. The tractors we had earlier seen had been replaced by tired looking donkeys dragging ploughs behind them.

Most of the houses were meagre affairs made of mud and thatch. The occasional brick building we passed probably belonged to a teacher or local merchant, Dave said, adding that the part of the country we were now passing through was in poor shape. There had been several years of inadequate rainfall and unlike the commercial estates, which had irrigation, the farmers here had nothing to cushion them against the vagaries of the climate.

While Gerlin had prepared me for the unreliability of the Land Rover she had said nothing about the fact that without air conditioning the heat in the cab became unbearable. That meant we had to drive with all the windows open, a problem on the road we were on because of the clouds of dust that billowed around us. Soon enough Dave and I were covered in a layer of sand and grit that made us look like ghosts.

'Don't be ridiculous,' Dave said, when, remembering my former trips through the desert, I wrapped a scarf around my head, leaving a narrow slit at the top I could peer out of. Although he laughed at first he looked increasingly uncomfortable as the day wore on, finally abandoning his sense of propriety to ask me if I had a spare scarf I could lend him.

Whether it was because of our resemblance to nomads from another part of Africa or because Europeans had not passed that way for a considerable period of time, our presence in one of the villages we stopped at attracted considerable attention. Overcoming their initial hesitation a group of children struck up a conversation with Dave, whose Shona after several years in a rural location was impressively fluent.

'What does the word 'Murungu' mean?' I asked him, after I had heard it repeated numerous times. It turned out to be the equivalent of the word 'Khawaja' I had heard every day of the three years I had been in Sudan. 'Foreigner,' 'white man,' 'European;' it was not uttered by the children in an unfriendly way, but was constantly repeated, as if they needed to convince each other that we had really appeared in front of them.

In many of the villages we had driven through that morning I had seen small groups of elderly gentlemen sitting under trees or lounging on benches, doing nothing more it seemed than contemplating whatever passed in front of them. There was one such group near the bottle store we stopped beside, and as we sipped our coca-colas and entertained the children, one man stood up to wave us over.

'I'll follow your lead,' I said to Dave as we walked towards them. I was thinking of Sekuru's words about the importance of greetings in his culture, the necessity of getting them right so as not to cause offence.

'If someone asks how you are,' he had told me, 'never tell them you're not feeling well, even if you're sick. That's considered bad manners in our society. Tell them you're fine and ask after their own health. The real conversation only starts when the greetings are over.'

I repeated the phrases I had learnt, shaking each of the men by the hand in exactly the way that Sekuru had shown me. Our audience seemed delighted, including the children who clapped after each successful greeting. They wanted to know where we were from, what we were doing in their village and where we were headed. I noticed how impressed they were when Dave told them he was a teacher in their district, in a community not far from their own. I remembered from Sudan how appreciative people were of foreign teachers who lived among them, and for a moment I envied him his popularity.

As we replied to their various questions a plastic bucket was handed to us. There was a white, milky liquid bubbling away inside it. I recognised the local beer that Sekuru had once offered me, something called 'Shake-Shake' that he claimed to consume with his friends in large quantities every weekend. Made from fermented maize it had a sour, sickly taste that was not pleasant. On the one occasion I had tried it, I had indicated that I would not do so again.

'If an African offers you beer, you can't refuse it,' Sekuru had insisted. 'Getting greetings wrong is bad manners. Refusing a drink is even worse.'

I had asked him about the matter of passing it around. 'Why do people not have their own private buckets they can stick their noses into? If everyone drinks from the same receptacle, aren't there germs that can be communicated that way?'

He had been irritated by my question. 'Sharing the same beer is a way of showing friendship and hospitality to others. And don't worry about the germs. Our local beer is strong enough to kill anything that falls into it. I've drunk it since I was a boy and as you can see I'm still alive.'

I ignored the warning in my guidebook that local beverages were sometimes laced with battery acid 'to give them an extra zing' and tried not to show my revulsion as I swallowed it down. My few quick gulps occasioned considerable applause and cheering. First the successful greetings. Then the beer drinking test. I felt as if we had passed an exam. 'Come and sit with us,' the man who had waved us over said, motioning his friends to make way for us on the log of wood that served as their bench. The children whistled in appreciation, as if we had been honored with the most prestigious seats in the village.

As we chatted away I noticed that the sizeable crowd that had now gathered around us was comprised of older men, women and children. There were no younger men at all. When I asked why this was so, the person beside me replied that all the males of working age had left, since there was nothing for them to do.

'What about farming?' I asked him. 'Doesn't that offer some employment?'

He pointed to some fields at the edge of the village and the small clouds of dust that swirled around them. Nothing was growing and I remembered Dave's earlier observations, not only about drought in the district but the general inability of the communal lands to sustain the populations that lived there.

'When my son was seventeen I told him to leave. There was nothing for him here. He went to South Africa and now sends money every few months. I haven't seen him since he left and that was over four years ago.'

Sekuru had told me a similar story, but that was about his own life fifty years in the past. 'Home in our country,' he had said, 'is where you grow up and where you die but not where you live your life in between.'

Talking to these villagers it was clear that little had changed. In the almost half century that had passed between the time Sekuru and his friends had left for the mines in South Africa, leaving home still seemed the only option for young men in rural communities. Women, children and the elderly were left behind. The irony was that the very people who disappeared were the ones whose contribution would be necessary if this cycle of deprivation were ever to be broken.

When we got round to the subject of where we were headed, the old men repeated the same warnings about Nyaminyami I was becoming familiar with: tsetse flies, sleeping sickness, malaria and marauding elephants. There were angry people too, one of them remarked, but added that if his own people had been evicted from their land in the same way the Tonga had, he would be just as angry.

If Nyaminyami was even harsher and drier than Hurungwe, and poorer than all the other districts in the country, why were we sending a teacher there? 'It's better to send someone here,' they said, pointing to a school at the end of the village which the children around us should probably have been attending.

I explained that we were responding to a request from the Ministry of Education. It was precisely because Nyaminyami was so poor and neglected that they wanted us to assist that district. But I said that I would discuss the deployment of more of our teachers to Hurungwe when I returned to Harare in a few days. That promise seemed to placate them.

Nyaminyami was still many miles away and some of them waved their hands towards some distant hills when we asked how much further it was to get there. They said that the road was in worse shape than usual, because of some recent rains. But pointing to our Land Rover they added that we had come with just the right vehicle to negotiate the terrain. Dave and I exchanged amused glances. These were the first complementary words about the vehicle I had heard since Gerlin had introduced me to what I would be driving, the principal 'headache' she was relieved to be leaving behind.

It was time to say goodbye, since we would require the rest of the day to get to Siakobvu, the administrative centre in Nyaminyami where we were headed. Neither Dave nor I were keen to travel at night along a road that would be barely distinguishable from the forest around it.

Some distance further on we lost the strip of tarmac that had guided us from Karoi. Meagre though it had been, it was still a road. When it petered out into a narrow track through the trees I had a moment of panic. Although I was glad to have Dave with me, I was mindful of the fact that he had never been to Nyaminyami before. In all my previous excursions into remote areas of Africa I had always had a local guide who knew where we were going. Was it wise to be on our own?

A battered sign a short while later offered some reassurance. It announced that Siakobvu was only forty miles away. But Dave warned me not to get overly optimistic. 'Forty miles on this road is like several hundred on any other.'

The track was severely corrugated, which meant that even at a modest speed the vehicle shook and rattled uncontrollably. The secret was to drive fast enough so you could catch the crest of each corrugation, but not so fast you couldn't stop in time to negotiate the large holes that would suddenly appear. With the dust coming through the window, the continuing heat of the day and the long drive still ahead of us, Dave reckoned that it would have been better to have stayed overnight in the village with our new friends, and attempted this route the following morning.

The landscape we passed through looked every bit as inhospitable as everyone had warned. There were fewer and fewer signs of cultivation the further we progressed. Occasionally we would pass a clearing in the forest where we would see a meagre hut and a family busy about its activities. Maybe it was our strange headgear that startled them, or the fact that they were not used to seeing vehicles, but unlike the other homesteads we had passed in Hurungwe no one raised their hands to greet us.

Parts of the forest were still smoldering from recent fires. Dave told me that this was how remote parts of the country were opened up for cultivation. With no access to machinery to clear the area, people resorted to 'slash and burn.' This meant cutting the trees and undergrowth with machetes and axes and then burning what was left so that the ash could fertilise the first crop they planted.

'The problem is that this land is so infertile it will only produce for a year or two. Once it's exhausted a family will simply move on to the next patch of ground and burn that too.'

One minute I remembered Dave talking about the damage that had been caused to the environment, the next minute we were off the road and I was staring through a cracked windscreen at a tree protruding out of the ground where I thought the engine should have been. Dave was rubbing his neck and cursing vigorously. A trickle of what I thought was sweat dripped down my forehead, until I rubbed it away and saw that it was blood.

'I think we've had an accident,' I said, stating the obvious.

'Bloody right we have,' Dave replied. 'Didn't I warn you to drive more slowly?'

He had indeed told me that the section of the road we were now on had recently been re-graded. He could tell that from the loose sand that had been pushed to one side. This might cause us to skid if I had to break suddenly. 'Best to be careful,' he had cautioned.

We had been approaching a bend at what I thought was a reasonable speed, but by the time I realised we were going too fast it was too late. I had lost control. The next moment we were in the forest with the front of our vehicle pointing towards the sky, and a strange spluttering sound coming from our engine.

I tried the ignition, hoping that we might still be in some shape to drive away. Nothing happened and I tried again.

'What are you doing?' Dave asked.

'I'm trying to start the car. Maybe it's not as bad as it looks.'

'Chris, this vehicle is not going anywhere any time soon. The engine is somewhere above our heads. It's broken, kaput, fucked. The office Land Rover has reached its last resting place.'

Taking his bottle he poured some water on my forehead to check my cut. 'You'll live,' he said, when I asked him if it was serious.

Once outside I could see that Dave was right. This was a vehicle that would not be going anywhere again for a considerable period of time. The front had been pushed up at a crazy angle by the tree we had crashed into. The radiator had punctured and there was oil dripping out of the engine. With only a small injury, Dave's stiff neck and our bruised nerves we could count ourselves lucky that it had not been much worse. The problem was that the accident could not have happened in a more isolated location.

Dave looked at his watch. The hottest part of the after-noon was over and he reckoned that we had only a couple of hours of daylight remaining. Earlier we had passed a tsetse fly control station where we knew there was a radio. But it would be dark by the time we walked there, and neither of us wanted to be stumbling around at night in a forest that was renowned for dangerous animals.

Another possibility was to explore the track in front of us, to see if we could find some habitation. Siakobvu, we guessed, couldn't be that far away. If we didn't find any-thing within an hour, there would still be enough time to return to the vehicle before nightfall. There we could wait out the evening and pursue the first option the following morning.

'Let's go,' I said. I had little expectation of finding any-thing, but neither did I want to sit around feeling sorry for myself. No matter its unreliability and Gerlin's advice to get rid of it, the damaged Land Rover was a depressing sight. I was worried too about what my new employer would say. Two weeks in Zimbabwe and I had wrecked our vehicle, not a good start to my tenure as country director. I wanted a change of scenery so I could think about something else. Dave was of the same opinion too.

The surrounding forest remained oppressively enclosed. Even when Dave climbed a tree to see if he could spot something, there was nothing but more trees stretching into the distance. We pushed on beyond the hour mark, neither of us wanting to remind the other of the deadline we had agreed on. Maybe around the next corner we would find a hut, a village, even a sign announcing that Siakobvu was only a mile away.

Instead, we stumbled across several large piles of half-digested grass and leaves, steaming away in the middle of the track in front of us. This prompted Dave to turn abruptly around and announce that it was time to retrace our steps.

'What is it?' I asked.

'These are elephant turds,' he replied, 'and judging by their fresh odour and appearance their owners aren't too far away either.'

As we scurried back in the direction we had come, I remembered Sekuru's and Fortunate's warnings about the wild animals of Nyaminyami. At the time it had all sounded exotic and exciting. I had even bought a book entitled 'Large Mammals of Zimbabwe.' It had glossy pictures of what it called the Big Five: elephant, lions, leopards, rhinoceros and buffalo. As I had leafed through its pages I had contemplated with eager anticipation my first encounter.

But that was supposed to take place from the safety of a vehicle, which you could drive away if the Big Five became too frisky. Meeting them here on an isolated forest road, with nothing but my own legs for propulsion, was not a prospect that enthused me. In the end it took us only half the time to return to our vehicle. This left us with enough daylight to transform the back of the Land Rover into a mini-fortress that would keep out the most determined of intruders.

'We need to thank Sekuru the next time we see him,' Dave said. He reminded me of how I had criticised him for insisting we take with us the mattresses, blankets, mosquito nets, extra food and water that were turning out to be so useful. When it got dark we lit the paraffin lamp that I had also wanted to leave behind. Even the walking stick Sekuru had handed to me, that I had threatened to throw out of the window, now provided me with an added sense of security. I quietly resolved not to question his advice on these matters again.

With a long night ahead of us there was nothing to do but

talk. Ignoring my nervousness about camping out in an area infested with wildlife, Dave steered the conversation in that direction. 'Have you heard of 'Maswera Sei'?' he asked me.

I shook my head, adding that as far as I knew these words meant 'How are you?' in Shona.

'It's also the name of a lion that has been terrorising this part of the country for the last few years. It has killed several children and some that have gone missing have been presumed eaten by the same animal.'

'Why is it called Maswera Sei?' I asked, despite my wanting to change the subject.

According to Dave it had acquired its name because of its habit of appearing early in the morning while boys and girls were on their way to school. It had even been known to wait for its victims outside their homes. One family had related how, upon waking up one day, they had opened their door to find 'Maswera Sei' sitting on the front step. It had said, 'Good morning', and then devoured one of their children.

I was convinced that Dave was pulling my leg, trying to make me nervous because of the predicament my poor driving had landed us in. 'I wasn't aware that lions hunted people,' I said, trying to sound knowledgeable. 'They prefer zebras and gazelles to human flesh.'

Clearly he had read more on the subject than I. 'When a lion gets old it can't hunt like it used to. Gazelles and zebras are too fast. Buffalo are too aggressive. That's when it will go for something weaker and slower. They say that when a lion gets a taste for human flesh it won't eat anything else. Have you never read about the famous man-eater of Malodi?'

As he related another story about an infamous lion that had terrorised railway workers in Kenya at the turn of the century, I wondered why he hadn't informed me about 'Maswera Sei' before we had started our journey. Why now, when we were stuck in the middle of a district notorious for wildlife, in a vehicle that was going nowhere and with nothing but a flimsy tarpaulin roof to keep out predators?

'Don't worry, he's only joking,' I said to myself, but when he pulled his trousers down a short while later to pee out of one of the windows, I realised that he was actually serious.

'There's no way I'm going out there with that animal around,' he said, when I asked him what he was doing. Half an hour later when I felt the same urge, I dropped my trousers and did the same.

Neither of us got any real sleep that evening. It was hot and oppressive in our cramped space and despite the mosquito nets we had rigged up around us, we could hear scores of insects buzzing around. The repellant I had plastered upon my face and arms didn't seem to work either. Whenever I woke up to scratch at another bite, I remembered Sekuru's prediction that I would return either with malaria or sleeping sickness.

As soon as the lantern was turned off, the forest seemed to come alive with all sorts of strange noises too. 'What's that?' Dave would say, claiming to have heard a rustling sound in close proximity to our vehicle.

'I didn't hear anything,' I would reply.

'Listen again. Can you hear it now?'

'Yes I can. What the fuck is it?'

Then we would shine a torch through one of the windows and make a loud banging noise on the side of the Land Rover to scare whatever it was away. It would take us quite some time to settle down again, our senses alert for the slightest indication of danger. On the rare occasion when I managed to close my eyes I would imagine waking up the following morning, opening the door of the vehicle and in front of me, licking his chops, would be 'Maswera Sei' anticipating breakfast.

When Dave nudged me awake again in the early morning, I thought he must have heard another animal. Tired and irritated I told him that even if there were a herd of elephants nearby I couldn't care less. I needed some sleep.

'Get up,' he insisted. 'I can hear an engine.'

Sure enough, there in the distance was the faint but unmistakable sound of a vehicle. By the time we had struggled out of our blankets, dismantled our barricade and exited the car, it had become noticeably louder.

The thought of our imminent rescue transformed the events of the previous day, the uncomfortable night and my companion's scary stories into something amusing. 'Wait till I tell my friends back home about our adventure,' I chuckled. 'I'm sure they won't believe me.'

From the rumbling sound it made as it got nearer we guessed that the vehicle was not a car. Dave thought it was an army truck. I said it must be a bus with comfortable seats, air conditioning and cool drinks. But when a strange looking machine with two men perched inside a cab finally rounded a bend in the road, I knew our ordeal was not yet over.

'I don't believe it,' said Dave. 'It's a bloody grader, the one that probably caused our accident.'

It seemed to take forever to reach us, even though Dave claimed that it was travelling at maximum speed because the metal bar it normally dragged behind it had been raised. The vehicle's occupants looked even more bizarre than we had the previous day, with ear-muffs, thick goggles, strange helmets and several layers of clothes to keep out the cold.

Switching off the engine, the driver climbed down a ladder on the side of his cab, walked over to where we were standing and whistled through his teeth when he saw the state of our Land Rover. 'You need to drive more carefully, sah,' he said, after completing his inspection. 'The roads here are very bad.'

The same person expressed no remorse when he told us that we were the second of his victims that week. A few days previously another vehicle travelling along the same stretch of road had skidded on the surface and overturned. No one had been hurt, but the car, like ours, had been a write-off.

'Can you give us a lift to Siakobvu?' I asked.

The driver and his assistant had a brief discussion. 'We're not supposed to carry passengers. It's against the rules. But since we don't want to leave you here either, we've decided you can come with us.'

Unfortunately, there was no space in the cab where the two of them were squeezed together. If we had no objection to being shaken around we could hold on to the ladders on the side and travel that way. 'That's the best we can offer.'

Dave looked worried. I was nervous. Not only did it look uncomfortable but dangerous too.

'Will another vehicle pass this way today?' I asked.

They shrugged their shoulders. 'Maybe yes. Maybe no. You could be waiting a very long time.'

'What about walking?' Dave persisted.

'It's not safe in this forest. Last month we saw some lions on the road. Have you ever heard of Maswera Sei?'

The moment he mentioned that name, I fetched my bag from the Land Rover, clambered up the side of the cab and took a firm hold of the ladder. 'We're not walking and we're not waiting. We accept your offer. We can leave whenever you're ready.'

It would probably have been quicker walking. For the rest of the morning we proceeded at a snail's pace, our only consolation that we were safe from wild animals, but from serious injury through falling off a moving vehicle, that was another story. Most of the time we had to concentrate on holding on, especially when we approached a bend in the road and the grader would lurch to one side, threatening to throw us off.

Enclosed within their ear-muffs and goggles, the driver and his assistant would occasionally turn to check if we were still there. Dave and I would wave in response, desperately hoping that we might stop for a few minutes to stretch our legs and relieve our aching arms. But they seemed determined to proceed, only halting a few hours later when one of them pointed to a nearby hill and said that Siakobvu was just behind it.

The most interest we had managed to stir in the homesteads we had passed the previous day were a few surprised stares from children clutching their mothers. But the closer we got to Siakobvu the response was different. As soon as they saw us, people dropped what they were doing to follow us into town. By the time we reached the central square, a considerable crowd had gathered.

The driver of the grader was enjoying the attention. He waved at everyone, occasionally pointing towards us as if we were some prize specimens he had captured. When he finally stopped the engine, he emerged from his cab to loud cheers. Neither Dave nor I understood a word of what he was saying, but the applause that greeted the speech he gave made it clear he was describing his own role in our rescue. Even the taciturn assistant, who had said little since we had first met him, received his share of recognition too.

One of our onlookers turned out to be a policeman, who approached us when all the commotion was over. Brusque and officious he did not share in the general enthusiasm that had greeted our arrival. 'All accidents have to be reported to our office,' he said. 'You'll have to follow me.' The driver of the grader was instructed to come along as a witness. The rest of the crowd was told to go home.

From the curiosity that our arrival prompted in a small cluster of wooden huts that passed for a police station, I guessed that Siakobvu was low on crime and short on entertainment. Within a few minutes the room we were ushered into was packed. There was a chief inspector of police, several other officers, a receptionist and someone who made tea. Even a nurse, who had been summoned to check the bruise on my head, asked if she could stay to hear our story.

'There's nothing much to tell,' I replied, when I was invited to relate what had happened. 'We skidded on the road, hit a tree and had to stay overnight in our vehicle to avoid the wild animals. We were rescued by our friend here this morning.'

Though pleasant enough, the inspector who kept on plying us with cups of tea, was adamant that a detailed report would have to be filled out for his superiors in Chinhoyi. 'There are several things I need to be clear about,' he said, in a tone of voice that suggested we were hiding something. From the way his colleagues nodded their heads in anticipation, I felt as if I were about to be interrogated for a major misdemeanor rather than a simple traffic accident that had injured nobody.

'Fire away,' I said, as casually as I could.

Several hours later we were still there. Most of the questions were about my driving ability. Did I have a licence? When had I done my test? Did people in Scotland drive on the same side of the road as those in Zimbabwe? How many accidents had I had before? What did Dave think of my driving? Did we have an argument beforehand? Had I smoked an illegal substance that might have impaired my judgment? Each of my answers had to be typed out on an old machine that had clearly seen better days. The secretary seemed unfamiliar with English too, and constantly asked me to spell what I had said.

The final upshot at the end of my interrogation was that I was to be charged with reckless driving. 'But what does that actually mean?' I asked, too surprised to be indignant. 'Will I be arrested?'

The inspector laughed, his colleagues joining in. 'Nothing like that. There's a small fine you have to pay. Your details are kept on record. After two years these will be deleted, unless you have another accident.'

I was tired and exhausted and the bump on my head was beginning to ache. I had no energy to argue but just wanted to find a place to rest, gather my thoughts and plan how we would get out of this mess and return to Harare.

Dave was more insistent. 'What happens if he pleads not guilty?'

'There'll be a court case in a few months, but my advice is not to contest this decision. The judge in Chinhoyi always agrees with what we recommend. If he gets upset he might take his license away too.'

'But what about the state of the road? What about the other accident this week? That grader bears some responsibility. If it hadn't been so sandy, we would never have skidded in the first place.'

'Everyone is supposed to take account of the road conditions,' the inspector replied, to nods of agreement from our onlookers. 'If it's sandy you slow down. If it's wet you drive more carefully. That's something he should have known.'

Although I could see that Dave was tempted to argue further, I could also see his hesitation. These were the same words, more or less, he had also fired at me when we had had our accident. There was nothing left to say.

'I'll pay whatever fine you want me to,' I concluded. 'But at the moment I need to rest. I had no sleep last night and my head hurts. Is there a place in town where we can stay?'

At an impromptu guest house, which also doubled as a beer hall, I snatched some fitful sleep on a creaky bed with no mattress and surrounded by crates of drink. Dave went out to explore. He came back fifteen minutes later, claiming to have seen everything that Siakobvu had to offer.

One dilemma had been solved, but several problems still remained. No one we had spoken to could tell us when the next bus would be leaving for Harare. There was no garage either where we could organise our vehicle to be towed to safety. I had tried to phone Fortunate, but the telephone at the police station returned nothing but a strange buzzing sound when I had dialed the number.

Then there was the issue of alerting my head office to what had happened. I imagined what my boss might say if he found out that after only a couple of weeks in country, I had already acquired a police record. Would he come to a decision that it was best to fire me?

'This is a fucking nightmare,' I said to Dave as we sat in our dingy surroundings, while noisy patrons danced outside our door. Though he did his best to sound upbeat and positive I could see that he was thinking the same thing too, and probably wondering what stroke of misfortune had prompted him to accompany me to Nyaminyami in the first place.

Later that afternoon we were sitting outside, avoiding the mosquitoes in the room and contemplating an unpleasant evening ahead of us. 'I wonder who that is,' Dave said, when several cars pulled up outside the guest house and a tall, thin man dressed in a safari suit emerged from one of them. I guessed he must be important from the whispers and stares of various bystanders, and the reaction of one of the waiters, who rushed off to find the manager as soon as he saw him.

I was surprised when he approached us and offered us his hand. 'Welcome to Nyaminyami, Mr. Chris and Mr. Dave. We've been expecting you.'

While I stood to attention, somewhat intimidated by his imposing appearance, Dave with his characteristic bluntness asked him who he was. 'And how do you know our names? I can't remember telling anyone that I was called Dave.'

'Because I know everything that happens in my district,' the stranger replied. 'I'm the administrator for Nyaminyami.'

Dave looked sheepish and stuttered an apology. I remembered what Gerlin had told me about the hierarchy of authority that prevailed in rural Zimbabwe. 'If you want to do business anywhere in this country, you'll need the blessing of the district administrator. These are people directly appointed by the President. If they decide that they don't want you in their territory, then it's best to go someplace else.'

With an informality that surprised me, he sat down on a bench beside us and asked me how I was. 'I heard you were injured.'

'It's nothing serious, sir. Just a small bump. I'm sure I'll be fine.'

'Nevertheless, it's best to let our doctor have a look at it,' he replied, and motioned to someone in the small entourage that was accompanying him to arrange an appointment at the hospital for me later.

Pointing to the establishment behind us, he then said it was inappropriate that we were staying in such accommodation. I had noticed that since his arrival the loud music had been turned down, something which our own earlier remonstrations had been unable to achieve. The manager had appeared too, hovering on the edge of our conversation. He looked much less assertive than when we had met him that morning. Despite our objections he had insisted on a ridiculous price for the one room that was still available.

'It's not quite what we're used to,' Dave said, loud enough to make sure the manager heard him, 'but there was nowhere else to stay. That's why we've ended up here, in a room with no windows, crates of beer around the beds and cockroaches hiding in all the corners.'

If that description was meant to prompt more sympathy, it was unnecessary. 'Don't worry,' the administrator said, 'I've already arranged for you to stay at the Government Rest Camp on the edge of Siakobvu. It's much more comfortable and clean. Unlike here you might actually get some sleep this evening.'

Things were looking up. He had already dispatched a vehicle to fetch the rest of our belongings from our Land Rover. These would be delivered to our new accommodation later. In a stroke of irony that prompted Dave and I to exchange amused glances he told us that he had also sent the grader to the scene of our accident, to tow our vehicle to the Government compound in Chinhoyi. 'It'll be safe there until you arrange its eventual return to Harare.'

I ignored Dave's whispered suggestion to ask him to have my charge of reckless driving withdrawn by the police. I didn't want to push our luck. When I thanked the administrator instead for what he was doing for us, he said that he was only carrying out his duty. 'You are here to send us some teachers. We don't want you to leave without completing that assignment.'

'But how will we travel around?' I asked, adding that the schools were scattered throughout the district and from what I could see there was no functioning public transport.

'Mr. Nyathi, come over here and introduce yourself,' he

responded, motioning to someone else in his group to come over and greet us. This turned out to be the district education officer. Instructed to make sure we had everything we wanted, he would drive us around for the next few days in a Ministry vehicle, show us the schools that needed teachers and answer whatever questions we might have.

One minute we were stranded in a remote town in the remotest district of Zimbabwe, with no friends or contacts and unsure of what to do. The next minute someone had appeared, issued a few instructions and our entire prospects were brighter.

'I have to go now,' the administrator said a short while later, tapping his watch. 'It was nice to meet you.'

As he sped off to his next appointment, Dave and I stared for several minutes at his departing vehicle, barely able to believe how our fortunes had reversed so completely in what had been no more than a ten minute encounter. The manager of the guest house looked uncomfortable as we brushed past him, telling us that we would not have to pay for the few hours we had already spent in his shabby room.

'Go and help them with their bags,' he shouted at one of the waiters who was standing idly beside him. 'Can't you see these are important people who are guests of our government. They are here to help the children of Nyaminyami.'

4

The People of the Lake

'What's that racket?' Dave shouted the following morning.

'What racket?' I replied, reminding myself that I was in the bedroom of a comfortable guest house on the edge of Siakobvu and not in a broken down vehicle in the middle of a forest with wild animals around us.

'Can't you hear it now?' he continued, as a thumping and banging came from somewhere above our heads. 'It sounds as if there is a herd of elephants upstairs.'

As we stumbled outside we could see that Jacob, the caretaker, was already up, busy over a charcoal stove preparing our breakfast. 'I see the baboons have woken you,' he said, pointing to a group of them clambering up and down one of the drainpipes on to the tin roof of the building where we were staying.

According to him they were regular visitors. Once, when he had temporarily abandoned his cooking, he had returned to find empty plates. They would eat anything and so he now kept a pile of stones within easy reach, which he would throw in their direction if they ventured too close.

'That one over there is the worst,' he said, firing a missile at a large brute that seemed to be presiding over the others, sitting on his haunches like a general surveying his troops. He bared his teeth when the stone clattered beside him, his irritation bordering on a menace that alarmed us. Both Dave and I edged backwards to the safety of the veranda, even though Jacob continued his cooking and said we should ignore them.

He then went on to tell us that a few months previously a baboon was reputed to have snatched a baby in one of the nearby villages. Fortunately the family had seen it happen and after chasing it a considerable distance, the baby had finally been dropped in no worse condition than when it had been seized.

The previous evening, he had told us about marauding elephants and hippos that attacked people. This morning it was about baby-snatching baboons. Slowly my benign perception of African wildlife was beginning to change and I was becoming much more wary.

'Don't worry,' Jacob said, when he finally signaled for us to sit down beside him to eat. 'They won't harm you.' I remarked to Dave that his pile of stones was not meagre and that there were several large rocks scattered among them.

Jacob was a member of the Tonga ethnic group that had been evicted from their homeland along the river and relocated to places like Nyaminyami in the 1950s and 60s. He had been the caretaker of the Government Rest Camp for the last ten years, which was where he had picked up his excellent English. Despite what my guidebook had said, he seemed willing enough to relate the history of what had happened. We had chatted away for over an hour, and though anger and bitterness was evident, it seemed that this was a subject he could have talked about at length.

'No one asked us what we wanted,' he replied, when Dave had asked him if they had been consulted about the decision to build the dam. 'One day, some men came to tell our chief that a large wall would be built across our river. They said that this would benefit the whole country, ourselves included, and that our people would be given land every bit as good as what we would have to leave behind.'

The water had risen slowly at first. Many refused to move, believing that it would never reach them. They were also worried that if they left, others would come in to take what was theirs. The flood plains along the river were rich and fertile and it was not the first time in their history that outsiders had coveted their territory. It was only when the water began to flood their areas of cultivation that they realised they really would have to leave.

Some moved west to Zambia. Others moved east to the escarpment on the Zimbabwe side of the river. A once homogenous community was split in two. 'I now need a visa to visit my brother on the other side of the lake,' Jacob complained. 'The last time I saw my family over there was several years ago.'

Of the promises that were made to compensate them, little materialised. People were settled on land that was dry and infertile, that had no roads and infrastructure to support them and that was heavily populated by wild animals. It was that same population of wild animals that now competed with humans for the scarce resources of the district.

'The dam created enemies,' Jacob had said, after telling us that on average about ten farmers were killed every year by elephant and buffalo trampling over their fields in search of food. Many more people were injured trying to defend their crops. 'It never used to be like that. We used to hunt an occasional elephant. But most of the time we kept to ourselves. The river provided what we needed. The forest was theirs.'

I asked if any of the benefits of Kariba dam had ever found their way back to the communities most affected by its construction. He had shaken his head. The villages in Nyaminyami were still without electricity, thirty years after the Tonga had been moved. He pointed out that the lights in the place where we were staying were powered by a generator he had switched on earlier. 'Kariba provides most of the country's power. Yet no one has bothered to bring us the electricity that was the reason we lost our homes.'

I had also read that the lake boasted a fishing industry, based on a small sardine-like fish called Kapenta. This was exported throughout the region and seemed to fetch a good price in Harare. 'Doesn't that bring some revenues to your communities,' I asked, 'and some employment for your people?'

Jacob explained that to catch Kapenta you had to fish at night, in sophisticated boats that had powerful searchlights. These lights attracted the fish to the surface, from where they were scooped up in mechanised nets. The fish were then taken to factories where they were dried or frozen, packed into boxes and dispatched onwards for sale elsewhere. 'No Tonga could ever afford the purchase of such a boat, let alone a factory to process these fish. Sure, some of our people are employed in the fishing industry but most of the money flows out of the district.'

According to Jacob, the tourist industry associated with the lake had also been captured by outsiders, people who had the resources to build hotels and safari camps. The managers and senior staff of many of these establishments came from other parts of the country. What were left were menial jobs for the locals.

In effect the majority of the Tonga had to derive a living from farming, but as we had seen, agriculture was a precarious if not risky business. No family cultivated more than a few hectares at a time for the simple reason that this was the maximum amount of land they could defend against invading animals.

'When you drove here yesterday, did you see small round huts in the middle of the fields?' Jacob asked.

I replied that we had, and had assumed they were im-
provised shelters where famers could escape for a few hours
from the heat of the day while they were working. They
seemed to consist of little more than a few poles stuck in the
ground, with thatch on top of them to provide some shade.

Jacob said that during the planting season people needed
to camp out in their fields for weeks on end. Unless their
crops were protected for twenty-four hours each day, birds,
baboons, elephant and buffalo would consume what was
growing in a matter of minutes. 'That's why most of our
children don't go to school during these months. If everyone
in the family doesn't help out, there will be nothing to eat for
anyone.'

As Jacob related his story, I was reminded of a similar
conversation I had had several years previously. It was in
northern Sudan in a place called Wadi Halfa. There, I had
encountered the remnants of a previously thriving community, that had been impacted by the construction of Aswan
Dam further north in Egypt. The rich culture and society of
the Nubian people along that part of the Nile had never
recovered. Their homes were flooded, their ancient temples
and monuments submerged. An entire population had been
scattered to other parts of the country, their history dismissed in the name of development and progress.

When I had visited the area several years after the dam
was constructed, people who had left were now trying to
return. They wanted to reclaim something of their past, even
though their previous livelihoods had been destroyed.
'What the Government gave in compensation,' a teacher
had told me, 'could never make up for what we had lost. It
wasn't just our land and homes that had been taken away, it
was our identity too.'

'Is Nyaminyami a name of someone or something?' I had
also asked Jacob the previous evening.

'Wait a minute,' he had replied, and had disappeared to the part of the compound where he stayed. He returned a few minutes later with an ornate walking stick, which had the head of a strange looking creature carved on the handle.

This turned out to be Nyaminyami, a large serpent that the Tonga believed inhabited the river in exactly the location where Kariba was constructed. The local legend was that separated from his consort on the other side of the dam, Nyaminyami was angry and would one day take his revenge. This included the destruction of the very structure that had caused all their problems.

Dave looked bemused as Jacob related this story and asked him bluntly whether people really believed there was a creature lurking in the depths of the lake, ready to wreak havoc when it took his fancy.

Jacob remained serious. 'Our chief told the people who were building the dam that it was dangerous to place it in that location. Something bad was bound to happen. The very year it was being completed, the Zambezi flooded. No one could ever remember it as high as that. Several workers were swept away and some of the foreign engineers too. Their bodies were never found. Our chief said they were devoured by Nyaminyami, because when people drown they always end up somewhere along the river.'

In recent years, the area had also experienced several earthquakes, none that were of a significant magnitude to threaten Kariba itself but strong enough to convince people that a vengeful river god was signaling his disquiet. 'We never had earthquakes when we lived along the Zambezi before. People are wondering why this is happening now, only after the dam was built across our river. There is a reason for these things.'

Dave could not resist responding. 'Because the pressure of all that water in the lake means that the ground is subsiding.

That's what is causing these tremors. It's common when dams are constructed. And the people who drowned were killed in an unfortunate accident. That's the only explanation.'

Jacob grinned and smiled politely. It looked as if he had had this conversation with a sceptical audience before. But as he rose to leave, informing us that our breakfast would be waiting before we travelled around the district the following day, he had some final words on the subject.

'When you crashed on your way to Siakobvu yesterday, do you really think it happened by chance? No, it's because one of you did something to offend someone. That meant your car was forced off the road at exactly the place where a tree was waiting. Why not at some other place, where there would have been no damage? It's the same when these people drowned in the river. It was because of something they had done. There is no such thing as accident or chance. Things happen to us because of our actions in the past and their consequences for our future.'

Mola was the largest village in Nyaminyami, one of the first settlements to have been established when the Tonga were forced to abandon their homes. Almost an hour's drive on the track that headed west from Siakobvu, it had the district's only secondary school.

On the bumpy ride there, we passed several groups of children marching in the same direction. According to Mr. Nyathi, who had picked us up from the Rest Camp earlier in the day, some of them would take up to two hours just to get to school in the morning. There was the same walk home in the afternoon. 'It's not uncommon for kids in Nyaminyami to spend more time walking to their classrooms than spending time inside them.'

Along the road we had driven in Hurungwe, long lines of

children had also been making their way to school. But one thing I noticed this time was that there were no stragglers. The children were bunched together in tight groups that only parted to make way for our vehicle.

'Why doesn't that surprise me?' I said, when Mr. Nyathi informed us that wildlife was again responsible. No one would risk being on their own with a man-eating lion reputed to be in the district. Quite often the children never made it to school at all, if they encountered elephants or buffalo blocking their path. If the animals didn't feel like moving there was nothing to do but return home and try again the following day.

'Good morning, sah!' a group of excited pupils shouted in reply when I greeted them in their classroom later that morning. Apart from the language, their different features and the trees rather than sand dunes outside the window, I could have been back in Sudan. There were too few desks and chairs. There were too many pupils for the textbooks that were available. There was the same open roof and broken windows, and a teacher who seemed little older than the pupils he was supervising.

I was aware of the same contradictions that had troubled me too. Just like the boys and girls I had taught in Sudan there was no doubting their desire to learn. How else could one explain their determined march to school every morn-ing and the fact that despite their poverty, families found money to pay for uniforms, exercise books and exam fees? But as their teacher rattled through a lesson with no attempt to find out if his pupils understood a word of what he was saying, I wondered if the sacrifices were worth it.

One girl presented me with a letter they had written the previous week, when they had heard that we were coming. 'Dear Sir,' it read, 'please send us a teacher to our beautiful school.' There was a drawing of a village with brick houses, a smart clinic, a church, fat cows and smiling people. It was the opposite of the mud huts we had encountered on the edge of Mola, the dilapidated health facility and the tired looking fields we had passed . I supposed that the message behind that picture was that education would help them realise the idyll it depicted.

As I thanked her class for their communication, however, I couldn't help thinking about something that Jacob had said the previous evening when we had told him why we were in his district. He also had a son and daughter at school. What he wanted above all was that they acquire the necessary qualifications that would allow them to leave behind the poverty and deprivation his own generation had suffered.

He wanted them to escape, but if school imparted skills that were only useful elsewhere, encouraging its brightest youngsters to leave, was it really serving the community in the way that it should? And if education was of little practical value to those that remained, how would Nya-minyami ever change? In those circumstances, was sending a teacher here the right thing to do? Would we be ex-aggerating the problem rather than contributing to a solution?

From the time we had spent with him, I felt that Mr. Nyathi was open enough to discuss these issues. As we moved to another location he told us that his Ministry was trying to promote an education that was not just academi-cally sound. It wanted to establish practical subjects too like carpentry, agriculture, sewing, craft production and small business development. 'But a big problem we have is the opposition of parents and the reluctance of pupils.'

This surprised me. 'If it gives children skills that will be useful in their communities, then why would they object?'

'Because of our past history,' he replied.

During the Rhodesian era there had been two systems of education, one for the privileged minority and another for Africans. The latter had had its share of practical subjects. But no one believed that this was because of any enlightened thinking on the part of the authorities at that time. 'It was because they wanted blacks to have skills that only suited them for more menial jobs. A school curriculum that encouraged critical thinking, open debate and academic excellence would have been seen as too much of a threat to the status quo.'

Although circumstances had changed, the period of time that had elapsed between then and now was too short for people to have forgotten the rationale behind practical education. "Give us what the whites had,' is what parents say, even when they know that many of their children will never pass the exams that would allow them to move up the educational ladder.'

The other constraint was financial. 'People often assume that practical subjects are cheaper to provide. They're wrong. You can't teach woodwork unless you have tools. You can't teach sewing unless you have machines. The Ministry of Education simply doesn't have the resources to ensure that every school in Zimbabwe is able to teach these subjects effectively.'

Mr. Nyathi confided that as a professional teacher he was sometimes troubled by the issue of quality and relevance in the education provided to children of impoverished areas like Nyaminyami. 'But every time I think about this, I remind myself that only a few years ago there were no schools at all in such locations. The focus of our efforts had to be the construction of facilities and the training of teachers. Once that is done we can tackle some of these more complicated problems.'

At another school a short while later, he steered us past

the classrooms and administrative buildings towards the forest that surrounded them. 'There is something else I want you to see.'

A short distance beyond the perimeter, among the trees, we stumbled across a series of shelters made of mud and wooden poles. On the drive to Mola earlier, Mr. Nyathi had pointed to similar structures. These were used to pen animals in at night to protect them from predators. I assumed that what we were now seeing was more of the same, but wondered why this had been included in our tour of educational facilities.

'You asked me how interested children are in going to school,' he said. 'Maybe this will answer your question.'

It turned out that this was a student village, where many of them resided. What we were seeing was their 'dormitory.' There were no latrines. A small stream at the bottom of a nearby ravine was where they fetched their water and washed their clothes. He showed us something that was little more than a hole in the ground, lined with plastic sheeting and newspapers, and a wooden cover on top that could be fastened from the inside. I found it difficult to believe that anyone could live there, but according to Mr. Nyathi these holes were among the more popular types of accommodation. 'They can be constructed in a few hours. They cost nothing. Children would rather spend the little they had on pens and exercise books than on something they consider is not a necessity.'

Even Dave, who sometimes assumed an 'I've seen it all before' expression, was shocked when we found one young boy inside such a shelter. He had been ill for several days with malaria, and apart from scraps of food brought by his friends, had received no other care or attention during that time. Only fourteen years old, he looked surprised when I asked him why he endured such squalid conditions. The

70

answer was obvious. 'Because there is no other secondary school near my village,' he replied.

Mr. Nyathi confirmed that Mola secondary school was the only one for hundreds of kilometers. Recently built, it had only been able to provide 'proper' boarding facilities for a handful of pupils. Apart from these, and the children that came from Mola itself, the rest had had to build their own accommodation. It was either that or no secondary education at all. 'Sometimes children are turned away, on the grounds that there is nowhere for them to stay, but they come back the next day saying they have found a relative in Mola who will look after them. More often than not this means they have ended up here.'

I had often been struck in Sudan by the determination of boys and girls to pursue an education. They walked long distances each morning. They studied at night under candles or smoky kerosene lamps. They worked at weekends and during holidays to earn some money to purchase books and uniforms. But I had seen nothing comparable to this, to the hardships that children in Nyaminyami were prepared to face to seize this one opportunity of getting ahead.

Dave had taken some photos. 'One day when I go back to my old teaching job and my pupils are mucking around in the classroom, tearing up their books and damaging school property, I'll show them these photos and tell them how ashamed they should be. I'll tell them that in another part of the world there are children living in holes in the ground, who would sacrifice everything to have a fraction of the opportunities they have been given.'

My doubts about the practical value of education, and the benefits it offered to impoverished communities such as Mola, would probably persist. But I too had been shocked by what I had just seen. It seemed churlish and dogmatic in these circumstances to deny Mr. Nyathi's request to assist this school and its desperate children. 'Sure we'll help,' I replied later, when a group of students asked me in their classroom if we could send them a math teacher as soon as possible.

'What would you like to see now?' Mr. Nyathi asked, after we had visited several schools, each one as desperate and needy as the next.

'It would be a pity to have come all the way here and not seen the lake itself,' I replied.

It was longer and thinner than I had expected. Even from the hill we were standing on, we could not see the southern shore. Mr. Nyathi informed us that from the northern end of the lake to the southern tip at Binga, was a journey of two days by ferry. Meanwhile, Zambia, directly opposite, seemed within swimming distance.

Closer inshore I could see the tops of hundreds of trees protruding above the water. Hadn't they been cleared when the dam was constructed?

Mr. Nyathi shook his head. No one had known where the lake would find its level. The result was that around its shores and beneath its surface, vast areas of forest were slowly rotting away.

I asked him how long they would take to disappear completely and was astounded when he replied that it would be several decades. In the interim, their presence created a navigational hazard since many boats had already been damaged and sunk. But the irritation they caused was not only physical, he added. They were a constant reminder to the people of the area of the homes they had lost, and that Lake Kariba was man-made and did not really belong there.

Chalala fishing camp looked quaint and picturesque from a distance. But up close, the term 'fishing camp' seemed something of a misnomer. Dave compared it to one of those frontier towns that featured in Western movies, a place that had sprung up overnight and attracted a flood of desperate people around it.

Unlike the gold, however, that had prompted the creation of such settlements in America and Canada, it was kapenta that was at the heart of this community. As we drove along the shore, we could see small, neat harbours with the sophisticated boats that Jacob had talked about the previous evening. There were rows of tidy offices too, and the warehouses and sheds where the fish were dried and packed for export. Fenced off behind high enclosures were the smart houses of the managers and supervisors who oversaw the entire operation.

It was the sprawling shanty town that stood out by contrast. It had spread itself out in all directions; up the sides of a hill, along the slopes of a ravine, with no obvious plan to inform its construction. This was where the majority of workers resided, in small, cramped huts made of tin and cardboard that looked as if they would blow away at the slightest gust of wind. The smell of rotting meat, fish and sewage forced us to close our windows, that and the thousands of flies that seemed to have taken over the community we drove through.

According to Mr. Nyathi, it was not only workers who comprised the inhabitants of the shanty town. A subsidiary industry of bars and brothels had also materialised to keep them entertained. I expressed my surprise that even at such an early hour several of the beer halls seemed full of patrons. 'That's because the fishermen go out at night. The only time they have to drink is during the day.'

Outside an establishment which called itself 'El Dorado Bar and Disco,' I suggested we go inside for some refreshments. I was also curious to see what was there, despite Mr. Nyathi's observation that it was nothing more than a place for people to get drunk. He was right. There was no pretence at decoration or atmosphere. Groups of men sat around their tables with empty bottles scattered around them, only stirring to signal someone at the bar to bring them more.

As we sat in our corner sipping our coca-colas I could see that there was a hard, determined quality to their drinking. There didn't seem to be much in the way of conversation passing among them either. Hardly an eyebrow had been raised when we entered and hardly an eyebrow was raised when we left. We had to step over the body of one young man near the doorway, who had simply sprawled out where he had fallen. None of his friends around a nearby table had bothered to remove him.

Chalala fishing camp, said Mr. Nyathi, was typical of others that had sprung up around the lake when the kapenta industry was established. They had been built entirely for profit, with no concern for the health or welfare of its residents who came from all parts of the country to work there.

'The problem is that no one wants to accept responsibility for the welfare of the people in what are called 'informal settlements.' The Government says it is up to the private companies that make all the money to invest in better conditions for their workers. The private companies say that it is not their problem and that the Government should step in, if it is so concerned.'

Meanwhile, the fishermen squandered their money on beer, women and gambling. According to Mr. Nyathi, they frequently failed to send anything back to the families they had left behind in the villages they came from. As he spoke, I was reminded of Sekuru's description of the compounds he had lived in when he was employed in the mines in South Africa. Mr. Nyathi agreed that what we had seen here was typical of what we would find in migrant worker communities throughout the region.

'Whether fishing for kapenta, mining for gold or picking cotton on large estates, you will see the same pattern repeat itself. Force people to live in these conditions and they will soon behave in the way they are treated. I don't blame them for getting drunk and trying to forget their lives. I blame the system that exploits them.'

At a clinic on the edge of the settlement, the last stop on our itinerary for the day, we found Sister Mutale. She was a large, imposing woman who glared at us from behind a pair of thick spectacles as if she were inspecting a couple of errant school boys.

'I'm too busy,' she replied, after we had been introduced by Mr. Nyathi and he had asked her to show us around. She only relented when he said that we worked for a charity and that our organisation might be able to help her.

'Don't get in my way then,' she said, as she rose to her feet. I worried that the patients would mind our tagging along, but as we trailed behind her I reckoned that even if they were unhappy with strangers coming to gawk at them, they would be too intimidated to say so.

'What is it that you need?' I asked, trying to be helpful.

She stopped for a moment to fix me with another penetrating stare. 'Several months ago someone came here and asked me a similar question. I'm still waiting for what he promised. I hope you're not here wasting my time, like he was.'

'Of course not,' I stammered. 'If we say we'll help, then we'll do so.'

'Good. Then write this down,' she said as we resumed our inspection.

They needed more staff. They needed more medicines and

equipment. They needed mosquito mesh for the windows. There weren't enough beds for the patients. The latrines were in poor condition and the pump that provided them with water needed repairs. Most of all they needed regular visits from the doctor across the lake. 'She's supposed to come here once a week. We're lucky if we see her once a month.'

'What's your most common medical problem?' I asked, trying to divert my attention from a gaping hole in the head of a young man sitting on a bench in front of us. As she instructed one of her nurses on how to stitch up the wound, she told us that he had been the victim of a machete attack in one of the beer halls.

'Fights are common. So are injuries at work. There's dysentery too from the poor water supply, but the things I'm most worried about are sexually transmitted diseases. Make sure you write that down,' she insisted, and in a voice that reverberated around the clinic she repeated the phrase for good measure.

'Most of the people you see here,' she continued, pointing towards the patients around us, 'came to my clinic last month with gonorrhea, syphilis and chlamydia. Most of them will be here next month with the same problem. Why?' she said with obvious exasperation. 'Because they don't use these.'

She pulled out of her pocket a condom that looked as if it had been pulled out on scores of other occasions. 'All they have to remember is to put one on before they have sex and they won't have to visit my clinic again.' The women giggled when Sister Mutale gave a display of how to fit a condom on to a wooden stick, another of the props she carried around with her. But the men looked sheepish and guilty, most of them looking away as she continued with the demonstration.

76

'We have one of the highest rates of sexually transmitted diseases in the province,' she concluded, 'and my boss continually tells me that I have to do something about it.'

Despite her brusque and off-hand manner it was clear that Sister Mutale ran an organised and efficient team. Four other nurses scurried around under her watchful eye. The clinic was spotless. Even the flies that had followed us that morning from the lake, didn't make it past the entrance. A large queue of patients stretched into the road, proof of what the community thought of the service she provided.

She warmed slightly when she discovered I came from Scotland. She had studied nursing in Glasgow for several years and remembered with affection the people she had met. When she told me that the nurse she had trained under was 'very scary,' I remarked that she must have been terrible to have intimidated someone like her.

'You should see me on one of my off days. You wouldn't want to be around me when that happens.'

'How did you end up in Nyaminyami?' I asked her, wondering how someone with her qualifications and training was now working in one of the remotest clinics in the country. I was sure that if she had wanted to, she could have had a more comfortable posting.

Again she was blunt, telling me that she hadn't become a nurse to have an easy life. For her it was a vocation. 'When my boss told me that they needed someone to run this place I said I was ready. That was a few years ago and I'm still here. I have no plans to leave any time soon.'

'Here's another patient I want you to see,' she said, as we continued our tour. The woman she showed us was lying on one of the few beds they had reserved for their more serious cases. Her leg was heavily bandaged. She was evidently in pain but insisted on sitting up when we approached.

According to Sister Mutale, the woman had been out

washing clothes on the edge of the lake a few days previously when she had been attacked by a crocodile. It had
managed to seize her and pull her into the water. It was only
when some other women heard her screams and threw
stones to scare it away that it had finally let go. But not
before it had taken a piece of her leg with it.

'I don't think we'll have to amputate,' Sister Mutale said,
as she inspected the wound, 'but she'll have a nasty scar for
the rest of her life. She's lucky to have survived. Once a
crocodile grabs hold of someone they usually hold on.'

Repeating the same observation I had heard throughout
my two days in the district, she confirmed that attacks by
wild animals accounted for a considerable number of the
patients they attended to. Such attacks ran a close second to
sexually transmitted diseases. 'Snake bites are the worst,'
she added. 'We have no medicine here and in any case it
would probably be too late by the time the patient arrives.
Some of the wounds I have seen are truly terrible. People
lose their arms and legs, and these are usually the lucky
ones.'

Sister Mutale was clearly not the kind of person you
wanted to fool around with and I was not about to offer
promises I could not keep. I mentioned that we had several
doctors in the country and were planning to send more. But
where they ended up was out of my hands. 'All I can do is
ask the Ministry to locate them in Kariba, but the final
decision is not mine. We also have a small fund to assist
projects. It isn't much but it will allow you to purchase some
medicines or repair some of the equipment you talked
about. That is the best I can offer.'

She seemed appreciative as we said our goodbyes, pointing out that whatever contribution we could make would be
welcome. But she had a final reminder too, in case I was
tempted to forget what I had committed to. 'I have your

name and address,' she said, pointing to the book we had had to fill in when we had first entered her clinic, 'and witnesses too. So don't think I won't come and find you if nothing materialises within the next couple of weeks.'

When we returned to the guest house later that afternoon there was someone sitting on the veranda. Over six feet tall, thin as a rake, with blonde hair and a beard, he was talking to Jacob and drinking a beer.

'Hello. I'm Soren from Sweden,' he said, shaking our hands. 'I'm your next door neighbor. Would you like a drink?'

It turned out that he was the other 'victim,' the one who had rolled his vehicle only a few miles from where we had wrecked our own. He had just returned from Harare after a few days recuperation. His organisation had provided him with another car and told him to return to Nyaminyami whenever he felt up to it. 'I got tired just sitting around, so decided to come back today.'

Nyaminyami had been home to Soren for the past year. Before that he had worked in a host of other countries in Africa. He had the grandiose title of 'community development specialist.' When Dave asked him what that meant he replied that he had the enviable task of driving around the district, spotting projects that he liked and throwing money at them to make them more profitable.

One of the things he had helped to set up was a programme to market local crafts. As we had seen from the carvings and basket ware on the side of the road, the Tonga were gifted artisans. But according to Soren they were poorly managed and organised, were at the mercy of middle men who ripped them off, and had little idea of how best to advertise their products. Soren had identified some outlets in Europe prepared to sell what they produced. Many families now received a higher income from carving walking sticks and wooden drums, than what they received from agriculture.

'Originally I wanted to set up some cooperatives,' he continued, 'similar to those I had established in Kenya. The profits from sales would be returned to the group and re-invested in more ambitious plans. But cooperatives here just don't work. Committee members would run off with the money. There were constant squabbles. People told me they preferred to work on their own. So individual families now get their money directly, and do with it as they please.'

'Why did it work in Kenya and not here?' I asked.

Soren believed that the social conditions necessary for a cooperative to succeed had disappeared when the Tonga had been evicted from their lands. Their communities were now divided and fragmented. Local traditions of solidarity and mutual help had been undermined. The chiefs, who were the guardians of many community practices, had been sidelined by a system of local Government that handed power to outside administrators and civil servants. 'In my view the Tonga can hardly be called a people any longer. Half of them live in Zambia. The other half here. Most of them dream of a life someplace else. To be honest, I don't know if they will ever regain their sense of identity and cohesion.'

'Don't you mind living here by yourself?' I asked, when Soren confirmed that apart from a French doctor who occasionally stayed in Siakobvu for a few weeks at a time, there was no other white person living in the town. Further down the road, at the fishing camps and safari operations near the lake, were other Europeans. But Soren said he could not abide their racial slurs against the local popula-tion, and their harping on about how wonderful things had been in the country before Africans took over.

'No, I like being here on my own,' he replied, pointing out that colleagues from his organisation who were living in Harare generally kept to a narrow circle of other expatriate acquaintances. 'They rarely mix with local people. But here I don't have a choice. I have to know my neighbors. Maybe because I'm on my own too, people are friendly.'

Soren's lifestyle intrigued me: his different postings to different countries with no fixed location he could really call home. He saw his family in Sweden once every few years, admitted that he had lost contact with most of his former friends and had no interest in 'settling down' any time soon. I remembered my friend Paul's warnings about my own nomadic future and wondered if he shared some of my occasional reservations. 'Don't you worry about what it will be like when you finally go home, to a place which is unfamiliar and where you mightn't fit in?'

He shrugged his shoulders. 'If you worry too much about the future, the present will slip away. I tried it once, going back home to work. I was offered a job in the head office of my organisation. But sitting behind a desk and filing reports didn't feel right for me. That's when I took this job and came back to Africa.'

When his supply of beer ran out, Soren suggested that we drive to Bumi Hills. There was an hotel there with a bar. 'But it's nothing like the beer hall you visited today. In fact you'll be shocked by the contrast it offers with the places you've seen so far in the district.'

What was meant to be a short drive took considerably longer. Half way there we got stuck behind a herd of elephants that showed no urgency in getting to wherever it was they were going. With an accident just behind him Soren wasn't interested in pressing his luck by trying to overtake them. 'We'll just have to wait.'

When the elephants abruptly disappeared into the forest,

leaving a trail of flattened grass and broken branches behind them, Soren switched off the engine. 'Listen,' he said. After a few minutes we could hear the sound of banging drums and the shouts of alarmed people. It went on for a considerable period of time. When the commotion finally died down Soren told us that either the elephants had been scared away, or the villagers had given up defending their crops. At this time of year, he added, these raids were a nightly occurrence.

Despite having seen the conflict between people and animals at first hand, Soren was convinced that their fraught relationship was avoidable. 'The fact is that if they were managed as a resource, as something that brought financial benefits to local communities, wildlife would be welcomed rather than resented as they are at present.'

A few months previously he had visited another district in the north of the country called Guruve. What he had seen there had turned him into a convert of CAMPFIRE, a programme that sought to harmonise the competing claims of people and animals on resources. The idea behind it was simple. Wild animals attracted curious tourists. Tourists paid money. Return some of that money to local people, and former poachers would be turned into gamekeepers.

'Zimbabwe earns a fortune each year from tourism. Visitors come to this country for two things: to see Victoria Falls and to see animals in the wild. But all of that money goes to the Government in taxes and to private safari operators and hotel owners in profits. Up till now the people who have lived in closest proximity to wildlife have suffered the most and benefited the least. That's why they turn to poaching. That's why they are angry. But change the nature of the relationship between people and animals and you have a solution.'

The programme had been running in Guruve for only a

short period of time, he added, but already results were impressive. From revenues that were diverted to the community a new school had been built, as had a clinic and an electric fence around their fields. The illegal killing of wild animals, that had been rife up till then, had dramatically declined. In a few cases poachers had even been reported to the police by the same villagers who had previously protected them.

Although some animal rights groups had raised objections, since part of the revenues came from safari operators who ran expensive hunting expeditions in the same area, Soren believed that such a programme offered the best possible option for those who wanted to see wildlife in Africa preserved and protected.

'There is considerable pressure among a population that is hungry for land to open up areas like Nyaminyami for farming, which of course would further reduce the territory available for wild animals. But if people received more of an income from having elephants and buffalo living beside them, than planting crops, this would mean that the land would be preserved as it is, rather than converted. For people who love wild animals I think this is the best deal possible'

As he had warned us, Bumi Hills hotel looked as if it had been manufactured elsewhere and transported thousands of miles to its spectacular location above the lake. Long before we actually arrived we had seen its blaze of lights in the distance, offering a stark contrast to the flickering fires that were the only source of illumination in the villages we passed. It was reputed to be one of the most exclusive destinations in southern Africa, with its own airstrip for important visitors. These had reputedly included a member of the British royal family and a former American president. I wondered whether our somewhat utilitarian clothes and untidy appearance would preclude us from entry, but Soren knew the guards who waved us through.

The bar where we ended up couldn't have been more different than the one in Chalala fishing camp that had shocked us that morning. Instead of a tinny radio there was someone in a corner playing a piano. Smartly dressed waiters fussed around the clients, continually asking if they could refill their glasses or bring them some snacks.

Soren told us that several months previously he had shared a beer with Clint Eastwood, who was making a film about an elephant hunter in Africa. 'I took his photo and sent it to some friends in Sweden. They were constantly teasing me that my circle of acquaintances in a remote African village must be pretty limited. I asked them if they had ever met any famous Hollywood actors in the bars in Stockholm. Since that time they haven't bothered to comment about my lifestyle again.'

On the walls of the hotel there were several old, grainy photographs that caught my attention. The pictures were of animals in boats and trucks being transported to different locations. The captions underneath them referred to something called 'Operation Noah.'

Soren explained that as the waters in the lake began to rise, shortly after Kariba was constructed, many animals became stranded on the islands that subsequently formed. The government had organised an ambitious programme to rescue them, aptly entitled Operation Noah. It had won considerable international acclaim and praise from various animal charities for the concern this displayed towards the nation's wildlife.

I remarked that there was no pictorial evidence, at least on these walls, of the Tonga being similarly rescued or transported to areas like the ones they had lost. Nor were there any photographs of their contemporary reality, such as the community at Chalala only a short distance away. 'I suppose that visitors to Bumi Hills, who pay a thousand dollars a night just to stay here, don't want their holiday disturbed by being reminded of such things.'

Part of the bar extended out on to a wooden platform built into the side of the hill. From there one could look down on a watering hole that was illuminated by flood-lights. Soren had heard that in order to ensure a spectacle every evening, food was discreetly scattered around the area to attract wild animals. Without having to set a foot outside the hotel, you could have breakfast, lunch and dinner in the presence of lions and hyenas a few yards below you.

As we sipped our expensive beers I found it difficult not to feel a mixture of amusement and irritation at the enthu-siastic guests who later turned up to watch the show. They seemed to have little sense that they were being duped. Perhaps it didn't matter. The hotel brochure that I had read offered its visitors 'an experience of wild Africa' but it assured them too that they would be pampered by polite staff, protected from bugs and insects, and provided with rooms that had hot baths and showers. Somewhat unkindly, I wondered what they would say when they returned home to their families and friends. I imagined that very little, if anything, would be said about the people who lived here, since the Africa that was being sold to them was a place where the locals were conveniently out of sight or only emerged to offer them coffee, cocktails and dinner.

Soren was more conciliatory than I, when I made a remark that if people wanted to see something really wild they should spend an evening at the beer hall in Chalala and watch the locals beating each other up or drinking them-selves stupid in quiet desperation. If rich people were willing to pay money to enjoy the illusion that was being presented to them in Bumi Hills, he said, that was fine by him.

'Every time I'm tempted to ridicule a group of rather spoilt, rich individuals who want to believe they are experiencing Africa in the raw, I remember that a fraction of what they are prepared to pay for such an illusion could provide electricity, schools, clinics and jobs for the people of the communities we drove through earlier. The only way that the people of Nyaminyami will ever emerge from the poverty that afflicts them is if tourism succeeds here and if they get a slice of that cake. That's why I can drink beer in this bar and chat with millionaires. I think of their potential contribution to this area's development.'

That perception was shared by the district administrator of Nyaminyami. A few days later we were sitting in his office, drinking tea and sharing our impressions. He was pleased that we were willing to assist the school we had visited by sending a teacher. When we mentioned our encounter with Sister Mutale and our decision to make a contribution to her clinic, he reminded us to keep our promise. 'She's not the kind of person you want to be enemies with.'

The administrator was as enthusiastic about CAMPFIRE as Soren, claiming that tourism held a real possibility of offering a solution to the conflicts we had witnessed if its revenues were distributed more equitably. The fact that the programme he had seen also encouraged communities to make decisions as to how wildlife revenues should be spent, was another positive feature in his eyes. 'If people are involved in decisions that affect them they won't just sit back and wait for handouts. The thing that impressed me most about Guruve, was the sense of responsibility I saw among the local population. We need that here, especially since people have become used to others telling them what to do.'

When I thanked him again for all the help he had given us,

he said that he hoped we would now become ambassadors for his district. We should remind our colleagues among the aid fraternity that Nyaminyami was one of the poorest areas of Zimbabwe and needed assistance. He had observed that aid often did not reach the people who needed it the most. 'Sometimes assistance is prioritised for parts of the country that are more accessible and convenient for field visits from Harare. I've said it to several representatives of organisations when I meet them at conferences and workshops on poverty eradication in this country. Whenever you feel that a location is too problematic and inconvenient to get to, remember the people you are missing out.'

As we rose to leave, he expressed regret about our accident and the disruption this had caused to our schedule. But echoing an observation I had already shared with Dave, he pointed out that if this had not happened, our time in Nyaminyami might not have been so instructive. 'When you phone your office in London you should mention that although you have returned to Harare without your vehicle, at least you have returned with a deeper insight into the place you visited.'

5

Trouble in Paradise

'Are you sure we should be travelling in this thing?' Dave said, when someone pointed to the bus that would take us back to Harare.

'What's wrong with it?' I asked, wondering if it was the bald tyres he was concerned about.

'It's the name,' he replied. 'It will bring us bad luck.' In bright blue letters on the back of the vehicle was a sign that read 'Tombs Buses.' Dave said that he expected to see a coffin painted somewhere on its side, but this was the only one on offer and we would have to take our chances.

'I've travelled on these buses for the last few years and never had an accident yet,' a fellow passenger replied when Dave asked him if he thought it was safe.

Some time later, when the driver decided he was unlikely to get any more customers, we were on our way. Within a few minutes we had managed to attract an audience. A young man, who was sitting on the seat in front of us, told us that white people generally didn't travel on public transport. That's why everyone was curious.

He seemed to have been appointed by the others to find out what he could about us. They wanted to know who we were, where we came from, where we were going and why we were travelling with them instead of in our own private vehicle.

'They've come from Nyaminyami,' he would shout to the people around us, before proceeding to the next question.

'They had an accident on the road and their vehicle is wrecked. The one on the right is a teacher in Hurungwe. The one on the left has only been in Zimbabwe for a few weeks. Yes, he's the one who crashed their car. He says he wasn't drinking either.'

The exchange was humorous and friendly and having provided the passengers with some entertainment we were plied with tea, coffee and sandwiches throughout the six hours it took us to complete our journey. 'This is much more interesting than travelling on our own,' I said to Dave, remembering how much of what I had learned about Sudan and its people had come from similar journeys on trains, buses and boats in that country.

Despite our interaction with the people around us, some of whom had given us their addresses so we could visit them in their rural areas, the closer we got to Harare the more troubled I became. There was still the small matter of a telephone call to my office in London, and despite the words of encouragement from the district administrator, I was unconvinced that my organisation would be sympathetic to the argument he had proposed.

'It's Chris here from Zimbabwe.'

'Hello. How are things out there?'

'I have some bad news, I'm afraid.'

'Oh! What's up?'

'You know the car we had, the old Land Rover. It was in an accident.'

'What happened?'

'I crashed into a tree.'

'A tree? Was another vehicle involved?'

'No, just the Land Rover. But the road was bad.'

'What condition is it in?'

'Not good. I don't think it can be repaired.'

'You mean we need a new car?'

'I think so.'

'Where do you think we'll get the money to buy one?'

'I'm not sure. Maybe the insurance will pay?'

'They'll cover the costs of some repairs, not the purchase of a new vehicle. Tell me, how long have you been in Zimbabwe?'

'Two weeks and two days.'

'You mean you've written off a vehicle only sixteen days after you started working for us? That's not good, is it?'

'No it isn't. But remember that the road was in a terrible state.'

It was a conversation like this one that played itself out in my head throughout our trip back, and although there were several variations they all ended up with the same result: termination, end of contract and a flight back to London.

At the office, Fortunate looked relieved to see us. 'Where have you been? I was worried sick about you.'

She was not the only one who had been concerned. Sekuru had pestered her every day once the deadline we had indicated for our return had expired. 'Something bad must have happened,' he would say to her whenever she told him to be more patient. Eventually they had agreed that if they had heard nothing from us by the end of that week they would contact the police to tell them we were missing.

'So where's our Land Rover?' Fortunate enquired, once she had greeted us. She had seen us get off the bus that had diverted from its destination at Mbare to deposit us in front of our office on the other side of town.

When I told her about our accident, adding that it was unlikely that our vehicle would ever be on the road again, she threw her hands in the air and uttered 'Hallelujah.' It was a blessing we had finally managed to get rid of it.

'I'm glad you're safe and I'm sorry you had an accident. But for years I've prayed for that vehicle to disappear. It doesn't present the right image. Now we can buy a proper vehicle and you can look more like the head of an aid agency.'

'Fortunate, you don't seem to realise the trouble I'm in. I've just arrived in the country and within a few weeks I've managed to write off the organisation's car. How will that look to the people who recruited me?'

There was only one way to find out and I was keen to get my telephone call over and done with as soon as possible.

'Were you hurt?' my boss enquired after I had given her a long, rambling explanation of what had happened.

'Well kind of,' I replied, talking up the injury to my head in the hope of gaining some sympathy that might mitigate her reaction.

'Well the most important thing is that you recover. Don't worry about the Land Rover. Gerlin complained about it for years and we should probably have got rid of it earlier.'

'You mean you're not upset?' I managed to splutter.

'Of course not. Accidents happen. We'll purchase a new vehicle in London and have it sent out as soon as possible. That will probably take a month or so. Can you make do with public transport until it arrives?'

No recriminations. No termination letter. Not even a formal warning. Public transport for a while didn't seem so bad either. Despite its convenience, a private vehicle limited my engagement with a host of people I could otherwise be interacting with. I remembered the advice of one author who claimed that the best way to explore another country was on foot. Public transport came second, while driving your own car and flying on an aeroplane could not be counted as meaningful travel at all.

Back home Sekuru Francis was relieved to see us again and keen to remind me that his warnings had been accurate. 'I told you not to go to Nyaminyami. That place is no good.

Why don't you send teachers to my home area? There are schools there that need your help too.'

He was less enthusiastic than Fortunate about the demise of our vehicle. It had served several country directors and he had become attached. Every day he had done his best to clean and polish it, and make it look presentable.

'So what will you drive now?' he asked.

'Nothing for a while,' I replied. 'I'll use public transport like everyone else.'

I could see that he looked shocked. 'But you're an important person. What will people say if they see you getting on a bus? What will they think of someone who doesn't have his own transport?' Although he didn't say so, I knew he felt his own status would be diminished too. What would his friends think if he worked for a boss who had no vehicle of his own to drive around in?

One month later I found myself on another bus, this time heading to Bulawayo, Zimbabwe's second city in the south of the country. 'Well at least it's not Nyaminyami,' Sekuru had said, still irked at my having to use public transport.

He insisted on accompanying me to Mbare early one morning to catch my lift. 'There are thieves just waiting to rob you,' he had said, when I told him that I was happy to go there on my own. As we made our way through a dense throng of people he held on to my bags as if they were stuffed with money, something I was convinced would attract more rather than less attention. He was only satisfied when he had personally placed them on the bus I would be travelling on.

'Make sure you deliver him safely,' he snapped at the driver, whom he had earlier accused of charging too much for the fare. Though I appreciated his concern, I was glad when he decided to go.

I had been keen to get out of the city again and visit the workers I was meant to supervise. My first meeting with them had not gone well and I remembered Gerlin's advice about the importance of establishing personal relationships. 'They are very different as individuals than when they come together as a group. That's why you need to get out and visit them where they live.'

The previous week all twenty-four of them had come to Harare for their semi-annual get together, and to interact with the new country director. On their own, they were friendly and polite, offered advice and information and enquired when I would come and see them. But all together in the same room, another dynamic developed that Gerlin's words of warning had not prepared me for.

'Aren't you a bit young for this job?' one of them said, after I had been asked to introduce myself and relate something of my past history.

'So what's Sudan got in common with Zimbabwe?' someone added, a question which I would have been hard pressed to answer.

'Why does the organisation appoint someone to manage us who has never worked here before? Some other people in this room applied for your job. They weren't even offered an interview.'

I was being scrutinised, tested and challenged to see how far I could be pushed. That's what had happened in every classroom I had taught in, an initial period of probing by the pupils to establish the limits of what they could get away with. Finding it here, among a group of adults who must have experienced the same thing in their own places of work at one time or another, surprised me. As I offered a series of defensive replies to the demands that were being thrown at me, I was struck by the contrast between the people I had interacted with earlier and this hostile group preoccupied with their grievances. Even Dave, whom I had counted as an ally, had become argumentative.

Gerlin had tried to explain something of all this beforehand. 'People have different ideas when they go to work in other countries. But if you don't leave your preconceptions behind you will end up being disappointed and unable to appreciate what another culture can actually offer.'

As the group continued to focus on everyone's failings – the Government's, donors', headmasters', decision makers' within our organisation and my own, I could see what she had been alluding to. Maybe Zimbabwe had not lived up to its promises at independence. No doubt our workers could claim with some justification that economic, racial and gender inequality still prevailed. But some of them seemed to have taken these failures as a kind of personal affront, as if they had every right to feel indignant that the country had not lived up to whatever expectations they had brought with them when they had come.

By the time they all departed I wondered whether I would be able to get through three years of these kinds of meetings. When my interviewer in London had asked me several months previously if I was mentally tough, I had thought of the difficult journeys I had endured in Sudan, the frustrations I had dealt with as a teacher, living without electricity or running water, the bouts of illness I had experienced. I had never imagined having to cope with difficult and querulous colleagues, and was not sure if I had the patience to handle them.

But Fortunate, who had been present throughout, was more philosophical. 'You need to remember that these occasions are the only opportunity for our workers to let off steam. Who else can they complain to? Don't take it personally. The sooner you get to know them individually, and the work they do, the better it will be. Why not start with a trip to Bulawayo. We have a wonderful doctor there whom you should visit.'

Gweru was at the half-way point of the ten-hour journey. Up till then we had driven through a landscape that seemed much like the one I was familiar with from my previous trip north. But beyond the town, the environment changed. It looked drier and dustier, and instead of irrigated fields there were stretches of land where there were no signs of cultivation at all. The spaces between the towns grew noticeably longer too and the people and homesteads we passed seemed poorer.

'It's not just drought that has affected us,' the passenger beside me replied when I remarked on the change and enquired about the lack of rains that had afflicted the south of the country. Freddie was from Matabeleland South, the province where we were headed. He was a teacher in a small town about a hundred kilometers from Bulawayo and just as I had experienced on other bus journeys, was more than willing to engage in conversation.

The two southern provinces of Zimbabwe, Matabeleland North and South, were predominantly populated by the Ndebele who comprised about 20 per cent of the total population of around 10 million. Freddie had told me he was Ndebele too and that most of the people travelling on the bus were from his part of the country. Unlike in Sudan, however, where facial features, tribal markings, stature and build, clothes and skin color distinguished one ethnic group from another, I could see nothing that differentiated him from the people I had so far encountered.

'Maybe you haven't heard our language,' he replied and uttered a series of clicks from the back of his throat that had nothing familiar with the Shona I was becoming accustomed to.

According to Freddie, his language was related to what was spoken in parts of South Africa, unlike Shona which was a Bantu language from further north in the continent. I remembered from what I had read that the Ndebele had pushed into Zimbabwe in the 19th century in a series of migrations prompted by internal conflicts in their own territory. They had finally settled around their new capital at Bulawayo, named after the chief who had founded it.

I was aware too that relations between the two groups had not been cordial, something that Freddie confirmed. There had been regular conflicts and because of their substantial military background, it seemed that the Ndebele generally came out on top. They expanded their territory and made forays into Mashonaland to seize cattle and women. It was only when their power was broken by an invasion of white settlers into southern Zimbabwe in the late 1800s that this chapter in the country's history came to an end.

I had been wary for some time of generalisations about African tribal conflicts, knowing that this had been used for many years by colonial apologists as a justification to intervene in the continent's affairs. I was aware too that the concept of a fixed ethnic identity based on a common ancestry or clan was not an accurate one and that many people migrated between tribal boundaries through marriage, political convenience or economic self-interest when it suited them. But while Freddie acknowledged that 'the boundaries between our two peoples were never rigid' he firmly asserted that the Shona were taking revenge for past humiliations.

'That is why the southern part of our country is so deprived today,' he said. 'Lack of rains may have contributed too but it is economic and political neglect that explains these impoverished looking villages we are passing through.'

As we were talking, the bus came to an abrupt halt a few kilometers outside a town we had recently stopped at. I thought we might have burst a tire or that the engine had seized up but Freddie pointed out of the window and said that it was neither of these. I could see some soldiers on the side of the road in front of a barrier that had been lowered to block our passage.

From the appearance and demeanor of the men that entered a moment later, I guessed we were in for a difficult time. Cold, unsmiling and with their guns openly displayed in front of them they had no need to demand the documents that were hurriedly thrust towards them.

One old man, who was too slow as he fumbled around, was told to hurry up and stop wasting their time. Another individual, whose papers were apparently not in order, was told to take his luggage and get off the bus. He was ushered on to the side of the road and from where I was sitting I could see another soldier poking through his bag with his gun, scattering his belongings carelessly on the ground.

They seemed uninterested in the passport I offered for their inspection. 'It's not you we are looking for.'

One of the soldiers interrogated Freddie on the seat beside me. Where was he from? Where was he going? What business did he have in Bulawayo? What was he carrying in his bags? It wasn't so much the content of the questions but the way in which they were delivered that revealed their true intent. As I has witnessed in Sudan and other places when I had the misfortune to encounter belligerent soldiers it was all about asserting authority, about reminding everyone who was in charge.

Half an hour later the door was shut and the bus allowed to proceed. The person who had been thrown off was still on the side of the road, remonstrating with the soldiers who were still questioning him. All around me I could hear a collective sigh of relief. 'There might be more of these between here and Bulawayo,' Freddie warned, 'so don't get too comfortable.'

I knew something about the tensions between the north and south of the country and the political problems that had beset post-independence Zimbabwe. But as Freddie proceeded to describe the history, background and scale of what was happening in his province it was clear to me that the gravity of the situation had barely been reflected in the material I had read.

Matabeleland, he said, had been under a state of siege for some time. 'It was worse several years ago but the road blocks and police raids have continued just to remind us that we are still under suspicion.'

The current conflict had ostensibly arisen because of a falling out of the two political parties that had brought the country to independence in 1980. But Freddie believed that the real reasons were more historical and deep rooted in nature. 'This is a continuation of the tensions and antagonism between the two parts of our country that has been there for much of our history.'

ZANU (PF), the Zimbabwe African National Union, was now the party in power after winning a clear majority in the 1980 elections. Under its leader, Robert Mugabe, it drew its support from the north and centre of the country where most of the population lived. Although it had some Ndebele members it was a party dominated by the Shona. By contrast ZAPU, the Zimbabwe African People's Union, headed by Joshua Nkomo attracted most of its support from the southern Matabeleland provinces.

Both movements had fought the war from different bases in Mozambique and Zambia. According to Freddie an interest in seeing a common enemy defeated had led to an uneasy but nevertheless working relationship between them. But a year or so after the end of the conflict, tensions had resurfaced. The two leaders had fallen out and dragged their respective parties with them.

ZANU claimed that Nkomo wanted to take over the country and that he was prepared to do anything to realise that ambition. Supplies of arms and ammunition were 'discovered' in several farms owned by prominent ZAPU politicians and leaders. This was proof, the government said, that the opposition was prepared to go to war again to seize power. Freddie was convinced that this was a smoke-screen, an excuse for Mugabe to eliminate his principal political rival. Fearful of losing his life Nkomo had fled, escaping across the border into neighboring Botswana and then on to exile in London.

The arrest, prosecution and imprisonment of the same politicians who had been accused of plotting a coup prompted some of ZAPU's former soldiers to take up arms. Returning to rural Matabeleland they engaged in several high profile attacks, with the aim of drawing attention to the plight of their leaders who were languishing in prison or in exile. 'It is true,' Freddie added, 'that several of the so-called 'dissidents' involved a criminal element. These were individuals who saw an opportunity to profit from the situation for their own personal gain.'

Things came to a head in 1984 when six foreign tourists were abducted when visiting the world famous Victoria Falls in the south of the country. There was a huge, international outcry when they were killed and a major decline in the numbers of tourists visiting Zimbabwe.

The Government response, when it materialised, was disproportionate to the scale of the problem. According to Freddie the entire population was held responsible for what had happened. A special army unit, trained by soldiers from North Korea, was deployed to the territory. 'The idea was to frighten us to such an extent that we would reveal the whereabouts of the dissidents, even when most of us had no idea who or where they were.'

Freddie himself had been arrested on several occasions. 'Why? Simply because I was a young man who looked as if I could carry a gun.' He said that he had been beaten as part of his interrogation. He had seen other people being tortured and killed. His cousin 'disappeared' after he had been arrested. Even now, several years later, the military who had taken him refused to reveal his whereabouts to the family. They were convinced he was dead.

Because of the secrecy that had prevailed during this period and the restrictions placed on journalists wishing to report on what was happening it was difficult to estimate the exact number of people who had been killed. I was shocked when Freddie told me that it was in the thousands rather than in the hundreds. 'That is the opinion of everyone else in the province. Most of us lost family members or relatives.'

'But wouldn't these kinds of numbers be reported in the international media?' I asked, remembering some reports I had read at the time. There had been nothing of the international outcry I would have expected in response to the scale of the problem that Freddie was describing.

'At that time Mugabe was very popular in your part of the world. The commercial farmers were happy. Foreign companies were investing in the country. No one wanted to upset him by calling for an independent investigation into what was happening in Matabeleland.'

As we reached the outskirts of Bulawayo, Freddie offered another explanation. It was one I had heard before. In Chad, where I had stumbled across a local war, I had asked some aid workers why the scale and nature of the crisis they were responding to had attracted such little international attention. 'Because African lives are cheaper than everyone else's,' one of them had said.

Freddie echoed a similar sentiment in a voice that carried no bitterness or recrimination. It was as if he we making an observation about the weather. 'When these tourists were killed by the dissidents it was in all the newspapers. We heard it repeated over and over on the BBC. But when our own people were killed in large numbers it didn't seem to attract the same attention. That's how it is here in Africa. Don't you know that by now?'

Mary was in her late twenties but looked older behind her tied back hair and severe spectacles. The hospital where she worked was not far from where I had disembarked from the bus. The grounds were neat and tidy. The buildings looked as if they had just been painted. The nurses in blue uniform seemed smart and professional too. 'She'll be in the staff room,' one of them had said, when I had asked her where I might find her.

The hospital administrator, whom protocol demanded I visit as soon as I arrived, told me what a wonderful asset Mary had been to their establishment. 'She works hard. The patients like her. She treats the nurses and orderlies with respect, something you don't often find among other medical professionals in our country. It's not just her attitude I appreciate but the example she sets to our junior doctors. I hope she stays a few more years with us.'

'I've no plans to leave any time soon,' Mary replied, after we had exited the administrator's office and I had asked her about her plans. Echoing much of what Dave had told me when we had first met, she said that she enjoyed the work, appreciated the challenges and valued the fact that her contribution seemed to be so highly regarded.

'My professional colleagues back home tried to dissuade

me when I first told them I was coming to Zimbabwe. They said that it would not be good for my career. My boss claimed that if I wanted to get ahead in my profession, then working in Africa would be a waste of time. But here I've been tested in a way I was never used to, and been given a level of responsibility I would never have had back in England. Quite simply, I enjoy being here. Why would I want to leave?'

'So why did you decide to come in the first place?' I asked, expecting to hear a story of some long standing commitment to Zimbabwe or a burning desire to make a contribution to health care in a developing country. With the accolades I had heard about her from Gerlin, Fortunate and now the hospital administrator, I presumed her motives would have been like her work: exemplary and laudable.

She laughed and looked a little embarrassed. 'You won't believe this, but I was running away. Zimbabwe was the first country that came up. It could have been Thailand, Peru or even Fiji.'

Mary had been active in student politics and had become involved in a campaign to free political prisoners in repressive countries: writing letters to their governments, demonstrating outside embassies and the foreign office, raising funds for the families of victims. 'We were particularly focused on Turkey. I think it was because we had some Turkish students in our class and they raised a fuss about the repression that was happening there.'

She giggled again, amused at some recollection of that period in her life. 'I suppose I was naïve and gullible. Many of us were. We had come straight from school to college and had no experience against which we could balance our emotions. Someone convinced me to marry a political detainee, whom I had never met before. That way he could get a visa to leave the country, come to the UK and escape persecution. The understanding was that at the end of a few months he would get his papers, we would get divorced and everyone would be happy.'

I expected her to tell me that they had fallen in love, that they had had a romance, that a relationship that transformed her life had ended abruptly because her 'husband' had returned to pursue his political commitments. Instead she told me that the person she had rescued from persecution had turned out to be less than honorable.

'Even though he got his residence papers he only agreed to a divorce on condition that I give him half of what I had. My lawyer told me that I would have to cut a deal. The marriage was valid. I hadn't agreed to it under duress or threat. In the end that's what I did. But I needed to get away, to have a new start somewhere else. That's when I saw an advert for doctors in Zimbabwe and that's how I found myself here.'

'But you didn't come to Bulawayo to hear my personal history,' she said, shortly after concluding her story. 'You came to see what I do. So let's go and visit some patients.'

I didn't like hospitals. The smell of disinfectant, the officious staff, the rows of beds with people in them looking miserable, the rows of seats beside them with relatives pretending to be jovial, always made me want to leave. I could remember my visit to a public hospital in Khartoum to have a test for dysentery. I had ended up in a waiting room that also functioned as an emergency ward. Some patients were lying on the floor in blood-soaked bandages, calling for attention from nurses who showed no interest in providing any treatment. Pursued by their groans and screams I exited after ten minutes, vowing never to enter a public hospital in Africa again unless I absolutely had to.

So when Mary announced that it was time for me to

accompany her on her ward rounds, I was less than enthusiastic. I knew she was doing an excellent job. Everyone
had said so. There was no need for me to verify this for
myself. 'Won't the patients mind me hanging around?' I
asked, looking for an excuse to head back to the staff room
where we could meet again later.

'Not at all,' she replied. 'They actually like it. They
appreciate the attention.'

I managed to lose some of my squeamishness because of
her calm and reassuring manner. 'Come and see this,' she
would say to me as if I were a fellow professional, pointing
to some evidence of a disease or condition I had never heard
of. Initially I held back, hiding behind the nurses who were
also accompanying us, but after a while I even ventured a
few questions.

While the patients she attended clearly appreciated the
time she took to greet them, they seemed disinterested in
hearing about what was actually wrong with them. Sometimes they would change the subject. One old man patted
her hand and said he didn't need to know anything more.
'Just get me better. That's what you're here for.'

When I asked her why this disinterest in hearing the
details of her diagnosis, she said that it wasn't so different
back home a few years ago. 'My mum was the same. I used
to ask her what the doctor had said to her during a
consultation. 'No idea' she would reply, swallowing the
tablets he had prescribed. 'The doctor knows what is best
for me, so why should I bother to ask him for an explanation?'

Throughout the wards that we had visited most patients
had family and friends around them. Some mothers had
even camped out on mattresses beside the beds where their
children lay. Mary told me that many of them came from
distant communities and had no place in Bulawayo to stay.

104

So the hospital took a lenient position and allowed them to remain with their children. 'It's better for the kids too to have their families close to them. Some of the doctors don't like it and the nurses say it makes the place untidy. But in the end we're here to make people better, not to run a smart hotel.'

Around the bed of one girl I noticed that no visitors were present. While none of the children in the ward looked happy, I was particularly struck by her sad and haunted face. She showed no interest when we approached, nor any reaction when one of the nurses began to remove the bandages around her arms and legs. Mary told me that she had been badly burned and was lucky to be alive.

'So why no family? Why is no one here when everyone else has visitors?'

For the first time that morning I thought I saw a break in Mary's professional demeanor, as if this was a case that had particularly affected her. The girl's story had been difficult to piece together, she said. When her mother had brought her into the hospital a few days previously she seemed reluctant to say what had happened, how her daughter had been so badly burned. It turned out that the girl was epileptic, had had a fit and fallen into a fire.

'Something was not quite right. Other children fall into fires, scream and their parents pull them out as quickly as possible. Sure they might get burned, but not as badly as this. It was one of the nurses who told me that epilepsy is regarded as a form of spirit possession within many communities. There is a fear that it is contagious too, that if you touch someone while they are having an attack then you run the risk of being possessed yourself. Maybe that explains why the girl was so badly burned and why, apart from a grandmother who occasionally comes to visit her, the rest of the family keep away.'

Mary said that she was constantly 'bumping against' traditional beliefs and practices. The ward we were in had a fair number of disabled children. 'The real problem is not their physical impairment. It's the attitudes shown by the family. When a child is born with a disability this is sometimes interpreted as a punishment, for something bad the parents may have done in the past. Then the child is hidden away because of the shame attached to their condition.'

I knew from my time in Sudan that local culture and tradition played a major role in the way in which sickness and health were regarded. Mary said that this was much the same in Zimbabwe too, and referred to a recent study by an eminent anthropologist which had shown that most people in the country continued to consult traditional healers.

'What confused me was that while consulting a *nanga* they will also visit doctors like me for more modern treatment. Why should someone visit both? A friend tried to explain it to me. When someone gets sick they have to do two things. Firstly they come to a hospital or clinic to get antibiotics or some other treatment. Secondly they have to go to a traditional healer so that he can tell them why this has happened to them, in particular what they have done or who they have offended to cause them to become sick in the first place. Unless they address that issue, the medicine won't work effectively.'

Mary was convinced that it made no sense to dismiss such beliefs out of hand. 'We can't just pretend that culture and tradition don't exist or wish them away by calling them primitive. We need to interact with traditional systems of health care so that both types of treatment complement each other rather than conflict.'

She had recently been invited by ZINATHA, a national association of traditional healers, to a workshop to promote better hygiene in the practices employed by its members when dealing with their patients. 'They use small knives to make incisions into the skin as part of their treatment. Sometimes these knives are not clean and wounds get infected. I thought it was a good idea to improve on what they are already doing and I was impressed by the fact that the people I interacted with seemed interested in what I had to tell them.'

That willingness to engage with practitioners from another health system was not shared by many of her colleagues in the hospital. They had criticised her for accepting the invitation, claiming that by doing so she had endorsed a form of practice that at best had no scientific justification and at worst actually caused harm. 'But I reminded them that traditional medicine has existed for centuries and that it would never have attracted so many patients if it had nothing to offer. If traditional healers were so open to hearing about what our system had to teach them, I found it unfortunate that my colleagues did not display the same openness. I told them how narrow minded I thought that was.'

The last patient we saw was a young man in his midtwenties who joked with Mary while she inspected his chart. I could see that he was seriously ill. Beneath the sheet that covered him was a thin skeleton and as we spoke he would regularly be seized by fits of coughing that left him gasping for breath. Blood tests a few weeks previously had revealed that he was in the last stages of AIDS. Mary told me later that she doubted whether he would last another week.

I had heard about HIV in Africa and in particular how it had ravaged communities in Uganda and Kenya. But the official word out of Zimbabwe was that there were only a few cases. A recent interview in the national newspaper with the Minister of Health reported that the country had managed to avoid the epidemic. 'Zimbabwe has nothing to worry about,' the Minister was quoted as saying.

Mary criticised the 'irresponsibility' of such statements. She was now seeing several AIDS patients a week and the numbers were increasing. 'In a few years' time I predict that most of the young patients who come to this hospital will be suffering from HIV related illnesses.'

'So why did the Minister say that there was no problem?'

Mary had discussed this with her colleagues and there were different theories. 'One person said it was because of personal denial. Politicians have numerous affairs and probably don't want to acknowledge that they are at high risk of contracting a sexually transmitted disease that has no known cure. Better to pretend that it doesn't exist.'

Someone else had claimed that it was out of economic expediency, that the government was ignoring or downplaying the figures for fear of suffering the same problems that had beset Kenya when it had disclosed its AIDS statistics. 'After a series of high profile articles and television reports on what was happening in that country the tourist numbers plummeted. Many visitors were worried that they would get infected by shaking hands with someone, or even being in the same room together. There is some speculation that the Government is worried about a similar loss in revenues, hence the pretence that there is no problem.'

Whatever the reason, Mary believed that any delay in admitting the presence of the disease, and alerting people on how to avoid it, would turn out to be a terrible mistake. Public information campaigns to promote condom use, open discussion by politicians and other influential people could save the lives of tens of thousands of people. But it had to be done as soon as possible.

'That's what Uganda has shown us. Unless we tackle the epidemic when it starts we will lose this battle. Some of us are worried that it is already too late, that the younger generation will look back on this period and say that we were guilty of negligence.'

6

The Bones of our Grandfathers

Several months and numerous bus journeys later, Fortunate received a call informing us that our new vehicle had finally arrived. We were to proceed to a warehouse in the centre of town to sign some papers and collect it. She clapped her hands when she saw the four-wheel drive Toyota Land Cruiser. Like Sekuru's friends, her colleagues in some of the other aid agencies had remarked that a boss who didn't have a decent car was hardly a boss worth working for at all.

At home Sekuru fussed around the vehicle, wiping it with his handkerchief and chasing away his dog who wanted to mark our new property. He was particularly impressed with the winch on the front to pull it out of mud or water if ever we got stuck. 'Now we can really show off,' he said. By the time it got dark he was still fidgeting with the different gadgets and I had trouble persuading him to postpone his inspection till the following morning.

When I woke up, he had already washed and polished it to a magnificent shine. Some of his friends were there too, walking around and nodding their heads in reluctant admiration. He had been teased for several months about my lack of transport. Now it was payback time.

'I'm coming with you,' Sekuru announced when I told him that I had to travel to the eastern part of the country later that week.

'But you've just been home,' I replied, reminding him that he had recently taken time off to visit his family.

'But something urgent has turned up again,' he responded. 'Now that you're travelling in my direction you can take me to my village.'

I didn't comment that he had never volunteered to accompany me before on my journeys around the country on public transport. In truth, I was glad to have him with me. The idea of driving on my own in a large, air-conditioned vehicle struck me as extravagant. Although I realised that Sekuru's principal motive for returning home was to arrive in his community in grand style, I also knew he would be able to tell me a great deal about the part of the country where I was headed.

Manica was Zimbabwe's most easterly province and had a border that ran for a thousand kilometers with neighboring Mozambique. The reason I was heading there was to visit some of the camps that had been set up to accommodate over a million refugees who had fled the fighting in that country. The Ministry of Health was tasked with providing services to the displaced population and had approached us to see if we could send them some physiotherapists and doctors.

Sekuru had never tired of telling me that his province was the most beautiful in the country and his people the most hospitable. When he had described mountains too, I thought he was exaggerating. In other parts of Africa I had heard about mountains that subsequently turned out to be little more than hills, but an hour or so outside Harare on the road heading east, I had to acknowledge that my skepticism had been misplaced.

In the distance along the horizon a row of peaks protruded from the ground like a set of perfect teeth. The tops of some were wreathed in cloud and mist just like the ones back home. 'Do you know that this part of the country was referred to by some of the whites who lived there as Little England?' Sekuru said, when I apologised for not having believed him.

At a place called Rusape the road began to climb steeply upwards towards Nyanga, our destination. The hilly terrain looked very different from the flat grasslands we had previously passed through but there was something familiar in the names of the private estates along our route. Although the maize, wheat and tobacco had been replaced by orchards of peaches, apricots, apples and tea it was still private property with signs to warn trespassers to keep out. Once again, I was struck by how much the road system in the country served the interests of large scale commercial agriculture.

Sekuru was reluctantly drawn on the topic of land distribution, probably because it still rankled and he did not want to show his irritation. But I told him I was keen to know more about the history of his people. If that meant telling me about injustices committed by my own then I was willing to hear what he had to say.

Almost an hour beyond Rusape he pointed to some nearby hills and a valley that ran between them. He said that this was the area where his family had once lived until they were forced to move to another part of the district allocated to Africans. Sekuru was unsure about the exact date but recalled that it was between 'the Great Wars' in Europe, sometime in the 1920s.

Although he was a boy at the time he could still remember the disruption and upheaval that had been caused. Entire communities had been evicted from these and other locations which had been designated for commercial agriculture. Simply put, Africans who had lived there for centuries had been removed to make way for European farmers, who then rehired some of the displaced population to work on the land they had just seized. 'The Government made us pay taxes so we had to earn money. The only way we could do so was either working on farms or emigrating to the mines in South Africa. Although the wages were poor there was no alternative. Our people were so desperate they were ready to do anything.'

One thing that surprised them, Sekuru continued, was the appetite of their new masters for land. 'They never seemed to have enough.' Some of the estates covered miles and miles of territory, parts of which were never even used. It was as if the act of possession was an end in itself.

'Didn't your chiefs own land too? I read somewhere that some of them owned large areas of the country and sometimes fought wars to acquire more.'

Apparently land wasn't owned by their leaders in the same way it was owned by the newcomers. As he described the role of chiefs within their communities, they sounded more like custodians than proprietors, allocating territory to members of their clan according to a set of customary regulations. According to Sekuru, the idea that a common resource could belong in any real sense to a single individual, who could then exclude others, was a foreign concept within Shona society. 'Our chiefs can give us land to cultivate but it is not theirs, or ours, to own or to sell. If land belongs to everyone then no one person can say it is theirs.'

I had read about communal resources and the criticism that lack of a title to land lead to abuse, since no one had a personal stake in ensuring that it was managed sustainably. Life in such societies, it was claimed, amounted to a free-for-all in which everyone competed to extract the maximum possible benefit. Something which belonged to everyone, so the theory went, belonged

113

to no one and quickly became exhausted through overuse.

But Sekuru dismissed this perception and said it was based on ignorance and lack of understanding on how their societies had functioned. For example, there were regulations on how many cattle were allowed in order to avoid excessive grazing on common grassland. There were prohibitions on the number of trees that could be cut, in order to prevent environmental damage. People adhered to these conventions because they perceived them as being in everyone's interest. 'Unlike the people who came,' Sekuru claimed, 'we never had any problems in sharing.'

'There is something else that the outsiders did not understand,' he continued. 'To us, land belongs not only to those who are living now. It also belongs to our ancestors, and they get very angry if they think we are neglecting them.'

'But how can people who have passed away be angry?' I asked, hoping that Sekuru would not take my question as a mark of disrespect. I had had conversations about traditional religious beliefs before and knew it was a sensitive topic, but he seemed happy enough to continue.

'A place where someone is buried is sacred ground. Unless it is properly looked after, the spirit of the dead person will come back to haunt us.' According to Sekuru, such things as illness, disease, lack of success in business, inability to have children and so on were all signs that an ancestor had been offended. Repeating what Jacob had said about our accident in Nyaminyami, Sekuru claimed that there was no such thing as bad luck. Every event and circumstance had a reason behind it.

This was something that Europeans had failed to appreciate, or deliberately ignored, when evicting Africans from the places where they had lived for generations. And once removed, they could not tend the graves of their fathers. 'I remember my uncle telling me that when he said this to the man who had come to evict them, he replied that our family should dig up the bones of our grandfathers and take them with us.'

A short while later, Sekuru pointed to a sign which announced our arrival in the communal lands where his family resided. There was no need for a sign at all. Just as when we had entered Hurungwe when travelling north from Harare a few months ago, the landscape changed to something different in an instant. It was stonier, drier and clearly less fertile. The huts of the local people became more frequent too and compared to the wide open spaces that we had just passed through, I could recognise what Sekuru had meant when he had earlier described his homeland as 'overcrowded.'

Off the main road and on a dirt track that Sekuru instructed me to follow, I crunched the gears before managing to engage the four-wheel drive. Winding down his window, Sekuru proceeded to wave at everyone, chuckling at every surprised stare as if calculating the kudos he was accumulating. 'Slow down. Slow down,' he shouted at regular intervals as we approached someone he knew, and I had to constantly sound my horn to announce our progress. By the time we reached the bottle store where we were headed, we had attracted a considerable crowd of curious spectators.

There was a loud cheer when Sekuru emerged from the vehicle. Even the local headman insisted that he shake our hands to welcome us to his village. Sekuru whispered that in the past he had rarely bothered to offer him the time of day. After the history lesson I had just received, I was surprised at my reception too. Shouldn't I have encountered coldness and hostility rather than this press of people welcoming me into their community?

Sekuru's home was a further fifteen minute walk from where we had to leave the vehicle. The crowd that had gathered followed us there. Whether because of their numbers or because it was customary practice to show reserve, the greeting between Sekuru and his wife seemed very formal; they shook hands like business acquaintances. Sekuru signaled to me to come forward and greet her. When she dropped to the ground on her knees in front of me, touched her head to the ground and clapped her hands, I was confused as to what to do.

'If you're unsure just imitate the other person,' Sekuru had once advised when I had told him that I found it difficult to remember all the greetings he had shown me. So I got down on my knees, lay down on the ground and imitated the gesture. Judging by the eruption of laughter around us, his wife's amused giggles and Sekuru's frown, I had committed a major blunder.

'There are many things I still have to teach you,' Sekuru said, as he helped me to my feet. 'This is not how a man greets a woman in our culture.'

His homestead covered a considerable area and included a vegetable garden, a wooden enclosure for his cows and goats, a container built off the ground to store his grain and a well that had been dug to one side of his property. There was a hut for the men of the family, another one for the women and children and a kitchen that exuded a steady plume of smoke through the thatch that covered the roof.

The hut for visitors was the grandest part of his establishment. Made of bricks and with a zinc roof, it was clearly a source of considerable pride. This was what he spent his wages on, Sekuru told me, pointing to a sofa and matching chairs, a television that didn't work because there was no electricity, and a sideboard that displayed the family memorabilia. There were photographs of a younger Sekuru when he had worked in South Africa, as well as cutouts of his favorite boxers.

As word of our arrival spread, a procession of Sekuru's relatives and extended family turned up to say hello. Again I was struck by the somewhat ceremonial quality to their greetings, and the importance that seemed to be attached to getting the protocols just right. There was a pecking order too and one that was not just determined by age, as I had first thought. A young man who couldn't have been more than twenty turned out to be Sekuru's 'uncle' and with one or two others, including myself as the honorary guest, was given a chair to sit on while the others squatted on mats on the ground.

It had been my intention to travel onwards to Nyanga later that day, but Sekuru informed me that it would be bad manners to refuse the family invitation to stay overnight. If I departed early the next morning there would be time enough to meet the Ministry official who would take me on to the camp I was scheduled to visit. 'We have already slaughtered a goat in honour of your coming. You can't think of leaving now.'

With part of the afternoon still ahead of us, I was curious to explore the village and its surroundings. But Sekuru had pressing family matters to attend to and when several crates of beer arrived from the bottle store, I knew he would not be available any time soon. 'Take Joseph,' he said, pointing to one of his nephews who had earlier introduced himself. 'He knows everything there is to know about the district and he wants to practice his English too.'

In his late twenties, Joseph had little need to practice his excellent English, which he had learnt at school and college and continued to improve through listening to the BBC World Service every evening. As we walked along one of the many tracks that criss-crossed the community, he told me that he worked for Agritex, an extension service set up by the Government to provide peasant farmers with technical advice and support. Most communal areas of the country now had this service and whenever possible the Government preferred to have advisers working in the same communities they originally came from.

'So what advice can you give to farmers who have lived here for generations? Surely you have as much to learn as to teach?'

'You're right,' he replied. 'If we go into communities thinking we are the experts who know everything, people will ignore us. I experienced this reaction initially. Some farmers said I was too young to advise them on anything. They asked me how many cattle I had, how much tobacco or cotton I had produced and how many children I had fathered. When I told them that as yet I had no cattle, tobacco or children they laughed and said that I should come back in twenty years after I had proved myself.'

But all farmers could benefit from advice and support if sensitively and appropriately offered. Commercial agriculture, Joseph went on to say, had become the driving force in the economy through the provision of a huge array of services and inputs. These inputs had largely been unavailable in communal areas until recently.

The Government had wanted to see that imbalance reversed. Now they provided peasant farmers with better seed varieties, organised vaccination campaigns for their cattle and constructed marketing outlets closer to where production took place. 'In the past, our farmers had to transport their produce many miles to the nearest grain marketing board to sell what they had. That was one reason why they hardly made any profit.'

I was surprised to hear that most of the maize in the country now came from communal areas as did an increasing percentage of cotton and tobacco. 'African farmers were previously seen as backward and ignorant, unable to contribute much to the economy. This was one of the arguments traditionally used to justify state support for commercial agriculture. But the last few years have shown that with the right type of assistance, we can be just as productive too.'

Joseph was keen to point out that there were limits to what farmers could achieve in areas like the one we were in. Poor soils, unreliable rains and overcrowding created real constraints to progress. In particular, he was worried about the over-exploitation of land and the damage and erosion that in time would threaten the very resource on which people depended.

'For example, there are too many cattle in this district. But it is difficult to tell farmers who hold their wealth in their herds that they should cut back on their numbers. Cattle have a special place in our society. They provide the basis of many of our transactions. When we get married, it is cattle that we exchange. When someone dies, it is a cow that is slaughtered. So when we point out that they eat all the grass and cause erosion, people shrug their shoulders and say they have no alternative.'

At a river that formed one of the boundaries to their community, Joseph pointed to where large sections of the bank had fallen away. 'A few years ago that was solid ground. Now it is disappearing. A large part of our country is being washed away, into Mozambique and the sea.'

Several attempts at preventing further environmental damage had been carried out. At different places along the river, there were structures made of wire netting, stones and wooden poles to strengthen the bank against the flow of water that undermined it. Joseph had supervised the construction of several of these and had never encountered any lack of community support in terms of contributing time and labour. These measures, he added, were not a solution to the problems of erosion that affected many communal areas of the country.

'Everyone knows that this land is carrying too many people. Each year its gets worse. We thank God that we now have clinics and hospitals, and that our children no longer die at a young age because of preventable diseases that were never treated in the past. But more children and longer lives also mean more mouths to feed. This place cannot cope with these kinds of numbers.'

So invariably, the issue returned to the vexed question of land distribution in the country. As with Sekuru I could sense an underlying tension as Joseph spoke, the frustration of several generations behind his well chosen words. 'A few kilometers down this road is a commercial farm, large parts of which are never used. People ask why it cannot be shared, why one person can own so much while they have so little. They are getting angry. They ask their chiefs and headmen why there was a war over land if nothing has changed. Mr. Chris, we are not a violent people, but I can tell you that there is an explosion waiting to happen in this country if something is not done soon. We cannot be expected to be patient forever.'

At a place where the river widened, we came across a gathering of several hundred people. Most of them were dressed in long white robes and wrap around headscarves. From their singing and collective hand waving in the air, I guessed we had stumbled across a religious service. Joseph confirmed that these were 'Vapostori' and that this site on the edge of their community was where they regularly came to pray.

Occasionally a member of the group was escorted into the river where an imposing looking gentleman, whom I assumed was some kind of pastor, was waiting to receive them. He pronounced a few words before dunking them under the water, after which they would emerge coughing and spluttering to return to where the others were waiting.

We stood at a discreet distance and Joseph told me what he could about them. The Vapostori were founded in the 1930s by a prophet called Johan Marange. Claiming to be in direct contact with God, his somewhat radical interpretation of Christianity and his message that anyone could experience direct revelation if they prayed hard enough, had stimulated a movement that now numbered tens of thousands of adherents.

'I think people were getting fed up with the cosy relationship between the colonial state and traditional churches. There were many local churches that developed around the time that the Vapostori were founded too. I know that Marange was regarded with suspicion by the authorities of the time. They saw him as politically dangerous and were worried that he would spread nationalist propaganda under the guise of being guided by God.'

There seemed something quite puritanical about their aversion to all things Western. Many Vapostori refused to send their children to school believing that what they learned at home and through religious gatherings from their preachers was more useful and important than anything they could pick up in a classroom.

There had been problems in recent years as well. 'All children are supposed to be immunised now against diseases like polio and smallpox. But many Vapostori won't allow their children to be vaccinated, claiming that prayer and fasting will cure any illness that affects them. Other parents got upset because they said that if one group wasn't immunised then they would bring these diseases back into the district.'

As we continued our walk, Joseph talked about a bewildering variety of churches and religious establishments that seemed to form a significant part of the social life of the community. He pointed to a building that belonged to the Catholics and immediately beside it another one frequented by the Methodists. Further on was a large hall constructed the previous year by Jehovah's Witnesses. There was even a small mosque to cater for the Muslim migrants from Mozambique and Malawi who had settled in this area in the past. Some religious groups had no formal structures where they gathered. Like the Vapostori, they practiced their rituals in the open air, near forests and streams.

'Is there conflict among them?' I asked, wondering how such a small community could accommodate such a large number of different denominations and competing ideologies.

'Not as much as one might think,' he replied. 'Another thing that might surprise you is that many people move quite happily between them.'

One of his aunts, he went on to say, frequented a Catholic service on Sunday morning. Then she attended a meeting of the Methodists later the same evening. The former offered literacy classes during the week while the latter provided training for women in craft production. 'She seems quite happy to sit through both services, listen to their preachers and sing their different hymns. The fact that she learns how to read and sew at the same time is an added bonus.'

Joseph said that many members of the community,

including those who were god-fearing church goers, continued to have an interaction with traditional beliefs and practices too. 'Haven't you noticed that no one is working in their fields today, even though it is the middle of the week?'

During certain days of the month called 'Chisvi' all agricultural work was suspended. It was believed that families who didn't adhere to this prohibition risked incurring the anger of certain spirits who would visit illness or misfortune upon them. 'In conversation, people may tell you that this tradition is based on nothing more than superstition. But you'll notice, if you observe carefully, that they won't work on these days either.'

Although some of the more established churches were openly opposed to aspects of traditional religion, particularly the use of beer in ceremonies and the practice of spirit possession, which they claimed was dangerous, many people saw no contradiction in reconciling their Christianity with an adherence to past culture and belief.

'I once asked someone in my own family how he could read his Bible during the day and then consult a spirit medium the same evening to see if he had angered his ancestors. His reply was interesting. 'Doesn't the Bible tell us to honour our parents? Well, that's not so different from traditional religion which says that we should continue to do so long after they are dead. The New Testament says that the spirit of Christ ascended to heaven three days after he was crucified. Our spirit mediums tell us that the soul of a dead person emerges from their corpse after a few months. Now, you tell me what's so different between them.' And the truth is, I had nothing much to say.'

Joseph's words were in keeping with something I had previously heard in Harare, from an African pastor who was addressing an NGO meeting on the principles of local development. He had said that while the Christian churches had brought a new set of beliefs into Zimbabwe when they arrived at the turn of the century, they had also been transformed in the process. Many of the ceremonies found today were almost unrecognisable from what had first been insisted upon by the missionaries who brought them. In his own church, he added, singing and dancing had originally been banned, but were now part of the regular service.

At the same time, tolerance for other beliefs and a willingness to see what was common rather than different, meant that ecumenism was more advanced in Africa than in many other parts of the world. 'That includes a generous accommodation of local belief and tradition. We were a deeply spiritual people long before Christianity came. It's wrong to think we were living in the dark ages before some missionaries came from Europe to save us. Sure, I'm a Christian pastor. I represent an international church. But that doesn't mean to say that I have to be dismissive of what was positive and important in the religious past of my own people.'

By the time we concluded our walk, it was late afternoon. Sekuru was in the same place as we had left him, his stack of beers now considerably diminished. 'We've been waiting for you for some time,' he said when we approached. 'Our goat is now ready to eat and we're all getting hungry.'

The gathering continued late into the evening, with everyone clustered around the fires that had been lit in different places within Sekuru's compound. There was a constant stream of visitors from different parts of the village, and just as in rural Sudan, I could see that the community needed little excuse to convene an impromptu party. Although the women kept to one side and presented a demure reserve when they interacted with the men, I noticed that their celebrations were considerably more animated than ours as the sounds of their singing and dancing drifted through to where we were seated.

Despite having my fill of sadza and goat meat, I was not allowed to refuse the sizeable plates of food that continued to circulate the entire evening. 'This piece is different,' Sekuru or one of his relatives would insist, handing me some new steaming morsel. 'You have to try it.' I could see that there was considerable importance attached to my being well fed and looked after and I was not inclined to disappoint Sekuru or his relatives by having the bad grace to say that I had had enough. Tactfully, and unobserved by the others, Joseph would remove the food I had hidden behind me and find some way of returning it to the communal plate.

By the time I went to bed around midnight, Sekuru was still in full flow. I said my goodbyes not expecting to see him or his family the following morning. But at six o'clock he was there, my car washed and gleaming, and his wife with him to wish me a safe onward journey.

I thanked them for their warmth and hospitality and asked them to convey my farewells to all who had made me so welcome. Joseph had been an excellent guide and minder and I asked Sekuru if it would be appropriate for me to leave him a token of my appreciation. 'One family member doesn't pay another for doing their duty,' he replied. 'Away from Scotland this is your home now.'

The bewilderment and confusion among the refugees I had seen several years previously in other parts of Africa were just as prevalent among those from Mozambique I encountered the following morning. Apart from a central area where Government buildings and the offices of different aid agencies followed some kind of plan, the word 'camp' seemed far too orderly and structured a nomenclature to describe the haphazard, chaotic spread of dwellings we found.

The latest arrivals, of whom there were thousands due to a recent upsurge in fighting, were living in temporary wooden shelters with bits of plastic on top to keep out the rain. They even lacked latrines, my guide told me unnecessarily, since the smell of human waste permeated the air.

Long before we had reached the camp itself, it had announced its presence. On the drive there we had passed through a large area of land that had been stripped of all vegetation. The trees had been cut down by the refugees to provide wood for cooking and construction, a fact which had angered many of the local residents who had seen their environment progressively destroyed over the ten or so years that these newcomers had lived among them.

'You can tell the new arrivals quite easily. These are the ones who are curious when a visitor arrives. The ones who have been here longer won't even bother to look at you. They have had so many visitors in the time they have been here that another one is hardly anything to get excited about.'

Tatenda seemed too young for the responsibilities he had been landed with. He had been appointed deputy manager of the camp only a few months previously. Polite, welcoming and keen to answer my questions he seemed at times to be as intimidated by the problems he was facing as were the people he had been appointed to look after.

When I asked him how many refugees were resident he confessed that no one knew the exact number. The difficulty of giving an accurate figure was not just because of the size of the population. 'There is a porous border between our two countries so people can cross quite easily. So refugees will come here for a few months. Then they return to their home areas to check on their property, if there is anything left. When the fighting erupts again, they come back. Some move as frequently as four to five times a year.'

He added that many of the refugees in Mozambique had families in Zimbabwe too and shared a common ethnic identity. 'Sometimes they will stay with their families on this side of the border, especially during the agricultural season when there is work available. But because their relatives are poor too, they cannot keep them the whole year. That's when they will come to the camp for a few months to receive food and other handouts.'

The situation in the refugee camp seemed as confusing as the conflict in the country next door. Regarded by many as one of Africa's worst wars, a serious claim given what it was competing against, it had not only affected Mozambique but all of the neighboring states as well. A total of around 3 million refugees were said to be living in Zimbabwe, Zambia, Tanzania, Malawi and South Africa. Every day the national newspaper had a front page article about the conflict. From these and other reports I had read, I had some idea about the history.

Portugal had granted independence to Mozambique in 1972. It had handed power to Frelimo, the liberation movement led by Samora Michel, which had fought against the colonial regime. The abrupt withdrawal of Portugal from its former colony was seen by the then Governments of both Rhodesia and South Africa as capitulation. Determined to maintain white control over their black populations, they were concerned that a successful African-ruled state next door would provide an inspiration to those who were challenging them in their own countries. In response, they had pursued a policy of covertly destabilising Mozambique so that that they could point to the resulting chaos as proof that Africans could not govern themselves.

In 1975, a group of Mozambican dissidents was created, armed and supported by the Rhodesians. When Zimbabwe became independent in 1980, the South African security forces took over the role of principal patron. Renamo, as it was called, claimed that it was fighting a war of ideals, that it was opposed to the socialist principles of Frelimo which would turn their country into a satellite of the Soviets. Capitalising on the Cold War sensitivities of the time, Renamo had little difficulty in acquiring the arms and resources it needed to conduct a long and protracted war. There were accusations that right-wing church groups in America supplied them not only with Bibles, but with guns and bullets too.

Whatever its ideological claims, it was clear that Renamo was bent on pursuing its opposition through fear and terror. Hundreds of clinics, hospitals, schools and administrative buildings were destroyed in the central part of the country where the fighting was heaviest. Roads and bridges had not been spared either.

'But how would such a tactic endear them to the population whose rights they claim to be protecting?' I had asked a Mozambican journalist I had befriended in Harare.

'Their intention is to destroy everything associated with the Government. Renamo can then claim that Frelimo has done nothing for the people, that since they took over at independence there has been nothing but chaos and bloodshed. By making the country ungovernable they want to present themselves as an alternative, even if it means killing and intimidating the very people they say they represent.'

The destruction of infrastructure not only deprived the local population of services such as health care and education, but disrupted farming too. This resulted in widespread starvation. The only refuge people could find was either in protected enclaves in Mozambican towns and cities, or across national borders in the countries next door.

The sponsors of Renamo also hoped that faced with these numbers of refugees the aforementioned states would feel less inclined to support the liberation struggle that was gathering pace in South Africa too. 'Mess with us and this is how you too will end up,' was how my Mozambican friend characterised the rationale behind the strategy of regional destabilisation.

At the offices of an international charity I was handed over to Marie, a nurse from France who had worked with the refugees for the past three years. 'You can help me,' she said after we were introduced, and pointed to a pile of photographs she was pinning on to a large wooden board. Around us there was a crowd of curious onlookers, mostly women, who would scrutinise each of the pictures as we put them up, commenting among themselves as to whether any of the faces looked familiar.

According to Marie, thousands of separated families were spread out across a number of camps in eastern Zimbabwe and southern Malawi. Every few weeks, or whenever there was a new influx of people, they would share their photos of lost children. If they were recognised by parents, relatives or other community members they would be reunited. 'But as you can see there are many more mothers than kids. That's because a lot of them simply didn't make it across the border.'

'Was it too far for them to walk?' I asked, thinking that the children had maybe ended up in orphanages back in Mozambique or with other relatives who were looking after them.

'I can see that you don't know much about African wars,'

Marie responded. 'Children are prized possessions because they make excellent soldiers. That's why so many of them are missing.'

She added that one reason why Renamo attacked villages was not just to create chaos and confusion. It was a recruitment exercise too, to replenish its troops. Kids as young as twelve and thirteen were now a large part of its army.

Marie had an impressive record of African conflicts behind her, and so I asked why children were so highly valued as fighters, even though some of them could hardly carry the weapons they had been given.

There were several reasons, she said. 'It's partly because children are more compliant than adults, who continue to harbour resentment about being made to fight in wars they want nothing to do with. That's something that can be exploited. There are stories of children in Mozambique being forced to kill their parents or other relatives. They are then told that they can never again return to their communities.'

She added that a large number of killings in Mozambique, carried out by both children and adults, were done using knives and machetes. 'It's not just because they want to save on bullets. Killing someone with an axe implicates you more in their death than shooting them from a distance. You can't claim lack of responsibility, or innocence either. That's what the army commanders want, soldiers who have lost any sense of allegiance to anyone but their comrades.'

She recalled a conversation with a young boy she had recently encountered. He had claimed to have killed over thirty people. He had etched the numbers on his belt and talked about his achievement as if trying to impress a teacher with some difficult homework he had completed successfully. Remorse over what he had done was a foreign concept. 'I did what I was told to do,' he had said, sounding like the ideal soldier.

As if to reinforce the terrible things that Marie was talking about, an old woman approached us. She handed us a photo and asked if we could help find her grandson. The photo, she said, had been taken the previous year. He was only eleven years old.

Their village, several days march across the border, had recently been attacked. The grandmother's daughter had been killed. Her son – in-law had been shot too. Somehow she had managed to escape, promising her dying daughter that she would take care of her grandson, but as they fled the burning village she had become separated from the main group. That was the last she had seen of him.

Marie pinned the photograph to the wooden board, more in hope than expectation that anything useful would come of it. 'There are thousands of people like her in this camp,' she said, in a voice that betrayed the stress and weariness she was clearly feeling. 'Each one has a story as harrowing as this one. You need a thick skin not to let it get you down. Maybe it's time for me to change my profession.'

As with Soren I was intrigued as to what motivated her long term commitment. What had prompted her to work in some of the worst places in the world?

'Because nothing else is quite so satisfying,' she said when I posed the question, not sure whether she would take offence at my asking. 'As you can see this life has its frustrations. But when I went back to work as a nurse in France I kept on thinking of what I had left behind. I missed the feeling of making a difference. Some of my friends said that I was addicted to suffering. I suppose there's an element of truth in that observation. Once you've been involved in humanitarian work, it can be difficult to return to normal life again.'

As we continued our tour of the camp, I couldn't help thinking that a considerable part of the misery we were seeing had been caused by people who had the same skin colour as our own. The defence of racial privilege was at the heart of many of the conflicts that had beset the countries in the region, including much of the destabilisation in Mozambique. The conflict in Zimbabwe had been about the same things too. Didn't Africans feel resentful? Why did they display so little antagonism?

'Because we are smart enough to know that not all people are the same,' Joseph had said when I had broached the subject as delicately as I could the previous day, referring to the land seizures by Europeans that had been such a prevalent part of the country's history.

He had pointed out that most members of his community were familiar with acts of kindness and charity practiced by their white neighbours. There was the missionary who had taught their children for years in one of the nearby schools. He had been evicted from the country by the Rhodesian authorities when he had dared to champion the cause of black emancipation. Some of the commercial farmers had helped them during a recent drought, providing them with free grazing for their cattle and seed to replant when the rains finally came. 'It would be a similar kind of racism if we were to hold all white people responsible for the problems that some have created.'

Marie echoed this when I asked her if she had experienced any hostile reaction from the refugees she was helping.

'No, and in the three years I've been here I've wondered about that too. I also believe that forgiveness and generosity by others is never something we should take for granted. Maybe that's why acts of solidarity are important; to help show people here that we are not all the same, that we are different from the ones that come to shoot up their villages in the early morning or supply the weapons and ammunition that allow others to do so. It's that belief at least that helps keeps me going when I get too depressed,' she said, as we entered a large enclosure in the centre of the camp where hundreds of malnourished children were waiting to be fed.

7

The Seat of the Gods

A few weeks after my visit to Sekuru's home I was back in his province again to check out a training centre run by the Ministry of Youth, Sports and Culture. Providing vocational skills to girls who had just completed secondary school it was located in the southern part of the mountain range I had seen on my original drive, amid a set of dramatic peaks near a place called Vumba. The friendly students and a persuasive principal had made it easy to agree to their request for assistance. They would have their fashion and design trainer in a few months' time.

Vumba was eulogised in my guidebook, described in flowery language as a location well worth a visit. Curious about this place in the clouds and with time to spare before continuing my onward journey further south, I decided to spend a few hours exploring. It wasn't just the cool, damp climate that intrigued me. It was a sense too of entering a place of privilege that couldn't have been more different from the desperation I had witnessed only a short distance away.

At a place called Leopard's Rock, which boasted a smart hotel, a nine hole golf course, a restaurant offering haute cuisine, and a botanical garden, Vumba offered from its lofty heights a spectacular view of war torn Mozambique only a few miles below us.

'I'll have tea and scones with raspberry jam and cream,' I said to the waitress at a cafe in the botanical garden. In

134

Zimbabwe, one minute you were in vibrant, intriguing, impoverished and chaotic Africa. The next, you were in 'Little England' being cooled by a breeze that smelled of pine trees and eucalyptus and sitting in a place where the only Africans to be seen were the ones serving you tea and scones.

'You don't look as if you're from around here,' an elderly white lady sitting at the next table interrupted my reverie.

'I'm not,' I replied. 'I'm just visiting for a few hours and then I'm on my way to Masvingo.'

'Is that a Scottish accent I detect?' she said, and when I acknowledged that it was, she asked if I would like to join her for tea. A fierce looking terrier, fastened by a lead to one of the chairs, took exception to my presence when I sat beside them. Although Hector was soundly admonished he continued to growl in my direction throughout the time I was there, to remind me no doubt that I was intruding on his territory.

As Mabel poured me a cup of tea, she told me that her father had come from Scotland. 'He was a MacDonald from a place called Oban. What's your name? Are we related?'

'I'm a McIvor,' I responded somewhat hesitantly. Our two clans had squabbled for centuries and I did not want to give Hector any further excuse to snap at my ankles.

It seemed that she was ignorant of our fraught history. 'I don't think I know any McIvors,' she said. 'It can't be a very common name.'

In her late sixties, Mabel lived in Harare but regularly came to Vumba to 'escape' the noise and clamor of the big city. She laughed when I asked her if she could tell me where I might find the 'noise and clamor' she was talking about. Almost a year in Harare and I was still searching for entertainment.

Her sister-in-law owned a small property a few miles

down the road, but the botanical garden was her favorite haunt because of its exotic flowers, the magnificent view and the scones served in its café. She was clearly a regular visitor, greeting the waitress who served us by her first name and enquiring after her children who had recently left school. In fact she knew all the staff by name, which in turn seemed to endear her to them. At regular intervals they would come over to enquire how she was and ask if she wanted more tea.

As we chatted away, I remarked to myself that Mabel was the first European resident of the country I had had a lengthy conversation with. It wasn't because I couldn't find them. Most of my neighbors in the suburb where I stayed were elderly white couples, but they generally kept to themselves and seemed aloof and distant.

There was a Mr. Townsend to my left. We had started off badly. Marching into my yard only a week after I had arrived, he accused Sekuru of stealing his chickens. Sekuru denied all wrongdoing and asked for proof that he was the guilty party. The 'evidence' consisted of some resemblance between Sekuru's dog and an animal that had recently raided Mr. Townsend's hen house.

'But there are scores of dogs that look like that one in this neighbourhood,' I said, pointing to Sekuru's mongrel. 'How do you know it's his that is responsible?'

'Because I've seen your domestic peering over my fence on several occasions and checking out my chickens. They're both guilty as far as I'm concerned.'

My refusal to admonish Sekuru seemed to irk him the most, as if I had sided with the enemy. On another occasion when I bumped into him at the local shopping centre, he asked me somewhat brusquely what I was doing in his country. He shook his head when I told him I worked for an aid agency. 'They'll take advantage of you, the Africans.

Believe me, I've been here all my life and know them better than you. Charity, development assistance, free hand outs: they're all a waste of time. The only thing this country needs is more hard work from lazy people.'

It was Sekuru who reminded me, with considerable generosity I thought, that one cantankerous neighbour was hardly the basis for making a judgment about the rest of the resident Europeans. From my reading I knew that there were about 200,000 whites who had remained in Zimbabwe after independence, about two per cent of the population. This was almost half the number that had been there before. Fear of what might happen after the fighting was over, concern about jobs and a possible decline in their standards of living prompted many to leave. Most had gone to South Africa but a fair number had emigrated to the UK, Canada, Australia and New Zealand.

It was a community that seemed difficult to penetrate, closed and insular and not particularly welcoming of aid workers either. Mr. Townsend's perception that I was a naive do-gooder who would be taken advantage of by ungrateful locals was one that seemed widely shared.

One expatriate colleague, who had worked as the head of a German aid agency in the country for many years, told me that a relationship of mutual distrust and suspicion was pervasive.

'The whites who live here believe that they know the country and its people better than we do. They think that our ignorance will be taken advantage of. Some of them resent our cosiness with the African population too, as if it is an indictment of their own past history and lack of interaction. Meanwhile, many aid workers categorise the entire European population here as a bunch of racists out to exploit the locals. Neither group really understands the other and I don't see much evidence of them trying to do so either.'

But Mabel was open, friendly and genuinely curious about the work I was doing. She displayed none of the frostiness I had anticipated when I told her I was the representative of a British charity. 'Good for you,' she said. 'We need more work of this kind in our country.'

'Now tell me,' she said, pouring another cup of tea, 'why haven't you joined the Caledonian society since you've been here?'

She seemed taken aback when I confessed that I knew nothing about the institution she was referring to. Hector gave another growl, as if my answer confirmed the low opinion he already had of me. 'The Caledonian Society is where Scots abroad can meet and interact with each other,' Mabel continued. 'I'm shocked you've never even heard of us.'

Apparently it was present in nearly every country on the globe that had ever hosted Scottish emigrants, a considerable number given our propensity to settle in other places. 'We're a generally sentimental people, as you must know, and I've never met a Scots person abroad who didn't want to retain some connection with their native land.'

Their membership in Zimbabwe numbered several hundred and every month they would gather at a venue in Harare to practice Highland dancing. Their highlight of the year was a celebratory Burn's supper on January the 21st. Sometimes they hosted visitors from other countries. They even sponsored a pipe band in one of Harare's private schools.

Mabel scribbled down a telephone number and told me to ring the Society secretary as soon as I returned to the capital. 'You mentioned that you're in need of entertainment and we're in need of new members.' I took the number and promised I would ring but did not add that Scottish dancing and sharing clan histories was not the type of entertainment I was really looking for.

Despite Mabel's 'sentimental' attachment to a country she had never lived in, she was also able to stand back and appreciate that there was a difference between what people imagined from a distance and the reality behind it. She had been to Scotland on two occasions to visit relatives, but had not been back for over twenty years. When I asked her why not, given that it seemed to feature so prominently in her social life, she confessed that what she had found was not what she had expected.

'Of course I knew the weather would be awful,' she said, 'but the country was different in so many ways from what I had always imagined. The stories our father had told us as children, his memories of what he had left behind, were colored by distance. That's what happens when you leave a place when you're young, isn't it? You only remember the good things. You romanticise the past. He never told us about the poverty and lack of opportunity that had forced him to leave, or the narrowness of some of his relatives. In that sense I suppose I was naïve to have believed everything he told us.'

Mabel said something else that intrigued me. Her visits to Scotland, she claimed, had made her more appreciative of the country she had been born in, as if discovering that Scotland was not really home had strengthened her attachment to Zimbabwe. I wanted to know more about her community and in particular how their lives had changed over the past decade. 'You mentioned a sister-in-law. Is your husband here with you? Do you have children?' I prodded.

Mabel's husband had died several years ago. 'He drank too much, I'm afraid, a common problem among our men folk. He wasn't that old when he passed away. We had three children, a lot of wonderful memories and he left me financially comfortable.'

For most of their marriage they had lived in the Midlands

Province, near a place called Kwekwe, raising cattle and growing tobacco. They had lived there during the war too and when Mabel spoke of those years I could see that she was angry. 'It was a stupid conflict and so unnecessary. I can appreciate that now. But at the time we couldn't see it. Ian Smith and his cronies played on our fears, and like sheep we followed in whatever direction they pointed.'

There was a personal tragedy too. Her son had served in an infamous military unit called the Selous Scouts and according to Mabel he had been irreparably scarred. 'There are deeper wounds than physical injury. He never spoke about the things he had seen or done but I knew they must have been terrible. I could see him change before my eyes so that in the end he was like a ghost of someone I once knew, who resembled my son but wasn't.'

After the fighting had ended he had left for South Africa, the same day the election results announced that Robert Mugabe would rule the country. 'The last thing he said before he left was that he would never be forgiven for what he had done, and that the rest of the white population wouldn't be forgiven either. We keep in touch but he's never been back since.'

Shorty afterwards her other two children had gone too, one to Australia and the other to England. 'Neither of them felt they had a future here after the war and at that time I didn't try to change their minds either, even though I knew I would miss them terribly.'

Mabel paused for a minute and I wondered whether this issue touched too raw a nerve. But when I told her that I was happy to change the subject she said that she was fine and that in any case these things needed to be discussed more openly, not buried away as they were among so many families.

'You see, when the rulers of our new country said that we

were welcome to stay, many of us did not believe them. After all, we had been told for years that they were communists, that they would cut our throats when they took over, that they would seize all our property once they assumed power. So, when my children talked about leaving, I encouraged them to go. Now I wonder if I did the right thing, if I should have done more to persuade them to stay.'

'Did you never think of leaving yourself?'

'In the first few years that was all I thought about. Should I stay? Should I go? My children wanted me to leave. 'There's nothing there for you,' they would tell me. 'Come and live with us. Get to know your grandchildren.' But leaving the things you are familiar with when you get older is not so easy. I kept on remembering too my visits to Scotland, the place I thought I might one day return to. There was nothing there for me either. At the same time, my friends who had emigrated to South Africa and England would write and say that it wasn't like what they had imagined, that these places weren't home. In the end I decided that I didn't want to feel like a stranger in another country. So I stayed put.'

'So how do you feel now, several years later? Has Zimbabwe turned out as bad as some predicted?'

'This might sound strange,' she replied, 'but in many ways I expected there to be more changes. Many of us live much the same lifestyle as we did before. At times I wonder if that is right and if we will be allowed to go on as we are for much longer. All I can say at the moment is that I've never regretted my decision.'

I wanted to hear more of her views on the relationship between whites and blacks in the post-independence period. The gulf between the two societies still seemed wide and I was interested to hear her perspective on whether this was so and why the lack of interaction.

'If you don't mind me saying,' I said, 'I don't see much reconciliation between the two races. I can see that people are polite enough to each other when they meet but it doesn't seem to go much beyond superficial pleasantries. From my outsider's perspective you still keep to yourselves and I can't help thinking that unless the fences between you are taken down you are storing up problems for the future.'

Again Mabel paused and I wondered if I had pushed too far. Perhaps the subject of race relations in contemporary Zimbabwe was not quite the thing she wanted to talk about over a cup of tea in the Vumba Mountains with a stranger. But again she insisted that I was not being too pushy.

'Of course you're right. There's not enough interaction, as you say. But you also need to remember that these things take time. We can't just wish our upbringing and social conditioning away, or pretend that history didn't happen. A lot of the whites who stayed on are old like me and maybe we are too set in our ways. It's probably a younger generation that will be more at ease with each other. Meanwhile, some of us do the best we can to get along. I suppose in a few years' time we'll see whether that has been enough.'

Mabel was keen to hear more about my work and so I told her about our projects and some of the places I had visited. I mentioned the refugee camp I had recently seen and tried to describe something of the desperation I had witnessed and what I had heard about the terrible situation in the country next door. As I related what was happening only a few miles away it struck me how remote it must seem. 'The seat of the Gods,' was how Mabel had characterised this small corner of Zimbabwe. From here the rest of Africa seemed as remote as if we were sitting in a café in London.

'My husband and I used to drive to Mozambique,' she said, after I had finished. 'A lot of us did in those days. There were hotels on the beach overlooking the Indian ocean, full of Rhodesians, South Africans and Portuguese. It always looked such a relaxed and beautiful place. I can't understand why these people would want to kill each other.'

When I recounted my understanding of the history of the conflict, and in particular how it had been started by the Rhodesian Secret Service and later fueled by outsiders who seemed ready to hand out money and weapons as soon as they heard the word 'Communist,' she seemed shocked. 'Were we involved in that too? I suppose you must think me terribly naïve for not knowing more about these things.'

I felt conflicted when Mabel said these words. I had thoroughly enjoyed our conversation and found her openness and curiosity, her interest in what I was doing, engaging. I genuinely hoped that I might meet her again. But part of me felt censorious too, surprised that someone who had lived here all her life could know so little about things that had happened, and were still happening, in her country. When I had mentioned my trip to Nyaminyami, and the poverty and desperation I had found in a community displaced from their homes so that the rest of the population could have cheap electricity, she had remarked that this was something she had been unaware of. 'It's never too late to learn,' I said, trying not to sound too judgmental or unappreciative of her hospitality.

It was time to leave. There was a long drive to Masvingo ahead of me and I would need the rest of the day to get there. Mabel wished me a safe onward journey and every success in the work I was doing. She hoped too that I would get in touch with the Caledonian Society when I returned to Harare. 'It's the same folks that meet every month. It would be good to see some new faces for a change.'

The waiter at the counter told me that the bill had been taken care of when I asked him how much I had to pay. 'Don't worry. Madame will look after it.'

As Hector continued to bark in my direction to make sure I was really on my way, I remarked that he seemed an unsociable animal and not at all friendly. 'I hope he doesn't give you a rough time too.'

He chuckled as I turned to leave. 'With us he's fine, sir. It's only strangers he can't stand.'

My descent from Vumba was as dramatic and almost as instant as dropping out of the clouds from an aeroplane. Up there, I had been dressed in a woolen pullover and thick jacket to keep out the cold. A short while later I was driving through a flat plain in short sleeves, with the windows of the car wide open. The pine plantations and apple orchards had been replaced by dry, dusty savannah broken by a few thorn trees. Once again, I was struck by the sharp contrast between the wealthy, private estates I had just encountered and the relative poverty of the communal lands I was now entering.

I was headed to Masvingo, the last major town in the south east of the country before reaching the border with South Africa. My journey was prompted by a letter I had received the previous month from an organisation asking for financial assistance. We received a lot of requests for help, mostly from individuals looking for work, a contribution to their study fees or information about how they could emigrate to the UK. Fortunate generally filtered this correspondence but sometimes she would hand me a letter that she felt merited more than a simple, apologetic rejection.

This communication had sparked my interest too. It talked about the erosion of traditional culture and religion in the country and how this in turn had been responsible for much of the environmental damage that was afflicting rural Zimbabwe. The organisation had been principally set up to work with church leaders and traditional religious figures in an attempt to solicit their support in protecting the region's natural resources. There was a brochure enclosed that included the aims and objectives of the organisation, some photographs of tree plantations they had established in districts around Masvingo and an address and telephone number in case anyone was interested in contacting them.

The person at the end of the line seemed surprised when I phoned, and took a few seconds to collect himself. 'You must excuse me,' he said. 'We send out a lot of requests for assistance and it's not very often that we get a response.'

After he provided me with the information I wanted, I told him that I was curious to find out more. 'When would be a good time to visit?'

We agreed on a date that was convenient for both of us. Mr. Shiri would book me into one of the local hotels and collect me at an appointed time to show me some of their projects. He would also introduce me to some other people in his organisation he was keen for me to meet. 'I'm sure God has put you in touch with us,' he concluded, which prompted me to remind him that I was making no promises at this stage and that my visit implied no commitment to supporting them.

Fortunate, who was a regular church goer, was enthusiastic about our potential involvement with an institution that had such a strong religious orientation. Sekuru was relieved that I was not returning to the wilds of Nyaminyami. 'At least there are no elephant or buffalo if you get stuck and I don't think Masvingo has sleeping sickness either.'

By early afternoon I had made good progress along the excellent road south, even managing to stop for half an hour at a place called Birchenough Bridge to admire what my guidebook described as one of the most impressive bridge constructions on the continent. But shortly thereafter I ran into a long line of traffic that was not moving.

When I enquired about what was happening from the driver of the car in front of me, he told me that a lorry had overturned blocking the route. Some people had been waiting for hours.

I joined a small crowd of people who were milling around, hoping to get some more information about when the road might be cleared. I noticed little of the irritation and frustration I would have expected if a similar inconvenience had occurred back home. 'How long will this take to sort out?' I asked one of them.

He shrugged his shoulders philosophically, in much the same way I remembered from Sudan whenever you posed a question about the future. 'Maybe this afternoon. Maybe this evening. Maybe tomorrow. It all depends on when the crane comes from Mutare to sort this out. Until then, there's nothing we can do.'

There were several accounts of what had happened: all of them to do with the incompetence of the driver, since no other vehicle had been involved. Despite a mass of tangled wreckage and spilled containers, he had emerged with little more than a few scratches and minor bruises. Someone pointed to a figure holding forth in the middle of another group of people. For someone who had just wrecked an expensive lorry and caused such mayhem, he seemed remarkably at ease.

Meanwhile, the residents of the area had decided to capitalise on the opportunity that had arisen. Women and children clustered around the cars offering tea, fruit, cooked chicken and other local food. There were pottery and baskets for sale. I noticed with some amusement that walking sticks were also on offer, an ironic reminder that it would have been quicker to walk to wherever we were going.

One enterprising entrepreneur had set up a stall selling

146

beer. A set of speakers blaring, noisy music provided the entertainment. Judging by the number of patrons he had managed to attract, I guessed that very few of the stranded travellers expected to be travelling any time soon. There was something of a carnival atmosphere about the whole event. Had these people no place to get to, or were they simply reconciled to making the best of a bad situation? I decided to wait no more than an hour to see what would happen. Then I would head back to Mutare, stay there the night and reconsider my options the following morning.

'No thanks,' I said to a young man with dreadlocks who knocked on the window of my vehicle a short while later, pointing to some stone carvings he was selling that I was too distracted to look at.

'Are you sure?' he persisted. 'For you, I have a very special price.'

'I'm sure,' I said, winding down my window. 'At the moment I'm not buying anything.'

'Where are you going sir?' he continued.

I pointed to the long line of traffic ahead of me. 'Well, I was hoping to go to Masvingo. But it looks as if I won't get there today. So I'll probably head back to Mutare and try again tomorrow morning.'

'But you can still get there today, if you want. I know another route that will take you past this accident.'

I pointed to the map I had spread out on the seat beside me. I had explored all the possible routes from Mutare southwards and could see no way of bypassing the one I was on. 'I don't think so. There is only one road to Masvingo and it's blocked. The only way I'll get there today is if that lorry is removed as soon as possible.'

'Excuse me, sir, but I know this district better than you. A few miles back along the way you came is a track to my village. If you follow it for another half hour, you'll come out on this same road again, but on the other side of this accident. You can reach Masvingo before it gets dark.'

Mindful of Sekuru's admonitions never to trust anyone, I asked him why the other drivers on the road had not taken this alternative. Some of them had been stranded considerably longer than I had and must have been just as anxious to get to where they were going.

'Because I don't think they will give me the money I am asking to show them the way.'

'And how much would that be?' I asked, expecting him to state an exorbitant sum. But the amount he came up with sounded reasonable, not much more than the price of the food and drink the vendors were selling to the occupants of nearby cars. Was I being duped?

As if guessing what I was thinking, he added that he was trustworthy and his only motive was to earn something to help his family. 'The people here know me,' he said. 'You can ask them about me if you want.'

I was tempted to take up his offer. I had a good vehicle and in four-wheel drive it could probably negotiate the route he had described. If the detour became too difficult I could always turn back. My potential guide seemed honest enough and I had warmed to his engaging manner. The prospect of waiting until the next day to get to Masvingo and having to revise an itinerary that would have already been organised was a prospect that didn't appeal to me either. 'Okay then,' I said, still not sure if I was making the right decision, 'but I'll only give you your money when I'm on this road again and the accident is behind me.'

He jumped into the front seat and some five minutes later pointed to a track that veered off the main road. There was no signpost to indicate where it led, but despite the ruts and potholes it was not much worse than the one I had driven on to get to Sekuru's home.

148

The Seat of the Gods

Tapfuma spoke good English, which he claimed to have picked up from listening to the radio. He pointed to his dreadlocks and said that he was a big fan of reggae music. Learning the lyrics of Bob Marley's songs, he said, was how he got most of his practice. 'I only had a few years of secondary school,' he replied, when I asked him if he had received an education. 'My parents couldn't afford to keep me longer, so I left before my final exams.'

Now he earned a living by carving sculptures out of the stone that seemed to feature prominently in the district we were passing through. It was a rocky landscape with dramatic looking boulders set precariously on top of each other. Apart from a few tired fields and some sorry looking goats, there didn't seem much to sustain the people who lived there.

'Do you make much from selling your work?' I asked. I had noticed that the carvings he had offered me seemed to be of good quality and must have required considerable skill.

'Some days I make a good sale. On other days I make nothing at all. It depends on whether there are tourists passing through the area.' The problem, he added, with selling on the side of the road was that people were generally looking for a bargain. They were rarely prepared to pay more than a few dollars for something that should have cost them considerably more.

At Tapfuma's village, which was little more than a collection of small buildings clustered around a beer hall and a church, he asked me whether I would like to see the place where he worked. 'It's only a short distance away and won't take much of your time.' His 'studio' turned out to be a small hut sited beside a quarry, which was how he accessed the stone he used for his carvings. It was a facility he shared with other young men from the area, some of whom were busy chiseling away when we arrived.

149

As we walked around, Tapfuma informed me that the rock they were working on was a form of serpentine that was common in that part of the country. It was one of the more popular stones for carving because although it was hard and durable it could be fashioned relatively easily as well. The only tools they used were some hammers and chisels, and sandpaper to smooth the surface of their sculptures. Tapfuma told me that they also used a floor polish called Cobra, to rub on to the stone when it was finished to bring out its different colours and textures.

'Have you ever thought of selling to a gallery?' I asked him, when we were in the car and bumping our way back to the main road which he assured me was only a few kilometres away.

'We tried that once. Someone came here and said he would try to sell our work. He took some of our carvings and told us he would return with the money. That was the last we saw of him.'

I remarked that I had been to several galleries in Harare. Much of what they were offering seemed little different from what he and his friends were producing. But they were fetching considerably more than the few dollars Tapfuma was requesting from passing motorists. One gallery owner had told me that he now exported stone carvings from Zimbabwe all over the globe. At a recent exhibition in London, he had sold all his pieces in a matter of days.

'I wonder how much the artists themselves received,' Tapfuma commented. 'From what I've heard, very little. At least one advantage of selling your work yourself is that no one can cheat you of what you are entitled to.'

At one of the galleries on the outskirts of Harare I had read in their brochure that most of the globally recognised stone sculptors now came from Zimbabwe. One of the most famous, Henry Munyaradzi, was working nearby and seemed happy enough to interact with the customers who were looking at his pieces. When I had asked him if I could interrupt him for a few minutes he had downed his tools and told me to go ahead and ask any questions I wanted.

One thing that had surprised me was his statement that neither he, nor most of the other sculptors he knew, had ever received any formal training. Nor did stone carving have a long, historical tradition in the country. Unlike wood carving in parts of West Africa, for example, which had been practiced by groups of artisans for centuries, stone sculpting in Zimbabwe seemed to have arisen in a matter of years from nowhere. 'I can remember carving bits of wood when I was a boy looking after my father's cattle. But no one showed me how to do it. To be honest, I didn't even know what an artist was. The idea that I would one day earn my living from sculpting rocks never occurred to me.'

It was only when he was considerably older that he had heard from a friend about a 'workshop' for African artists at a place called Tengenenge, some few hours' drive north of Harare. It had been set up by a white farmer on the edge of his property. Henry had visited, had liked what he had seen and had been accepted into the small community. Over the next few years he had then produced his sculptures, many of which were now displayed in prestigious galleries in different countries.

What struck me most was his considerable humility and his subdued, almost apologetic manner. Here was one of the reputably most famous sculptors in the world dressed in dirty overalls, sipping tea with a stranger and politely and patiently responding to questions that he must have been asked hundreds of times before. I guessed that part of this probably came from his modest background and upbringing in a poor rural community. But what impressed me too was the way in which he described his own formidable talent as something that had been granted to him as a gift, a skill that he took little personal credit for.

'When I'm working on a piece of stone, I forget who I am,' he had said. 'It's as if someone else takes over and moves my hand in a particular way.'

He was currently working on a large rock that would form the material for his next piece. I had asked him what it would be and how he planned to turn it into the figure he envisaged before he started.

He seemed surprised at the question. 'I can't say at the moment. I'll only know when it's near to being finished. It's not me who decides what it will be.'

'What do you mean?' I had asked, wondering if it was the gallery owner or some patron of the arts, who had commissioned a certain sculpture, who dictated the final product.

'Some sculptors know in advance what they want to create. They will work on a piece of stone to turn it into the figure of an elephant or a giraffe or the head of a person. But that's not me. I never know beforehand what will come out at the end. It's almost as if the stone decides for itself, as if there is something buried inside it that wants to get out.'

He added that in his view this was the difference between an artist and a craftsman. The latter 'imposes his will' on the stone to make something that he wanted to sell. It might be of high quality, well-crafted and worth a lot of money. But it wasn't the kind of art that Henry practiced. 'Of course I enjoy selling my work. That's how I make my living now. But it's not a commercial intention that drives me to carve something in stone. Even if no one bought my pieces I would still feel obliged to make them.'

Tapfuma said that he could partly appreciate what Henry had been talking about. But being an artist in the true sense of the word, someone who was faithful to their talent, was a luxury he and his friends could not afford. 'If it doesn't sell, we don't eat. It's as simple as that. Sure, I get fed up with carving the same figures every week. But that's how it is at the moment and so we produce what our clients demand.'

But as he spoke I could sense some frustration behind his words. It made me wonder how much 'luck' there often was in someone becoming an established artist and having the wherewithal to pursue the talent they were given.

Henry had acknowledged that if he hadn't stumbled upon Tengenenge and been given the encouragement and freedom to make whatever he wanted, he would never have progressed to where he was today. Tapfuma, meanwhile, was imprisoned by the economic reality around him, his poverty and circumstances dictating how his skills were used. 'I imagine there are hundreds of people like me scattered across this country,' he had said, 'wishing that they had the chance to express themselves in the way they really wanted.'

Half an hour after we had left his village, and in keeping with his promise, Tapfuma pointed to some tarmac ahead of us and announced that this was the road to Masvingo. It seemed that I would make my appointment after all.

'Didn't you believe me?' he asked, noticing my look of surprise.

I laughed and told him how Sekuru, my minder, was constantly reminding me to be careful about the people I met and not trust them until I knew them better. 'Generally it's good advice, but at times you have to take a risk too. This time I'm thankful that I did.'

'This is too much,' he said, when I handed him more than the amount we had originally agreed. But I insisted, knowing what the extra money would mean to him. He had told me that he had just had a second child and that he and his wife were struggling to meet the costs of healthcare and other basic necessities.

He finally accepted, but insisted that I take one of his sculptures as a token of his appreciation. 'God has given me a better day than the one I had expected. This accident has brought good luck not just to me but to the people of my community.'

I thanked him too, not just for having saved a day of my time by showing me an alternative route to Masvingo. As we had chatted away I had been reminded again that it was away from the main road and off the beaten track that Africa seemed to reveal itself more fully. He had been an excellent guide. I had seen a part of rural Zimbabwe that I would never have encountered if he hadn't knocked at my window and ignored my attempts to brush him aside. An inconvenience had turned out to be an opportunity to learn something new. Maybe my African friends were right when they claimed that there was no such thing as an accident, that seemingly random events always had a purpose behind them.

8

Spirit Mediums in Masvingo

Mr. Shiri was the head of a church I had never heard of before, but he looked like a pastor, with a grey suit, white collar and a pair of earnest spectacles that accentuated his air of pious commitment. He was effusive too and gave me a warm hug, as if I were a long lost relative or a new recruit just admitted into his congregation. 'Welcome to Masvingo,' he said. 'We've been looking forward to meeting you.'

The 'we' turned out to be a welcoming committee of the organisation they had set up to turn their province into the Garden of Eden they claimed it could be. I shook hands with several other ministers. According to Mr. Shiri, they had cast aside their doctrinal differences 'for the sake of an endeavour that is bigger than our divisions.'

All of them were friendly, but on the periphery of the group hovered an aloof, more reluctant figure. Mr. Mutasa was introduced as the representative on their committee of traditional African religions. 'If it weren't for him,' Mr. Shiri added, anxious to draw him into the fold, 'we wouldn't be where we are now.' Mr. Mutasa nodded in my direction but unlike his companions, never came forward to shake my hand.

'Here's the timetable for your visit,' Mr. Shiri continued and handed me a typed list of activities. I noticed that the last entry read, 'Day Seven – Return to Masvingo town and

Discussion of Next Steps.' This must be an error. They couldn't be expecting me to stay an entire week!

'But there's a lot to see and it's a big province,' Mr. Shiri replied when I pointed out that his timetable had a mistake. 'Surely you will want to know everything about us before making a decision whether to help.'

'I was expecting to return to Harare this evening,' I spluttered, noticing immediately how my statement caused a ripple of surprised stares and looks of concern among the gathered party. It prompted a wry smile on the face of Mr. Mutasa, as if I had just confirmed what he had warned his colleagues about before my arrival.

'Less than a day! Mr. Chris, you can't be serious.' Mr. Shiri replied. 'How can you appreciate what we are doing here in such a short period of time? Don't you want to know what others think of us? Who will give you an honest opinion in only a few minutes?'

I was about to reply that my time was not my own and that pressure of work in Harare necessitated my return. But something made me pause. The criticism I had just heard was one I had leveled myself several years previously in Sudan against the representatives of an aid agency who had descended on the community where I was working as a teacher. They were there to come up with an intervention strategy for the thousands of people affected by drought. They too had stayed less than a day. I had asked them how they could make such a decision without meeting the people they were supposed to help.

They shrugged their shoulders and said that they had things to do in Khartoum.

Now here I was manifesting the same behavior. I reminded myself that taking time to understand local communities and make informed judgments about what was required to help them was part of my job description. But

156

servicing the bureaucracy of my organisation: writing reports, managing a budget, checking accounts, attending planning meetings, producing proposals, contacting donors, sending letters of thanks to our supporters back home and so on, left me little opportunity to interact with people in anything but a tokenistic manner. Who indeed would give me an honest opinion if they knew I was only prepared to offer them a few minutes out of my precious schedule?

Before I had joined the organisation, I made a decision to try and avoid the disparaging label that was being used to characterise professionals in my chosen field of work. One author had coined the term 'development tourists' and the title had stuck. It referred to workers in charities who made fleeting visits to easily accessible locations and then made snap judgments about what was in the best interests of the people they were meant to assist. Very often the only people they spoke to were Government officials just as ignorant about what was happening in these locations, or a few leaders who had been primed beforehand in terms of what to say. The most vulnerable and needy were rarely accessed because the aid workers had no time to find them. Now I was conducting myself in a similar fashion to those I had vowed never to emulate.

'Wait a minute, Mr. Shiri. Let me make a call,' I said, and asked the hotel receptionist to put me through to our office in Harare.

After several minutes, I managed to speak to Fortunate on a crackly line. 'What meetings do I have scheduled over the next few days?'

She recited a list of appointments with the representatives of several other agencies, a meeting with officials in the Ministry of Education and a visit to the offices of a donor we were asking for money. All of these could be postponed to another time. 'Please contact them and schedule appointments for next week. I'm staying in Masvingo longer than I expected.'

'Don't forget you have the monthly report to write for head office,' Fortunate reminded me. 'They need it the day after tomorrow.'

'Ring them up. Tell them that my vehicle has broken down and that I'm stranded in a remote part of the country. They'll have their report when I return.'

'A week is too much but I can offer you a few days,' I said to a relieved Mr. Shiri, who assured me I had made the right decision.

His companions looked pleased too, apart from Mr. Mutasa who was as inscrutable as ever. 'You could spend weeks with us and you would never understand what we are trying to do,' was what he seemed to be thinking, which made me all the more determined to prove him wrong.

Our first stop was a community several hours drive from Masvingo. My vehicle could not transport the entire entourage who had come to meet me and there was a discussion as to who should be included in the travelling party. I noticed that Mr. Mutasa volunteered to absent himself but that Mr. Shiri was adamant he come with us.

'He seems a bit hostile,' I said, taking the opportunity as we walked to the car to ask Mr. Shiri whether there was something I had said or done to make his companion look so morose.

Taking me aside he placed a friendly hand on my shoulder and assured me that it was nothing personal. 'I'm not sure if you know anything about the history of spirit mediums in Zimbabwe. If you do, you will be aware that they were often persecuted by the colonial authorities.

Mr. Mutasa was imprisoned for much of the war and this explains some of his resentment towards white people. But because of his influence and his knowledge of traditional religion, he is extremely important to what we are trying to achieve. You'll see what I mean when we visit the communities. Just be patient.'

The tree planting project they wanted to show me was on the road south, somewhere between Masvingo and the border with South Africa. There was no need for Mr. Shiri to point to the consequences of the deforestation that his organisation was concerned about. Clouds of dust swirled around whenever the wind picked up and there were stretches of countryside with nothing but dry, thorny scrub and a few withered looking trees. On a few occasions we stopped so I could inspect the flaky, crumbling soil that now sustained the livelihoods of thousands of farmers in the communal districts of the province.

At a fenced off area of land near to the village where we were headed, Mr. Shiri pointed to a sign that read 'Keep Out' in English, Shona and Ndebele. That warning had clearly been ignored. The fence had been torn down in several places. Some boys, who came up to greet us, were encouraging their goats to eat the young trees that had recently been planted. They seemed proud of themselves and displayed no evidence of feeling guilty at having been found trespassing on private property.

'I hope this is not one of your projects,' I said to Mr. Shiri as we walked around to see for ourselves the state of disrepair the plantation had fallen into.

He shook his head. 'We wanted to show you what we are trying to avoid.' The Government, he continued, through its forestry department and with the help of several donors had established a number of plantations like this one. The idea was laudable, namely to reforest parts of the province with trees that would not only protect the soil from erosion, but also provide local communities with a resource they could use in the future. Wood was commonly used as fuel for cooking and heat and to construct houses and furniture.

'So why has it so spectacularly failed?' I asked.

'They're the wrong trees for a start,' Mr. Shiri replied. 'These ones here are imported from Australia. They grow quickly, that's true, but one problem is that they require too much water. Villagers are complaining that their wells are drying up in areas where these trees are being planted.'

'The wood also doesn't burn very well,' another of Mr. Shiri's companions explained as we continued our tour. 'That means they're not suitable in terms of providing fuel for cooking. Women complain that they still have to walk long distances to fetch what they need. As far as they're concerned these plantations have not helped them.'

'Has no one pointed this out to those who are responsible?' I asked. 'Surely the forestry people can see the problem for themselves.'

Mr. Shiri shrugged his shoulders. 'Sure, we speak to Government officials all the time. They promise that they will do things differently, that they will plant other types of trees more suitable to the environment and more in line with what people need. In private they tell us that this project was designed and financed by an outside agency and no one wants to irritate the donor who is supporting it.'

He went on to say that at the heart of all that was wrong with the programme was a failure to consult local people about what they required. No one had thought to ask them their opinion. One day the villagers had woken up to find an area of their land enclosed by a fence, signs erected telling them to keep out and trees planted that they had never asked for. It was hardly surprising that a few months later, wire from the fence had been 'stolen' for use by the villagers for other purposes, and their goats encouraged to move in.

'It's true,' a member of the community concurred with what Mr. Shiri had just said. A delegation had come out to greet us and after the formal introductions and hand-shakes they were ready to share their concerns and displeasure at what had occurred. 'No one asked us for our opinion. The only time we were called to a meeting was when someone came one day to tell us what would happen. He wasn't interested in our questions or our request to move the plantation away from our fields. We knew that these trees require too much water for what we have in this area.'

'And we all know what will happen next,' added another. 'That same person will come here in a few months and tell us that we are lazy and ungrateful for having let these trees be destroyed by our animals. They won't accept any responsibility themselves. The truth is that if they had done this differently we might have had something that everyone could have been happy with.'

There was an obvious sense of frustration, but watching the faces of the villagers I fancied I could see another emotion too in the way that some of them smiled when their leaders spoke. Being ignored, being spoken down to, being told what to do by outsiders was how it had always been and always would be in the world they inhabited.

'We are poor farmers, peasants, and illiterate people in the eyes of the educated and privileged. How else can we expect to be treated?' was what their expressions seemed to be saying.

I had seen the same thing in meetings I had attended in Sudan, when farmers had been harangued by Government officials who claimed that their agricultural traditions and practices were backward. After an hour or so of having to listen to criticism of what they had been doing, and instructions on how it should be done, a glazed, blank expression would appear. Occasionally, too, there was that same wry smile of bemused, philosophical resignation at being spoken down to, as if they had nothing to offer, as if their years of experience were of no account. It was little wonder that once these 'experts' disappeared, their advice was ignored.

A drive of a further hour brought us to another location and according to Mr. Shiri a different way of doing things. From some distance away I noticed how green the area looked, the colour standing out against the drab brown of the landscape we had been passing through. Close up, I could see that several of the hills near the village were densely wooded, unlike the other communities we had seen where most of the environment around them was bare. Despite the fact that we were in the middle of the dry season, a stream emerged from some rocks close to where we finally stopped.

For the first time that morning, Mr. Mutasa came up and spoke to me. His manner had changed as dramatically as the landscape that now confronted us. 'One thing you'll notice here is that there are no foreign trees. We haven't planted anything that doesn't belong to this country.'

As we inspected the area he pointed to different varieties and recounted their properties. 'You can eat the leaves of this one,' he said. 'They cure diarrhea. If you boil the bark of that tree there it can be used to treat malaria.'

I had noticed that there was no fence and asked how the forested area was protected against goats, remembering the previous village we had visited and the marauding animals that were eating everything.

'That's the point,' Mr. Shiri replied. 'You don't need a fence if the community looks after their environment.

Because they see the value of this area, they keep their animals away.'

He went on to explain that before a single tree had been planted they had spent time with the community to discuss their value. 'We also talked about why that stream over there was slowly drying up. It was because the rains when they came simply washed down the hills and flowed away. With some tree cover the water can sink into the ground and now that stream flows all year round. We never did anything without the participation and agreement of the local community. Because they see this forest as their own, they do everything they can to protect it.'

'It's not just about pointing out the practical value of trees,' Mr. Mutasa interjected. 'Very often people know about all that and still cut them down. You have to appeal to something stronger.'

'What do you mean?' I asked.

'The hills around this village were traditionally set aside as sacred ground. That's because one of the most important chiefs of this district was buried here many years ago. We call such places in our language 'Murambatemwa.' These places are supposed to be protected. That means: no hunting, no grazing of domestic animals and no cutting down of trees. If these rules are broken, the spirit of the chief will return to punish his people. Our role is to remind the community of these traditions and the respect they should show towards them.'

Mr. Shiri nodded in agreement. Practical reasons as to why trees were important were not enough to motivate people, he said. 'For people in my church it is the Bible that inspires us. God made us stewards of his earth. If we ignore that duty then it is clear that we risk punishment.' Planting trees and putting up fences was the easy part, he added. It was getting the community behind them that was difficult.

At the village itself a small crowd had gathered, having been informed the previous week about our visit. I noticed the respectful and deferential manner Mr. Shiri and his companions displayed when greeting the village elders, and how this in turn seemed to be appreciated by everyone who was there. I had no sense that the community had been orchestrated beforehand into repeating what I had just heard. But they universally concurred with what Mr. Shiri and Mr. Mutasa had said. While they could recount the practical value of their forest and the benefits it delivered, it was the respect inspired by culture and belief that seemed to inform much of their motivation in looking after it.

'Our ancestors are angry at the way we have treated the land,' claimed the village headman. 'That is why we have drought in the province.'

'God is angry with us because we cut down our trees and never replaced them,' was another phrase I heard.

As we continued our tour I took the opportunity to speak to some members of the community on my own. It was clear that they appreciated the participative and respectful manner that had been adopted by Mr. Shiri and his colleagues. The promotion of indigenous trees, suited to the terrain and with which they were familiar, was also welcomed.

An older person I spoke to lamented the fact that Government forestry officials seemed to have little knowledge about indigenous tree varieties. Nor did they display any curiosity to find out what they could about them. 'If they want to help us they should listen more and do less talking. There are things that we can learn but not from people who treat us like fools. They should remember that it is only we ourselves who can solve our problems.'

'So what's the schedule for tomorrow?' I asked Mr. Shiri as he walked me back to the hotel later that afternoon, after we had said goodbye to the others. I had noticed that his 'timetable' indicated our attendance at some religious gathering and I was curious to know what this was about.

'Tomorrow is an important day for us,' he replied. 'We have organised a meeting in one of our communities with an important spirit medium. As I told you before, their support is important.'

It turned out that in order to get to where the meeting would take place we would have to leave Masvingo as early as five o'clock the following morning. I said that this was fine by me but when Mr. Shiri asked if I intended to wear any red clothes, I had to ask him to repeat the question.

He laughed. 'Don't worry. I'm not interested in what you wear. It's just that spirit mediums are sensitive to this colour. It's something to do with the sight of blood that upsets them.'

I replied that my only shirt of that colour was back in Scotland where I had left it. But were there other kinds of restrictions I needed to observe? As a European and an outsider would my presence be welcome?

I had noticed that despite a slight softening in Mr. Mutasa's manner when we had inspected his trees, the rest of the day he had remained aloof and reserved. He had barely interacted when I had asked him some questions. It might well be that his hostility was 'nothing personal' as Mr. Shiri had said, but by virtue of my race, background and colour I could probably expect more of the same tomorrow. In fact, it might be worse if I was now gate crashing a ceremony that was so culturally sensitive.

I reminded Mr. Shiri of what he had told me earlier when I had asked him about the importance of spirit mediums in Zimbabwean society. He had talked not just about their healing powers, their ability to help sick people or those who had had a misfortune, but about their role as guardians of belief and tradition. It was because of this that they had conflicted with the authorities for much of the time the country had been ruled by outsiders. The latter were determined to stamp out traditions that were seen to be hostile to their own control of the population. That was why cultural leaders had become principal targets of persecution.

The most famous in recent history had been Ambuya Nehanda, a spirit medium from the north of Zimbabwe. I had been surprised to hear that she was a woman, since my experience in other parts of Africa had led me to believe that the principal religious figures in most societies were men. Her pronouncements helped to prompt an uprising among the Shona in the late 1800s, irked at the seizure of their lands by the European population. The war dragged on for several months resulting in the deaths of scores of settlers and hundreds of Africans. Ambuya Nehanda was caught, tried for the murder of a European Commissioner and eventually hanged, a measure which raised her to the status of a national martyr.

Some of the laws that were subsequently passed in Rhodesia had been about limiting the influence of spirit mediums and local chiefs. But partly as a result of these measures, their reputation and status among the population had been enhanced. It was the name of Ambuya Nehanda that had been carved on the weapons of many of the African fighters in the recent war, and her face that was now printed on several of the flags that fluttered on top of Government buildings in the capital.

Curiosity was fine but I had to be sensitive too. 'I don't want to cause any offence or embarrassment,' I said. 'I appreciate that this is not about me personally, but if you were to tell me that my presence tomorrow would be inappropriate, I would fully understand.'

Once again Mr. Shiri reassured me. 'We talked about your coming tomorrow and Mr. Mutasa was present too. We all agreed that it is important for you to see as much as possible of what we are doing here. We all appreciated your respectful manner today and your willingness to listen. Do the same tomorrow and you'll be just fine.'

As he took his leave, informing me that he would come to the hotel to pick me up at the appointed time, he added that the only other thing I would need the next day was a sturdy pair of shoes. 'The place where the meeting will be is some distance from the road. We have a long walk to get there.'

There were five of us in the group the next morning as we walked along a narrow track that was barely visible in the forest we passed through. Mr. Mutasa had not arrived at the hotel with the others and I had worried that he had boycotted the meeting in protest at my coming. Maybe this had been a mistake after all, and Mr. Shiri had been too polite to say so. But now I had no chance of pulling out. With no signs of habitation amid the featureless landscape, I would be lost in five minutes if I tried to return to where we had left the car.

An hour or so later and seemingly in the middle of nowhere, the track we were on emerged into a clearing where a crowd of people had already gathered. We had seen no one else since we had set off that morning and yet suddenly here they were, an entire community waiting patiently in the middle of the bush.

We were ushered towards some benches by an individual who seemed to be in charge of the arrangements. The atmosphere was less solemn than I had expected and there was none of the tense formalities I had worried about. People came up to shake my hand and find out who I was. Mr. Shiri did the introductions. The warm response went some way to reassuring me that I was not out of place or that my presence was unwelcome.

It was the sudden and intense hush that finally settled over the crowd that focused my attention on a figure that emerged from the trees. Dressed in a black gown and a headdress made of feathers, which partly concealed his face, he stood completely still and fixed everyone with a steady, hostile stare. There was someone beside him, carrying a drum and a small, ceremonial axe. He too remained motionless. It was as if they were both sizing up the situation and making a decision as to whether they would proceed.

'What are they waiting for?' I whispered to Mr. Shiri after some fifteen minutes had elapsed. In all that time the crowd had remained silent as both figures remained motionless without uttering a sound.

'They are waiting for the ancestral spirit to arrive,' he replied. 'But sometimes this doesn't happen if the circumstances are not right, if something keeps them away. Just be patient. This could take some time.'

A short while later, however, as if they had reached some kind of decision, the attendant began to tap the drum he was carrying and move slowly forward. As the sound intensified, the rhythm was picked up by members of the audience. Some of the men began to clap their hands and stamp their feet. The women began to ululate, producing an eerie, penetrating sound that I remembered from Sudan at similar emotionally charged gatherings. Meanwhile, the spirit medium began to shake his head and roll his eyes, uttering strange barking sounds from the back of his throat. 'That's a good sign,' Mr. Shiri said. 'The mudzimu, his spirit, has possessed him. Now he will speak.'

I was quite happy to sit where I was and observe what was happening from a distance. There was something alarming in the nervous, jerky movements of the medium and his contorted features. As they waved their sticks and began to jump around it looked as if some of the people around me were also becoming possessed. Clouds of dust billowed into the air from their stamping feet and everyone was jostling and shoving to get closer.

'Don't you want to hear what he has to say?' Mr. Shiri asked, as he took my arm and pushed me forward. 'There's no point in coming all this way and then missing the important part.'

Up close, the spirit medium looked more pensive than stern. He seemed exhausted too, as if the effort of hosting his 'mudzimu' had drained him of energy. He was uttering a series of sounds which his attendant would then translate as his response to the questions that were being directed towards him. Occasionally he would pause, take some snuff from a box that his attendant held towards him, snort some into his nostrils and then resume where he had left off.

Although I did not fully understand what was being said, I gathered that the medium, when asked, endorsed much of what I had heard the previous day. The ancestral spirits were angry about the disrespect their descendants had shown towards the land they should have taken care of. It was this that explained the drought and misfortune that had affected their district in recent years. The solutions were simple: respect their traditional leaders, honour their ancestors and replace the trees that had been cut down. If all those things were done, circumstances would improve.

With that message it seemed that the spirit medium finally exhausted his energies. Almost immediately, his face relaxed and the strange, jerky spasms and movements stopped too. A second later, he was whisked away by his attendant, back into the forest from where he had come.

One minute I had been caught up in an atmosphere charged with religious fervor. The next, as if a switch had been turned off, calm and order were restored. The people around me, who had worked themselves up into a kind of frenzy, returned from whatever place they had momentarily occupied. They shook hands, clapped each other on the back, discussed in groups what had just been said and slowly began to filter away along the tracks that would take them home.

Mr. Shiri and his companions were pleased. The message that had been delivered was one that would resonate among the neighbouring communities, making their job of convincing people to protect the environment and plant more trees that much easier.

As we walked back along the track, I had time to reflect on what I had seen that morning. I had no sense that this was a stage act, a means to convince a gullible community that it should behave in a certain way. Although I could not relate to the beliefs and customs that underpinned this event, it had been too intense and emotional to be considered a sham.

Remembering too the cold, hostile stare that the spirit medium had fixed on the crowd when he had first appeared, I felt partly reassured about the hostility I had experienced the previous day. Maybe from the perspective of the persons they became when their spirits possessed them, there was good reason to feel disappointed with the way in which people behaved. Maybe it was not only me who irritated Mr. Mutasa.

By the time we reached the car I had made up my mind. What I had seen over the last few days was that if you wanted community support, whether in protecting trees, digging latrines or constructing a school, you had to understand and speak the language that people could relate to. For outsiders, technical advisors and Government officials that effort seemed particularly hard. To them, it probably meant abandoning their position of prestige and authority, their appointed role of expert who has nothing to learn from those they were helping. Mr. Shiri's organisation was one of the few I had seen that seemed to have made a genuine effort to engage the community in an equal partnership. In the dealings I had seen they had shown an exemplary respect for local opinions and had clearly engaged with the culture and beliefs that determined people's behavior. In return they had won the hearts and minds of their so called beneficiaries, an achievement which was rare in many of the development projects I had witnessed in my short career in this field. It was an easy decision, therefore, to agree to their request for more resources.

'We will provide you with some funds,' I said, as we drove back to Masvingo. 'I thought at one stage you might benefit from an external advisor, one of our expatriate workers who knows about forestry, but I can see now that this would be a waste of time. There is nothing more that such a person could teach you.'

'You can't leave Masvingo without visiting Great Zimbabwe,' Mr. Shiri said, after we had concluded our business a few days later and signed an agreement for the transfer of funds. He added that the word 'Zimbabwe' was derived from the Shona 'dzimba dza mabwe' which translated as 'house of stone.' How could I not visit the very place that the country had been named after?

I had planned to travel to Harare early the following morning but decided to delay my return by taking a detour to see the country's most impressive ruins. Following the directions he had drawn on a piece of paper, I found myself the next day driving along a narrow, pot-holed road and wondering if I had taken a wrong turn. Since I had left Masvingo I had seen only one small sign that had something resembling a monument painted upon it. If this was the route to the country's most prestigious historical landmark, shouldn't it have been in better condition?

As I drove on I recalled previous disappointments when visiting some of the continent's tourist attractions. Frequently I had ended up in front of something tired and unexceptional, which bore little resemblance to what I had been led to expect either from a guidebook I was reading or the recommendations of fellow travellers. Once there I would be invariably pestered by caretakers and custodians, more anxious about soliciting a bribe than looking after whatever it was they were meant to supervise. In contrast it was the unannounced that had often impressed me the most, like the pyramids I had stumbled upon in northern Sudan when all I had expected were a few broken stones in the desert.

It was at these pyramids near a place called Merowe that I had met Thierry, a French archaeologist who was scratching away at a patch of ground to uncover a lost Nubian city. That was the first time I had heard of Great Zimbabwe too. We had been talking about why Nubia was less well known than Egypt as a site of previous civilisations. Thierry had claimed that one reason was a bias in his profession against acknowledging that Africa south of Egypt had ever produced anything of note. Although this prejudice was now changing, it had been assumed for a long period of time that black Africans could simply not have created complex societies.

The ruins of Great Zimbabwe, he told me, were a perfect illustration of what we had been discussing. They clearly displayed evidence of a culture that boasted significant achievements in architecture, trade and social administration. There were even fragments of pottery from China and Persia that were said to be more than six hundred years old. But for much of the period after Great Zimbabwe had been 'discovered' the Rhodesian authorities had insisted that such a civilisation could never have emerged locally. Members of the archaeological fraternity had come up with all sorts of theories to explain it away. This had included claims that it was founded by lost Phoenician sailors, itinerant Arab traders and even the survivors of Atlantis.

It was only in the 1960s that, begrudgingly and belatedly, an acknowledgment was made that Great Zimbabwe was the site of a powerful Shona kingdom that had once controlled much of what constituted the country today, and large parts of Mozambique as well. After my conversation with Thierry, I had promised myself that if the opportunity ever arose I would visit the ruins to see what all the fuss had been about but first I had to find them.

It was only when I came across a large bus with tinted windows and a sign that read 'Majestic Tours' that I guessed I was on the right track. It had taken up most of the narrow road and had disgorged a group of tourists beside some stalls selling crafts and other local knick-knacks. I knew that I must be near when I saw, amid the spears, drums, wooden carvings and colorful cloth, some T-shirts which read, 'My friend visited Great Zimbabwe and all I got was this lousy T-shirt.'

With no hope of squeezing past the bus, I had to wait until the passengers it let off decided to get on again. My heart sank when the vehicle then pulled off in the same direction I was headed. I had naively imagined having Great Zimbabwe to myself for a few hours, with the freedom to explore it on my own and meditate on its history and past significance without the noise and interruption of others.

Perhaps because of its setting, Great Zimbabwe seemed

all the more stately and impressive by contrast. One minute I was driving through a typical rural area with goats, cattle, fields of maize and tired looking donkeys on the side of the road. The next minute it had appeared; a large, sprawling area of impressive stone walls, towers and enclosures that clearly hinted at the thriving metropolis it had once been. Thierry, my guidebook and Mr. Shiri had all enthused about this place, claiming that it was a must see for anyone visiting the country. I had been skeptical because of my past experience but this time I was prepared to admit that from a first impression Great Zimbabwe merited every bit of the reputation it had acquired.

The minimum size of group for the several guides that were available to show visitors around was twenty-five people. I ended up with the 'Majestic Tours' party, which included couples from England, Holland and Germany and an elderly gentleman called Bernie who came from Australia. Seeing I was 'unattached,' like himself, he decided we should benefit from each other's company. In exchange for telling him where I came from, what I was doing in Zimbabwe and what I thought of the people and places I had so far seen, he gave me an outline of his own back-ground, circumstances and former travels. This included his lack of enthusiasm for piles of broken stones which adver-tised themselves as ruins. 'I don't see what all the fuss is about,' he said. 'If they have fallen down then they probably weren't much to begin with.'

On another occasion I might have been happy to ex-change pleasantries with a complete stranger, and even swap our respective life histories. But anxious to preserve the privacy and intensity of the emotional experience I hoped Great Zimbabwe would offer me, I tried to maintain a cool and frosty reserve. But Bernie was persistent and had an impressive capacity to ignore my signals. He kept up an endless chatter while I pretended to read what my guide-book had to say. By the time that Amos, our guide, had introduced himself and started his presentation we had become a couple like the others, albeit in a marriage I was keen to terminate.

First on out itinerary was a small museum. Inside it there were examples of the pottery, jewelry, iron working and other carvings that had been excavated over the years among the ruins. There was the porcelain from China that Thierry had mentioned, coins from Arabia and Persia, and an impressive range of other artifacts. This included the famous stone birds of Great Zimbabwe, replicas of the eagle that now featured on the flags and banknotes of the country as the national emblem.

Of the eight stone birds that were originally found at the site, seven had been whisked off to other countries, including one that was presented to Cecil Rhodes, the founder of Rhodesia. There was a widespread belief that until all the birds had been returned, peace would remain elusive in Zimbabwe. All of them had now been repatriated, apart from the one that had been presented to Rhodes. The *bataleur* eagle, which the carvings depicted, were birds of good omen in Shona culture and venerated as intermediaries between humans and the spirit world they were said to be in touch with. The fact that one was still missing continued to rankle, especially since it was resident in the home, turned museum, of the very person who had orchestrated the seizure of the country in the late 19th century.

I was also intrigued to discover that a one David Randall McIvor, an amateur archaeologist who had excavated among the ruins in the early 1900s, had fought a lonely battle to credit the Shona as the originators of this impress-ive civilisation. The artifacts he had found were in keeping with indigenous traditions. He was brave enough to challenge his colleagues, who either through conviction or coercion maintained that such a level of sophistication could never have emerged from local people.

His conclusions were ridiculed by the authorities too, who censored any reference to indigenous origins in the guidebooks, school textbooks and other material that mentioned Great Zimbabwe. McIvor was not a common name, as I knew, and having a namesake who had maintained scientific objectivity and racial impartiality in the face of intense opposition and bias filled me with pride. I had difficulty preventing myself from announcing there and then, either to Bernie or anyone else who would listen, that David Randall McIvor and I were members of the same illustrious family.

As our guide explained Great Zimbabwe's complex administrative structures and widespread trading agreements with other countries, I was struck by the irony of our presence there. Here was a group of Europeans from societies which had been convinced for generations that Africa was backward, ignorant and in need of our civilising influence. Yet at a comparative point in history, Great Zimbabwe had hosted a culture as advanced as most of those in our own part of the world. I wondered if this was appreciated by the visitors around me, most of whom brushed past the exhibits as if they were items on a stall that they had no interest in buying.

Somewhere among the ruins, and in front of an impressive conical tower that would have required considerable technical ingenuity to construct, a member of our party asked the question that I had anticipated would materialise sooner or later. Could Great Zimbabwe really have been constructed by Africans? Wasn't it more likely that it had been built by some other people?

Our guide fielded the question as well as he could, despite

the obvious skepticism of the questioner. 'There is nothing to suggest that Great Zimbabwe was built by any other people. All the archaeological evidence points to a civilisation founded by the inhabitants of this area.'

'But I read somewhere that this place was built by Phoenicians who sailed down the coast of Africa.'

'That theory has been disproven,' our guide replied. 'There is nothing to suggest that Great Zimbabwe was anything other than local.'

As we moved on to the next section of the ruins, I listened to the comments of some of the people around me. 'You've seen what we've driven past this morning. Africans can't even construct decent houses. How could they have built a stone city like this one?'

I remembered the words of Thierry when I had asked him why there had been this antipathy towards acknowledging Great Zimbabwe as the site of an indigenous African civilisation. 'It's easier to colonise a people if you believe they have never produced anything worthwhile. These ruins confront our prejudices and preconceptions. That's why Great Zimbabwe has made people so uncomfortable.'

'Yes, I often get asked these kinds of questions,' Amos replied when I managed to find an opportunity to speak to him. 'Despite what I say I can see that some of our visitors don't believe me.'

I asked him if this bothered him. 'Why should I get upset?' he replied. 'It's not my problem if people don't want to believe what is in front of their eyes.'

'You can have some time on your own now,' he said, after our allotted hour was up. Making an excuse about having to leave for Harare, I abandoned Bernie to the other members of his party and found myself a quiet location on one of the walls where I could have a moment of reflection alone. I ended up thinking about something that

Amos had also said in response to another question that one of our party had asked.

'How did Great Zimbabwe decline? How could such an advanced society have collapsed and left nothing but these stones behind?'

There were several theories to explain what had happened. The kings who had ruled Great Zimbabwe were said to have exacted heavy taxes, which provoked their subjects to rebellion. There were regional conflicts too, and rival seats of power that wanted to take over the immense territory that Great Zimbabwe controlled. The location of the city so far inland was also inimical to trade. Rival maritime kingdoms or those located on navigable rivers could better import what they needed to sustain themselves, but the theory that Amos thought was most likely was one that pointed to a contemporary problem too.

There was considerable evidence to show that Great Zimbabwe had been impacted by a lack of respect among its population for the environment in which it was sited. Trees had been cut to excess. The soil had eroded. The rivers had dried up. Quite simply the land could no longer sustain the inhabitants of such a large metropolis. Without food the people became hungry, the rulers lost the support of their citizens and one of the country's most impressive empires fell away, leaving nothing but these ruins behind as a testimony to its past glory.

As he spoke, I guessed that Amos was also thinking of the current problems that were affecting his province: the destruction of trees and the resulting deterioration of the environment, the abandonment of villages by younger people, the inability of agriculture in the communal areas to adequately feed the population upon them. It was the same theme I had been exposed to over the last few days, when during my travels with Mr. Shiri and his colleagues we had seen how an inability to manage the resources of a particular location inevitably came back to haunt the population dependent upon them.

Having seen what Mr. Shiri's organisation was trying to do, I was a bit more optimistic than Amos when it came to contemplating the future. 'What happened here is something we can learn from,' he had concluded, 'but I'm not sure if we are wise or smart enough to recognise what history can teach us.'

9

Further Afield

'You've been here for over a year now,' Sekuru said to me one evening as we sat on the veranda contemplating a glorious sunset over a couple of beers. 'When are you going home to see your mother and father?'

He seemed shocked when I told him that I wouldn't go home just yet, that I was curious to travel and see the region. He reminded me that there was nothing worse than neglecting your parents. 'Travel can wait. Your family can't.'

'I have to go back to London next year for a meeting,' I reassured him. 'I'll go and see them then.'

Then I changed the subject. On a previous occasion when he had asked me who was looking after my parents, my answer that they were looking after themselves had not satisfied him. 'Who stays with them when you are not around? What about your brothers and sisters?'

I had told him that like me my siblings were scattered in other parts of the globe. My brother was working in Saudi Arabia. My sister had emigrated to Canada. 'Our families are not so different,' I had remarked. Hadn't he and his brothers left for South Africa when they were younger too?

'One of us always stayed behind,' he replied somewhat tersely, as if I had insinuated some neglect on their part.

He had then asked me if there were any aunts, uncles, cousins or nephews in close proximity to where my parents resided. When I told him that they were on their own and that we had lost touch with our cousins in Scotland many years ago he shook his head and said that such a thing was impossible in his culture. 'The worst thing that can happen to someone here is to die away from your family and to be buried among strangers. Who will look after your grave? That's why if we are seriously ill we will make every effort to return home as soon as possible, even if getting there kills us.'

I had tried to explain to him the workings of the modern, self-sufficient, nuclear family. Living with your parents once you were of an age to stand on your own feet was considered something of a joke in the part of the world I came from. I explained to him too that my parents had chosen to end up in the far north of Scotland, miles away from any relatives. They had provided us with a good education and pushed us to go to university. 'They can hardly criticise us for leaving home to realise the ambitions they fostered. In fact, when I told them I was coming to Zimbabwe they were pleased that I had found what I wanted to do.'

He was still not satisfied. 'But if their children are far away what happens to old people when they can't look after themselves any longer?'

'Many of them go into a home, where they receive professional care.'

'You mean a home run by strangers?'

'Yes, but they are professional people,' I explained, seeing where this conversation was headed. 'They are paid to look after them and see that they are well taken care of. Their children visit as regularly as they can.'

'But how can someone outside the family provide what an old person needs? You can't buy respect or affection. I can't think of any worse place to end up,' he concluded, and I could see his surprise that the 'developed' society I came from could treat people in such a fashion.

At Sekuru's home when I had visited he had introduced me to an 'uncle' who lived with them, a gentleman in his nineties who seemed alert, engaged and a key figure within the family. The children fussed around him. Visitors would make a point of engaging him in conversation. Sekuru regularly consulted him, so he told me, for advice on important matters. 'If you live to be ninety then you've done something right,' he added. 'It's only a fool who would ignore you.'

The centrality of old people in community and family affairs was something I had seen in Sudan too, a role rarely attributed to the elderly in the UK. Truth to tell, one reason I steered away from conversations on this topic was that I could see Sekuru's point. I had no real rejoinder to the shock he had expressed, nor his constant reminders that I should keep in touch with my parents.

'So which part of the region do you think I should visit?' I asked him, hoping that my statement about seeing my family later that year would persuade him I was a decent son after all.

'Why don't you go to South Africa,' he said. 'I've never been to London but I imagine it's much the same. If you go there you'll feel at home.'

Sekuru had a fixed idea that London was the size of an entire country and that places outside it were little more than suburbs of a gigantic metropolis. It was the same concept he had of South Africa, which he had once described as a country of cities.

'What do you mean?' I asked him.

'South Africa is developed and development means cities, doesn't it? It's only poor countries like Zimbabwe that have large spaces in between their towns.'

If South Africa was so much like London then there was little point in my visiting, I told him. 'I want to see something different. In any case my organisation isn't keen for us to travel there.'

Zimbabwe's southern neighbour was constantly referred to in disparaging terms in the newspapers, radio and television, much of whose coverage was devoted to what was happening in that country. Even the demure and unassuming weather lady would announce when the main news was finished, 'A cold front is spreading northwards from the racist Republic of South Africa. Expect rain and strong winds tomorrow.'

The prominence of South Africa in the news wasn't just because of the weather it exported. It hovered like a menacing presence over the political, economic and social landscape of the region. A few months previously we had watched pictures on television of bodies being removed from a house in Bulawayo. The dead were members of the ANC, the liberation movement headed by Nelson Mandela. They had been killed by South African commandos helicoptered into the country to carry out their executions.

It wasn't only South African exiles who were targeted. On another occasion there was a serious shortage of petrol in Harare and other cities. The queues lasted for days and fuel was rationed to such an extent that you received barely enough to drive to the next petrol station to see if the queue was shorter. The problem was due to a cut in supplies transiting through South Africa. A journalist had informed me that such events were common. 'It's a reminder of who controls the transport network in the region. The message is simple; step out of line and we can turn the tap off at any moment.'

'So if you can't travel to South Africa then where will you go?' Sekuru asked.

'I miss the sea. It's strange travelling the length and

breadth of this country only to end up at a border with more land behind it.'

Although Mozambique had a coastline that was close, the war made travel there all but impossible. I had no intention of repeating an experience I had had in Chad, when I had turned up in the middle of a conflict and it had taken a month to traverse that country.

'What's that place with all the blue beside it?' Sekuru asked, pointing to somewhere on the map I had spread out on the table in front of us.

'That's Namibia,' I replied, 'and the sea beside it is the Atlantic Ocean. But it's on the other side of the continent and judging by the distance it would probably take me a week to get there. Besides, it's having a war too.'

Sekuru shrugged his shoulders as he rose to leave. 'Then there's only one solution,' he said. 'If you want to see the ocean, then fly back to Scotland, visit your parents and enjoy the view from your family home.'

At the airport in Lilongwe I regretted that I had chosen neither of Sekuru's options. A few months after our conversation I had decided on impulse to visit Malawi instead. Although it didn't have a coastline it had a huge lake that covered some twenty per cent of the country. If I couldn't find an ocean then at least I could have the next best thing.

There was a direct flight from Harare every Wednesday and Saturday. 'You can purchase a visa at the airport,' the travel agent had informed me. What she didn't tell me was that if you were dressed 'inappropriately' or your hairline extended a fraction below your collar you could be refused entry. I had been whisked out of the arrivals queue by two security officers and ushered into a room to have my situation 'regularised.'

A short, thin gentleman sat down on the chair opposite

me while his larger companion placed himself in front of the door, as if to make sure I wouldn't escape. The former did all the talking. The other said nothing for the thirty or so minutes I was in the room, occasionally fixing me with an unpleasant stare that made me feel uncomfortable and jittery. 'Don't get nervous,' I said to myself. 'You'll only sound guilty.'

'Malawi,' said the thin one 'is a civilised country, thanks to the efforts of our great leader.' He pointed to the only decoration in the room, a large, framed photograph of Hastings Kamuzu Banda, the so called 'life-president' of the country. 'We don't want hippies or the wrong sort of visitor passing through here. They bring drugs and pornography and influence our young people in a bad way. That's why we won't let them in.'

'I'm not a hippy and I don't carry drugs,' I spluttered, handing him a card with my name, address and position printed upon it, hoping that this would convince him I was respectable. He proceeded to scrutinise this for a few seconds before placing it on the table and resuming where he had left off.

'Hippies have long hair and your hair is long too. How can you blame us for thinking you are the wrong sort of person to come into our country?'

At this point, I found it difficult not to laugh. Hippies had hair past their shoulders, thick beards, glazed eyes and wore jeans with patches on them. Ten years previously I might have fitted that description. Now I could be mistaken for a bank clerk. 'Excuse me sir,' I said as politely as I could, 'but I don't think you can describe my hair as long at all. In fact where I come from it would be considered rather short.'

It was the wrong reply. Taking out a tape measure from his jacket pocket he told me to sit still, to look ahead and not bend my neck. Then he placed the measure on my shirt collar and counted the centimeters to where my hair ended. 'You see,' he said triumphantly, pointing to the mark he had made on his tape. 'Your hair is longer than it should be.'

I shrugged my shoulders apologetically and said that I had not been informed about this restriction before I came to his country. Had I known I certainly would have had it cut before I travelled. 'I meant no disrespect,' I said, summoning up as much sincerity as I could.

My apology seemed to placate him. Out of another pocket he produced a piece of paper with a list of 'prohibitions' typed upon it. I should have been familiar with that list, he said, before I came to Malawi. It was displayed in all their embassies, including the one in Harare. Travel agencies were also supposed to have copies so that they could alert tourists beforehand about the country's regulations. 'You can read it now if you like.'

Most of the prohibitions were about dress and appearance. Women who wore trousers would not be let into the country. If they wore a skirt it had to cover their knees. Men with long hair, bracelets and flared trousers were encouraged to stay away. Anyone caught carrying communist literature, girly magazines or a copy of 'Africa on a Shoestring' would be barred from entering. Thankfully I had a different guidebook than the one mentioned. 'Why is it banned?' I asked.

He frowned. 'That book is very bad. It says terrible things about our leader and the system of Government we have in this country. You're not carrying a copy, are you?' he asked, and I shook my head and pretended that I had never heard of it.

After reading his list I handed it back to him and said that my travel agent had clearly failed to discharge her duty. She had given me no such document. In any case, the only prohibition I had infringed was the one about my hair and for that I repeated my apology.

'Where are you from?' my interviewer now asked, leafing through my passport.

'I'm from Scotland but I'm now working in Zimbabwe.'

Mention of Scotland seemed to prick his interest. 'We like people from Scotland,' he said. 'Do you know that our President spent many years there as a doctor?'

'Of course I do. Everyone in Scotland does. It was a great honour for our country to have him.' Even as I lied part of me was thinking that for anyone who knew anything about Hastings Banda, his presence in our country was more of an embarrassment than an honour. Although I had not read 'Africa on a Shoestring' I knew that the life-president had the reputation of being one of the continent's worst dictators.

Happy to exploit what seemed to be a more genial atmosphere, I reverted to the subject of my hair and what we could do about it. 'Can we sort something out?' I asked.

'The problem is if we let you into Malawi people will say that we are not doing our job,' he replied, not unsympathetically. 'They will say that border officials are ignoring their own regulations.'

'But there's a simple solution,' I said, in a flash of inspiration. 'In my bag I have a pair of scissors. Why don't you let me go to the bathroom and cut off the length of hair you are worried about? That way no one can ever accuse you of ignoring the rules.'

They had a brief discussion. The big gentleman looked worried as if agreeing to my request might land them in trouble. But my interviewer seemed more supportive and judging from our interaction to date, he was the one who made the decisions. In the end he agreed. There was a bathroom next door. Once I was finished I was to return for an inspection. If their measuring tape indicated that my hair was the appropriate length they would let me into the country.

In front of a mirror I cut off the offending centimeters. Afterwards I could see no real difference in my appearance and wondered what all the fuss had been about. Did all the officials in Malawi carry measuring tapes around with them? If so, it was bureaucracy carried to an extreme.

'That looks better,' the thin one said when I returned. 'Now you look respectable.'

I was about to head for the 'Arrivals' desk when he placed a firm hand on my shoulder and announced that there was one more thing I had to do. I was convinced I was about to be asked for a bribe and mentally calculated what I could afford on my tight budget. What he said surprised me even more.

'Some visitors to our country have complained about their treatment. That book I mentioned earlier even claims that people are harassed at the airport. You need to sign this form to say you have been satisfied with our behavior. Then you can go.'

I read the statement in silence. There was a passage on the professional standards that Malawi was famous for and its long history of hospitality. I was to declare that my treatment at the airport had been in line with those standards and to acknowledge that the officials, whose names were listed, had discharged their duties in an exemplary manner. As quickly as I could, I scribbled my signature before they found a reason to change their minds.

'Welcome to Malawi,' the thin one said, shaking my hand. 'We hope you have a pleasant stay.'

Most Presidents were honored with monuments and landmarks after they left office, but in the case of Hastings

Banda it was different. His picture was plastered all over the brand new, glistening airport he had named after himself. There was a plaque too, thanking the generous South African government for picking up the tab. This surprised me. Governments in the region generally distanced themselves from their large apartheid neighbour and its policies of racial discrimination. Malawi, however, seemed more than happy to advertise its cozy relationship.

I had been to enough airports in Africa to know that most of them were isolated bubbles of development, an exception in countries that often lacked roads, electricity, running water and other basic amenities. But the contrast when I exited outside was even more stark than usual. Outside the doors that sealed in the cool, air-conditioned atmosphere, Malawi abruptly announced itself in all its poverty.

Beyond the perimeter fence a few meters away there was the start of a miserable looking village. Some women were carrying water on their heads from a stream that meandered through their fields. Children in ragged trousers and no shirts ran around kicking a football that looked as if it had been made from rolled up newspaper. They screamed and shouted in excitement when the aircraft I had arrived on took off again with a sudden roar.

But where was the metropolis that the airport was supposed to serve? A sign announced that Lilongwe was over twenty-five kilometers away. Maybe because of my delay the public transport that I had assumed would have met the new arrivals had disappeared. The taxi rank had no taxis. A place marked 'bus stop' had no buses and when I asked a security guard when the next one might arrive, he said that it was only scheduled for the following morning. 'You can always hitch,' he said, pointing to the road that led to Lilongwe. 'That's what we all do when there is nothing else.'

The irony of standing outside a glitzy, modern airport

with my thumb in the air trying to cadge a lift was not lost on me. Nor was it lost on Dermot who stopped half an hour later to pick me up. Before I had a chance to tell him, he guessed the reason I was there. Taking a look at the back of my head he asked me if I had been apprehended by airport security. 'That's the principal reason visitors get stranded out here. They either have to change their clothes or trim their hair. You're lucky they let you in. Frequently they put you on the next flight out of the country.'

Dermot had no such problems with his appearance. He was a priest from Ireland who had lived and worked in Malawi for the past ten years. He was returning to his mission in a town not far from where I was headed. When I told him I was travelling in that direction he offered to take me most of the way there. 'It's not out of Christian charity,' he laughed when I thanked him. 'If I don't have company, I'll fall asleep while I'm driving.'

Like the airport, the road out of it had only recently been built and was as well-paved as anything I had driven on in Zimbabwe. But again, I was struck by the contrast it offered to the impoverished looking settlements on either side. 'How can the country afford that airport and this road?' I asked. In my guidebook Malawi was listed as the sixth-poorest country in the world with a per capita annual income of only several hundred dollars, barely enough to buy a few meals in a London restaurant. I knew too that there had been famine and starvation the previous year. Zimbabwe had sent maize to its struggling neighbour, both as a gesture of solidarity and to avoid an influx of refugees into its own territory.

In response, Dermot pointed to a sign as we entered the outer suburbs of Lilongwe. It stated that the road had been financed through the donations of several countries. South Africa was mentioned. So too were Taiwan and Israel, names I would never have expected to see in that part of the world. 'So what's in it for them?' I asked. As far as I knew Malawi had no strategic resources that might have prompted such generosity.

'They're buying a vote,' he replied. 'Whenever the United Nations wants to issue a communiqué to condemn something that South Africa or Israel has done, Malawi either objects or abstains. Last year the president made a state visit to Pretoria, the only African leader in recent history to have done so. The cost of this airport and this road is Malawi's political integrity.'

'But that must make Banda unpopular among his peers.' I added that one of the few points of agreement there seemed to be among the continent's leaders was their universal opposition to apartheid.

'But none of his African brothers can build a road or an airport in his country, can they?' Dermot responded. 'In the struggle between principles and pragmatism the President has chosen the latter.'

As we drove through the city, I could see numerous new buildings in the course of construction, roads being dug up and in one location hundreds of flowers being planted. It was as if Lilongwe was being invented from scratch and it was only in the outer suburbs, cramped and squalid for the most part, that there was any hint of a previous history.

I had read that Lilongwe was a recent capital. A few years previously, that honour had resided with the town of Zomba in the Malawian highlands further south. For some reason, the people there had managed to irritate the country's ruler. Lilongwe had been chosen as an alternative because it was close to his home area.

The relocation was clearly costing a lot of money. 'Why rebuild the whole city?' I asked. 'Aren't there more urgent priorities for the country, like feeding its people?'

Dermot shrugged his shoulders, indicating that whatever the reason he thought it was a flimsy one. 'The most common view is that the President wants to present an image to the outside world of a country that is modern and progressive, where people from outside can come and do business in an environment that looks like their own. Visitors will soon be able to drive from the airport to the centre of the city without having to see anything that makes them feel uncomfortable.'

He added that this 'pretence of modernity' was not just confined to smart public buildings and first-world roads. 'Most of Malawi's education budget is swallowed up by elite schools, where Latin and Greek is part of the curriculum and where local languages are prohibited. The President seems to think that by creating a small group of privileged people the rest of the country will eventually follow.'

Dermot seemed willing enough to discuss the politics of the country when I asked him for his opinions, but he was cautious too. 'This conversation remains in the car,' he added, fixing me with a stare that left me in no doubt how serious he was.

I had mentioned to him that I occasionally wrote for an African magazine published in London and that they had expressed an interest in an article about Malawi. He told me that I needed to be careful not to display the notebook I was carrying in public. Journalists were regarded with suspicion and without an official permit I could be arrested. 'If a policeman asks what you are writing, tell him it's a letter to your mother back home.'

As we were talking, we passed a group of women walking on the road. The face of Hastings Banda stared back at us, imprinted on the bright yellow cloth they had wrapped around their buttocks. There seemed no place in the country that was private, from which his gaze was excluded. I recalled that there were portraits of Robert Mugabe in public buildings in Harare. President Nimeiri had the audacity to print his features on bank notes in Sudan. But when Dermot told me that there was a law in the country which stipulated that a photograph of the President had to be higher than any other object on the wall on which it was displayed, including clocks, I realised that his personality cult had been carried to an extreme.

At one point in the conversation, I used the word 'dictator' but Dermot was keen to point out that it was not only repression that kept the President in power. 'Terror is there. That is true. When Malawians speak ill of their President they don't have the luxury of being expelled from the country. For them it's jail and sometimes worse. But you also need to remember that the first African face that Malawians saw when the British handed over power was the face of Banda. Many people here perceive their freedom as a gift he won for them.'

Dermot added that Banda had been astute in appropriating certain aspects of culture and tradition that resonated among his population. For example, he had given himself the title of Ngwaza, a Chiweshe word variously translated as Chief of Chiefs, Great Lion and Conqueror. 'Through that title, he is claiming that his authority and leadership has a longer history than his struggle with the British. It dates back to a pre-colonial past when chieftainships were handed down between certain families who had special powers and were divinely chosen. When he waves his stick and loses his temper some of his people see that as an expression of his concern for them, like a stern parent worried about his children.'

Despite the politics, the repressive regime, the spies and informers, the skewed development and the periodic famines that gripped the country, Dermot was not pessimistic about Malawi's future. We were passing a school and judging by what I could see, it was packed with pupils. On the road out of the village there were also scores of children, carrying books and bags. When Dermot told me that some of them would have walked miles that morning to attend classes, I was reminded of Nyaminyami where I had seen similar levels of determination.

'There are lots of churches in Malawi, including my own,' he continued. 'I don't know any of them that hasn't invested in education. The Government seems quite happy for us to build schools, but I don't think they realise that education raises a population's expectations and gives them ambitions that a repressive system can never satisfy. That's the hope I see for a brighter future.'

As an ex teacher, I was flattered by Dermot's estimation of the value and importance of my former profession. But from past experience, I had my reservations too. I expressed the same doubts I had shared with Mr. Nyathi in western Zimbabwe when he had shown me some establishments that were in need of our teachers. 'Surely it depends on what children actually learn. In many countries, school is not a place where children are encouraged to think for themselves or where their curiosity is rewarded. They go to a classroom to copy down exactly what the teacher tells them. In fact, schools can end up as places where children are taught to conform rather than to question. I believe that some Governments see education as a means of better controlling their populations.'

But Dermot was insistent. 'Even if the curriculum is restrictive and the quality of teaching poor, learning to read and write is a precondition of any kind of emancipation. A child's concept of the world and their place within it is different if they have sat in a classroom with other children trying to learn, than if they only know the inside of their home and the fields they have to look after. In that sense all education is subversive,' he said, sounding more like a revolutionary than a priest. 'You need to have more faith. God works through these things in ways that neither you nor I could ever fathom.'

His passion was evident, and for the first time since we had spoken that morning I could see something of the missionary in him. But it was not his church and its ideology that seemed to inspire him, it was his vision of a society that people would one day live in.

What surprised me too was a statement he made that freedom and development were not just entitlements to be transferred by one group of people to another. Many of the anti-colonial struggles in Africa had foundered, he claimed, because once liberated people seemed happy enough to hand over what they had won to another oppressor. The education he had earlier talked about not only provided people with skills and opportunities, but a sense of responsibility too, a realisation that your own future was in no one else's hands but your own.

I had assumed that as a man of the cloth and the representative of a hierarchical church, his remarks would have been more along the lines of 'We know what is in the best interests of the people and it is our duty to guide them.' But somewhere on the long road to Lake Malawi he said that one thing he had learned in his many years as a priest was that God never made the most valuable things in life easy for anyone. 'Struggle is necessary, he said, 'otherwise individuals will never learn to appreciate the true value of something. Once they've won their freedom for themselves, they won't be inclined to lose it either.'

My interrogation at the airport and the copy of the country's prohibitions I now carried around with me had led me to assume that Malawi's tourists would all have cropped hair and be wearing clothes more appropriate for a church service than a vacation. So when I stepped off the bus at Cape Maclear, my first impression was that we had erroneously crossed the border and ended up in a different country. The first people I encountered were two bare-chested Australians, with hair past their shoulders and jeans with holes in them. They were carrying beer bottles in each hand and judging by the way they lurched down the street, these were not their first of the day either.

'Gosh mate, that haircut is a bit severe,' one of them remarked, pointing to my head when I asked them for directions to a place I could stay.

'I was apprehended at the airport,' I replied, not mentioning that my hair had not been that much longer to begin with.

'Have a beer,' said the other one, handing me a bottle. I took a swig of something that left me coughing and spluttering in the middle of the road. The two Australians laughed hysterically, then slapped me on the back and told me I was a good sport. I had just sampled the local 'kachasu', they said, a beverage made from cane sugar and other ingredients the principal purpose of which was to get you drunk as speedily as possible.

'The best place in town is where we're staying,' one of them replied to my original question. 'That's where we're going now, on our way back from buying this stuff. We'll take you there.'

As we walked down the street, the Australians holding onto each other to make sure they didn't keel over, I looked sheepishly around me. If the locals had been warned by their President about the loutish behaviour of ill-mannered foreigners, here was a prime example of what he had been talking about. But everyone seemed intent on their own business, hardly casting a glance in our direction.

I was further astounded when my new companions waved to someone in uniform who was idling outside a small office marked 'Police Station.' The man waved back and shouted a greeting in reply.

'Don't worry,' one of them said when he noticed my looks of concern. 'We met him a few nights ago and he drank both of us under the table.'

The place where they were staying was run by two brothers called George and Ernie. From a dog-eared copy of their prohibited guidebook, one of the Australians read me a flowery paragraph that enthused about its easy going atmosphere, the quality of the food and its location in one of the most scenic parts of the country. A few years previously it had consisted of nothing more than a couple of beach huts to cater for occasional visitors. It had grown and expanded since then and had now assumed a legendary status among seasoned travellers, so the guidebook claimed, adding that as a result it was frequently booked out too.

The two brothers, who according to the Australians were identical twins, apparently derived considerable amusement from asking visitors if they could spot any differences between them. My new companions had to guess which one of them was now at reception. This time they were able to do so because they remembered the floral shirt that Ernie had been wearing as they headed into town earlier that morning. Apart from the clothes, they said, there was nothing to distinguish between them.

'Sure we have a room for you,' Ernie replied when I introduced myself and told him I needed a place to stay for a few nights. But I worried about the lack of formalities. There was no request for my passport or other identification, and no form I had to fill out with my details. I would pay when I left and no deposit was required up front either. Food was available in the restaurant, Ernie replied when I asked him where I could eat. But when I quizzed him further about opening hours he shrugged his shoulders and told me that it depended on when their chef felt like cooking.

'Help yourself to anything you want from the fridge,' he said. 'All you need to do is write down what you took and put your name beside it. We'll total up when you leave.' He held up a tattered exercise book on the front desk that looked as if it had been used by the hundreds of school children I had seen earlier that day. As the two Australians volunteered to take me to where I would sleep, I wondered if 'George and Ernie's' was perhaps too easy going for what I was looking for. I reconciled myself to the fact that I would probably have to find somewhere else to stay.

'What do you think?' the Australians said as we emerged from reception and onto the beach. The view of the lake, the clear sparkling water, the islands shimmering in the distance and the forested hills behind us were as impressive as the guidebook had enthused . The accommodation seemed to be of a much higher standard than I had feared too. The 'huts' had mosquito mesh on the windows, solid roofs and electric lights strung around them. Maybe I had landed on my feet after all.

To get to my room we had to pick our way through a large number of bodies lying on the sand. As we stepped between them I was struck again by the sharp contrast between what I had imagined I would find in Malawi and the reality. Earlier that day I had been told that women who exposed their knees were not welcome in the country and would be asked to leave. But there was considerably more than bare knees on show among the women sunning themselves on mattresses along the length of George and Ernie's beach. What had all the fuss been about at Kamuzu Banda airport, I asked myself. Was I really in the same country?

Tired after my long journey, I turned on the fan in my room, flopped down on the bed for what I thought might be a few minutes rest and woke up several hours later to a banging on my door. It was the Australians who had come to invite me to a party with their friends. Maybe they felt guilty about their earlier prank. Whatever the reason, they ignored my arguments that I needed to sleep. 'Don't tell us you came all the way to Malawi just to lie in your bed,' they said, pushing me out of my room.

A large bonfire had been lit at one end of the beach and a crowd of about twenty people had gathered around it. Most of them belonged to the tour group the Australians were part of. I had seen the bus they travelled around in earlier, a colorful affair with 'Wild African Adventures' printed on the side of it. It had started off in Kenya, had made its way through Tanzania and had stopped off in Malawi for a few days. Their final destination was Cape Town, which they hoped to reach a few weeks later after a detour through Zimbabwe.

I had met touring parties before and had struggled to find anything appealing in traversing Africa's roads in a cramped vehicle, surrounded by strangers you could never escape from and with whom you had to share your most intimate moments. What had struck me too was their limited interaction with local people. As an independent traveller you could stop off at any town or village you liked and change your plans if it suited you. But as a member of a group it meant that you were bound to an itinerary, had to leave at an appointed time and according to a schedule that was decided for you. Having the freedom to respond to the unpredictability of Africa was for me one of the preconditions of enjoying the continent.

The Australians were not unrepresentative of the rest of

the group they were travelling around with. Their hair might have been a shade longer than that of the other men, but compared to the standards indicated in Malawi's list of prohibitions all of them had infringed the required regulations. I noted that one or two had earrings. I even spotted a pair of flared jeans on a gentleman sprawled helplessly on the ground.

Meanwhile, the women I had seen earlier that afternoon had partly wrapped themselves up against the fresh wind that blew off the lake, but none were dressed in anything that could be described as prim and proper. When one of them handed me a pipe and asked me whether I wanted to smoke some local 'chamba' I asked the question that had been nagging me ever since I had stumbled across the Australians earlier that day. 'No offence, but how on earth did the authorities let you into this country?'

They were familiar with the same set of rules I had been presented with at the airport. They had read the relevant pages in 'Africa on a Shoestring' too, and despite the risks associated with carrying that book around with them waved their copies towards me like churchgoers showing off their bibles. But 'Wild African Adventures' had managed to negotiate a safe and hassle free passage for its travellers across the length and breadth of the country. In return for a few bribes here and there, they were ignored and left alone. It was only 'fools' like me who entered Malawi through its prestigious new airport and fell foul of overzealous officials.

'People know that tourists can always go elsewhere,' said the young woman who had offered me a smoke. 'If they get too rigid about their rules everyone knows that this country will lose money.'

By now flat on their backs, it was the Australians who summed up the collective thinking of their group. 'Malawians are easygoing. They couldn't care less what we do.

No one has ever come up to us to complain about the way we dress, our appearance or behaviour. If they objected, why haven't they said so?'

But that perception of the locals as being laid back and indifferent to the behaviour of outside visitors was not something that resonated the following day when I interacted with some of them. Ernie had told me that there was a guide in the neighboring village who would take me out to the islands for a small fee. I had walked several kilometres along the length of the beach and then been escorted by a noisy group of children to the home of the person he had referred me to.

Joshua had a variety of different occupations, apart from tour guide. He was a farmer, a fisherman and the owner of a store that sold basic commodities. His English was good; he had picked it up at school and improved through interacting with visitors who wanted to hire his services for a few hours. Judging by the deference that was shown him as we walked through his community, he occupied a position of considerable importance too.

The boat we would tour the lake on was little more than a hollowed out tree trunk cut from the nearby forest. It looked unsteady but Joshua informed me that his 'canoe' was perfectly safe. He had lost no customers as yet. The secret, he said, was to hold yourself as still as you could in the centre of the boat and just relax while someone at the back and another at the front propelled it through the water.

Encouraged by the shouts of the children who had accompanied us, I climbed in followed by Joshua and one of his relatives. With a few swift strokes we left the village behind us. It was difficult in the hot sun not to move around and try to find a more comfortable position. Fortunately my companions had an uncanny knack of compensating for my every movement. As we glided along, I began to relax while Joshua set up a running commentary on the fauna and flora of Lake Malawi.

It was on one of the islands where we stopped to have lunch that we got around to discussing the behaviour of tourists. Joshua knew all about the Government regulations. He was aware too that they were irregularly enforced and seemed to depend on the whims of officials and their susceptibility to being bribed. But while his definition of what constituted appropriate appearance and behaviour was more generously drawn than the prescriptions I had been handed at the airport, he was clear too that visitors should show some sensitivity to the cultural norms of his country. 'It's bad manners to go into someone's home and not respect the people who live there.'

What concerned him in particular was the influence that visitors had on young people in his community. 'For many years we were told that Europeans had to be looked up to. If we wanted to be civilised, we had to behave like them. Nowadays some of our children see visitors who are drunk in public, who openly smoke 'chamba' and who lie on our beach with hardly any clothes on. Despite what we tell them, they think it is okay to do these things themselves.'

What he had also noticed was that the display of relative wealth and privilege that had come with tourism in close proximity to their village, had also had negative consequences. 'Now we have young people loitering around our community who say that they don't want to fish or farm. They say there is more money selling drugs to tourists. In the case of some of our girls, they sell sex. I don't think that visitors understand that there is no such thing here as privacy. Everything you do is seen and heard. So you have to be careful how you behave and how you influence young people who might look up to you.'

'So is tourism a bad thing for Malawi, something you would rather not have?' I asked him.

'I personally can't complain,' he replied. 'I can support my children to go to school because of the extra money I earn as a guide. But one question we often ask ourselves is where most of the money that is supposed to come from tourism actually ends up.'

He then echoed something that Jacob, the caretaker of the guest house in Nyaminyami, had said too when we were discussing who controlled the economy of his district. 'The hotels here are owned by outsiders. The beer you drink at the place you are staying is imported from South Africa. The bed you sleep on is not made in this community. Sometimes our women are employed to clean your rooms and wash your clothes. But I believe that tourism could do much more if it was better organised and if it was focused on helping local industries and employment too.'

In the late afternoon, when the heat of the day had passed and after Joshua had exhausted his considerable store of information, we made our way back towards the shore. It would be dark by the time we would get to the village and I asked him how we would find our way home. He pointed towards a line of lights shimmering in the distance that had just been turned on. According to him these were the hotels, guest houses and other facilities that had been constructed along the shoreline to cater for visitors to Lake Malawi. 'We know where our villages are just by looking at these lights' he said. 'Since we have no electricity ourselves we just aim for the darkness between them.'

10

A Drive to the Coast

'Watch out for land-mines on the side of the road,' the Namibian border official advised us as we were about to leave. His casual manner, the offhand way this remark was tossed out, as if he were commenting on the weather, made me initially think that he was joking.

'Sorry, could you repeat what you just said?' I asked.

'Keep to the road, sir, and you'll be fine. It's several months since we had our last incident.'

Before I had made my decision to drive to Namibia I had visited the embassy in Harare. 'Is it safe to travel in your country?' I had asked the young woman who was responsible for issuing visas.

'Of course,' she replied. 'Why wouldn't it be?'

'Because you've just had a war.'

'Don't worry about that sir. We have peace now. Visitors are welcome.'

A few weeks later we arrived at the eastern end of the Caprivi Strip, a long ribbon of Namibian territory that bordered Angola and Zambia to the north and Botswana in the south. To get to the town of Rundu at the other end was a drive of almost a day. I had read that the road was in poor condition and that it was best to fill up with diesel before starting, since there was nowhere in between where you could find fuel. Now it seemed we had landmines to contend with too.

'Haven't they been signposted' I asked. 'Aren't they marked so people can avoid them?'

The border official seemed surprised by the question, as if the answer was obvious. 'What's the point of having land-mines if everyone knows where they are? That way they could just walk around them. They were meant to kill people.'

I was tempted to ask him about the 'incident' he had referred to but Paul, an Irish friend who was accompanying me, pulled me aside and said that it was best to leave immediately if we wanted to reach Rundu before dark. 'Besides, we'll only worry if we find out what happened. Do as he says. Stick to the road and we'll be fine.'

It was over a year since my conversation with Sekuru when we had pored over a map of southern Africa. He had pointed to the Atlantic coast and suggested that if I was so determined to see the ocean I could always head for Namibia.

In the intervening period, peace had broken out in a country that had seen decades of armed conflict. I had read my history before I had travelled and was not surprised to discover that the issues were much the same as those that characterised other struggles in the region. A small group of privileged whites controlled the land, the economy and the politics. The black majority had no vote, were marginalised in the poorest agricultural areas of the country, had limited access to education and health care and formed a source of cheap labour for the mines and farms that generated Namibia's considerable wealth.

South Africa was also implicated, since in effect it was the *de facto* ruler of its northern neighbour. Namibia had been a German colony until the conclusion of the First World War. It had then become a protectorate of South Africa, a mandate which the United Nations revoked in 1960, calling for free and fair elections and a peaceful transition to majority rule. Unwilling to cede control and have an example of a black ruled state on its periphery, South Africa refused. Instead it had installed a puppet government and had introduced the same system of apartheid politics to keep the African population in a state of subjugation.

Fed up with having their peaceful overtures refused and their leaders imprisoned, the nationalists eventually took up arms and the inevitable war followed. Over twenty-five years later a peace accord had finally been signed. Elections were held in which SWAPO, the movement that had been at the forefront of the struggle, won a convincing majority.

Shortly thereafter I received a call from my boss in London indicating that our organisation was thinking of establishing a programme of assistance. Our presence in Namibia would be welcomed by the new Government. Would I be interested in going there for a few weeks, to meet up with some contacts and provide some recommendations as to how to move ahead? I had mentioned to him on a previous occasion that I wanted to visit. This way I could combine work with satisfying my curiosity at the same time.

I had found a friend who was as interested as I to explore a country that until recently had been off limits because of the conflict. Paul was a teacher from Ireland whom I had met at a workshop in Harare. He taught in a secondary school in Gweru in the centre of Zimbabwe. We had mutual friends back in Dublin and our paths had crossed several times since. 'Sure, I'd be delighted to go with you. I have a break in June for a few weeks. Why don't we go then?'

Our journey had started inauspiciously. Half way between Harare and Bulawayo I had pulled into a lay-by and indicated that it was time for him to take over. We had a long day ahead of us and it was best to drive for a few hours each before we became too tired to concentrate. He seemed surprised when I stopped and opened the door. 'Sorry, but I never said I could drive. I didn't realise you were expecting me to help out on that front. If it's any consolation I'm a good navigator and I know how to change a tire too.'

I turned moody for a while. We had two to three weeks of constant driving ahead of us. Now I had become a chauffeur to someone who had the luxury of gazing out of the window at the passing landscape while I had to focus on the potholes in the road. I realised later that I was responsible for this misunderstanding. I had never bothered to ask him whether he had a license. In any case, Paul was good company and if nothing else he could keep me awake if I began to fall asleep at the wheel.

There was very little danger of my falling asleep along the Caprivi Strip. The road was patchy at best with bits of tarmac here and there where you could pick up speed, but these would terminate abruptly and without warning, so that frequently I would have to brake hard as the road changed to a corrugated track that shook and rattled the vehicle even at a pedestrian pace.

Though the war may have been over, evidence of militarisation was still everywhere. The other vehicles we encountered were mostly army trucks of one sort or another, all driven with the same reckless abandon I was familiar with in Zimbabwe. This time I was even more nervous. To avoid them I had to swerve off the road, imagining each time I did so that we would disappear in a cloud of smoke, having detonated one of the landmines we had been warned about.

Paul was quite blasé, pointing to the donkeys and cows we passed at regular intervals. 'If it was really dangerous there would be bits of these animals scattered all over the landscape. That border official was exaggerating.'

At the height of the conflict thousands of South African troops had been stationed in Namibia. There were tens of thousands of local conscripts too. For a population that numbered little more than three million people there had been a disproportionate number of soldiers to civilians, even by African standards.

Evidence of what this occupation meant was everywhere. Along the length of the Caprivi Strip there were watchtowers at regular intervals, more numerous along the western part from where the SWAPO fighters had infiltrated from Angola. Any settlement of any size was dominated by a military barracks, usually placed at a strategic height above the territory it supervised. One barracks we passed was bristling with military hardware: tanks, guns and even helicopters. In a nearby field some farmers were struggling with a wooden plough to break the surface of the soil in preparation for the forthcoming rains. The contrast in power and technology could hardly have been starker, nor the irrelevance and futility of what all this 'progress' had been focused on.

But soldiers had money too. In one of the stores we stopped off at to purchase a drink, the owner lamented the opportunities that were disappearing with the departure of the troops. There was no one else in the store and I had asked him if he had customers at other times. He had shrugged his shoulders. 'Once the soldiers go, no one else can afford a Coca-Cola in this village. People can afford to eat. That is all.'

It was dark by the time we got to Rundu. At the entrance to the town we were stopped by an army patrol manning a roadblock. Remembering roadblocks I had encountered elsewhere, I took a deep breath and opened the window.

The soldiers were cordial enough when they requested our passports and this time their guns were not pointed in our direction. 'Why are you driving at night?' one of them asked. 'Don't you know it's dangerous?'

I replied that we had driven from Katimo Mulilo earlier that day, that the road had been worse than we expected and that there was no way we could have driven faster without damaging the vehicle.

'Why is it dangerous?' Paul asked. 'I thought the war was over.'

'The war might be over but that doesn't mean that peace has come. There are still guns in this part of the country. A car like yours is worth a lot of money.'

At a place called 'The Travellers Rest' we had a choice of whatever rooms we fancied. We were the first customers in several days. Samuel was the hotel manager, a young Namibian in his early thirties. He managed reception, poured beer for us at the bar and even made us a sandwich. There was nothing else on the menu that was available, he said, the cook having left a few weeks earlier.

'Why don't you have more customers?' Paul asked. The quality of the furniture and the hotel décor indicated that the place had seen better days.

It was the same story we had heard earlier. Army officers had been the principal clientele for a number of years. 'Some weekends they would take over the entire establishment,' Samuel said, shaking his head at the contrast between then and now. 'They got a bit noisy and drank too much, but one thing was that they always paid for the damage afterwards.'

For a while before the elections of the previous year, the hotel had been busy too. This time the soldiers belonged to a United Nations peace keeping mission, there to ensure that the uneasy ceasefire was maintained. According to Samuel, however, they were rowdier than the local troops, drank more beer and what was even worse, never paid for the damage they caused. 'One thing they did leave behind was a lot of illegitimate children.' In northern Namibia, he claimed, there was a generation of UN babies that had been abandoned by their fathers when their tour of duty had ended.

As yet the source of his custom had not been replaced, but Samuel was hopeful. With peace there was every chance that tourists would come to this part of the country. He was curious to know too whether our presence heralded an influx of foreign aid workers. 'We have heard that international charities will come to Namibia to help us. Please tell them that if they come to Rundu this hotel is the best place to stay.' He pointed apologetically to the sandwich he had prepared for us. With more customers, he added, his chef would return.

'Don't get me wrong,' Samuel was keen to point out. 'I'm glad that the fighting is over. I lost friends. For years we prayed for independence.' But the question that was now uppermost in people's minds was what the conflict would be replaced by. War had terrorised them, had destroyed communities and killed family members and relatives. But it had brought business and employment too, and outsiders with money to spend. Now that it was over people were waiting to see what dividends peace would bring.

'Many of us are worried about what will happen to the thousands of soldiers on both sides of the conflict. They can't all be assimilated into the new army. What will the rest of them do? These are people who were trained to be killers. If they don't get what they want, they will take it for themselves. Thefts and robberies are becoming more common. Some say that it is former soldiers who are behind it all.'

It wasn't just bottle stores and hotels that were running out of customers. Shortly after Samuel had poured us another beer we were approached by a group of giggling girls in short skirts and heavy make-up, asking if we could buy them a drink. They looked as if they were in their teens, one or two barely out of secondary school. There was something diffident about them too behind their bravado as they approached us. Despite their request for something stronger we asked Samuel to serve them Coca-Colas.

They seemed happy to sit beside us, even after we had declined an offer of a private massage back in our rooms. Samuel didn't chase them away either. Apart from bed, breakfast and alcohol the soldiers had demanded a supply of girls. Samuel told us that if he had refused them, the army would have taken its business elsewhere.

The girls seemed happy to chatter, asking us where we came from, what we were doing in their country, our first impressions of Namibia. Finally they talked about themselves. They had tolerable English that they had picked up in school and from interacting with foreign soldiers. Whenever the conversation got stuck, Samuel translated.

'Oh, please take me with you to Scotland,' one of them pleaded when I mentioned that that was where I came from.

'It's cold and wet and you wouldn't like it.'

'But it can't be worse than here,' she replied, casting her arm in a circle that seemed to encompass not just the empty bar and the vacant hotel, but the town that surrounded us as well.

It was a judgment that resonated with her friends. 'It's getting worse,' one added, echoing the same refrain I was now becoming familiar with. 'When the army left, so did our customers. I wanted to become a secretary. How can I pay for my studies now?'

Although our conversation never touched directly on their means of earning a living they hovered around the subject, as if they were keen in some way to justify why they had fallen into their profession. 'I have a young son to look after,' a pretty woman with an engaging smile said. 'His father left me. How else am I supposed to support my child?' she continued, answering a question we had never asked her.

It turned out that she was only nineteen years old. Her son was four, which meant that she was only fifteen when she had had him. 'Weren't you a bit young to have a child?' I asked.

'I fell in love with someone. Then he disappeared and now I'm on my own. Don't you want to look after me?' she teased, running her fingers through my hair to the laughter of her friends.

Men's fickleness and lack of responsibility was a topic they unanimously agreed on. 'African men are the worst,' one of them asserted. 'They make you all sorts of promises but, as soon as a child appears, that's when they dump you.'

Samuel felt obliged to respond. 'It's not just Africans,' he interjected, keen to ensure that blame was apportioned fairly. 'All men are the same. Foreigners too. Think of all those babies the UN soldiers left behind.'

As they chirped away, occasionally asking us to replenish their drinks, I thought about some statistics. The army in Zimbabwe was said to have an HIV prevalence rate over three times the national average. I had recently read that the South African defence forces had been tested too. Over one quarter of their number was HIV positive. It was likely that these same figures were present in Namibia and I wondered what precautions these young women had taken to avoid a disease that was ravaging this part of the continent.

At one stage in the evening one of them had taken a packet of condoms out of her bag. This was after I refused another offer to spend some time with her alone in my room. 'Don't worry, Mr. Chris,' she had said. 'I've come prepared. Nothing bad will happen to you.'

I thought about how back in Zimbabwe, women complained that their husbands and partners never agreed to use condoms. There were taboos and misconceptions about them that limited their acceptance; one of the reasons why sexually transmitted diseases, including AIDS, were becoming so prevalent. 'I thought that African men didn't like using condoms,' I said, wondering how insistent she might be if a client refused to wear one.

'If we talk nicely to them they agree,' she replied, somewhat unconvincingly.

Her friend was more honest. 'Men here say that wearing a condom is like eating a sweet with the wrapper on. If we insist, they tell us to go and find someone else. Then it depends on how desperate we are for money. Most of the time it is only God that is protecting us.'

They were still sipping Coca-Colas when we left them, a group of young women on a night out, chattering away, talking about their families and their children, commenting on a new dress that one was wearing, what they might do that weekend. As we said good night they teased us again, asking if we had changed our minds about their earlier offers.

'Is there something wrong with me?' one of them said as she twirled around, showing off her figure, her lips brushing my ear.

'Of course not,' I stuttered, as I rose to walk chastely to my room. 'You're very attractive. But tonight we're tired, and tomorrow we have an early start.'

Grootfontein was almost the same distance from Rundu as the journey we had made the previous day, but instead of twelve hours we were there in three. The road was perfect: tarmac throughout, broad, straight and signposted at regular intervals. 'Another legacy of the war,' Paul said, read-

213

ing from his guidebook. 'Apparently the South African air force used to land their jets on some of these roads, so that they could refuel near to the area of combat.'

Closer to town, the dry, thorny landscape we had passed through earlier was replaced by irrigated farmland. These were large estates, presided over by houses that were as grand and imposing as anything we had seen back in the country we had come from. 'We've returned to Zimbabwe,' Paul said, echoing what I was thinking.

At a small restaurant in the centre of Grootfontein the portly gentleman behind the counter said good morning to us in German. There was sausages and sauerkraut on the menu. The smell of ground coffee and freshly baked *apfel-strudel* transported me back to similar cafes in Bavaria, where I had spent holidays every year visiting my mother's family.

As we were eating our breakfast Paul nudged me, pointing to the other side of the square. A group of African women had suddenly appeared, immediately noticeable because of their colorful costumes. They were Herero, one of the predominant tribal groups that lived in this part of the country. I was no expert on Namibia's different ethnicities but they looked exactly like the women showcased on the tourist poster I had seen at the Embassy in Harare. 'Welcome to Namibia,' was the caption, 'a country of colour and tradition.' Beneath the photo, I had read the name of the group the women belonged to.

Colorful and exotic as they were, it was unlikely that the costumes they were wearing had much to do with indigenous tradition. The dresses were heavy, shapeless and impractical. Even from a distance, I could see that the women were wilting in the heat.

I had read that the occupation of the country had been particularly brutal. In the carve up of the continent that had taken place in the late 1800s, Germany had been given South West Africa. The colony had been neglected for several years until diamonds were discovered in the southern part of the territory. This had led to a massive influx of migrants hoping to make their fortunes.

One obstacle to doing so was that they were in competition with the people who were already there. As in Zimbabwe the indigenous population was pushed out of the more fertile areas, not only so that this land could be appropriated for commercial agriculture but to help create a pool of labour that could be used in the mines and farms that needed workers. Forced evictions were carried out by an army sent from Berlin. It was not only land that was seized but livestock such as cattle and goats, another means of ensuring that the locals would become so desperate they would be forced to accept whatever meagre wages their new masters chose to pay them.

By 1904 the Herero had had enough and rose in rebellion. They were followed by the Nama further south a year later. The response, under an infamous German general called Louis Von Trotha, was excessive even by colonial standards. Entire villages were put to the torch. Men, women and children were slaughtered. The Herero moved eastwards towards the desert to escape the German army but in a particularly brutal act of genocide all the wells were poisoned.

It was estimated that around eighty per cent of the Herero were wiped out in the space of a few years. The rest ended up in camps in Botswana or as little more than slaves in the farms and mines that were emerging throughout their former territory. The repression of those years was codified in all sorts of rules and regulations, including an infamous decree by the German Colonial League that the testimony of at least seven Africans was required to challenge the claims of one white man.

The process of colonisation had had the official sanction of the various churches that had been established to convert the natives. From what I had read, very few ministers had raised their voices to object on Christian grounds to what was happening during that time. Much of it indeed was justified under the guise of bringing civilised values to a backward people. This included standards of dress and appearance. The heavy, dull and shapeless uniforms worn by pious German matrons at the turn of the century had been imposed on local women as a mark of progress.

Later, the Herero had added some colour to what they had been instructed to wear. At some point it had become distinctive and a mark of their identity. It seemed ironic to me, if not unfortunate, that these costumes were now appearing in posters advertising local culture and tradition when they could just as easily be seen as symbols of former control and the enslavement of a people.

Close to where we had parked the car, Paul, who had taken seriously his role of tour guide, announced that we were only a short distance away from the town museum. It was listed in his book as worth a visit but I was reluctant to delay our departure much longer. We had a long drive ahead of us to Etosha National Park, where we planned to stay for some days, and I had no intention of arriving there after dark. 'But it'll only take us a few minutes to look around,' he argued. 'Besides, what's the point in coming all this way if we don't take some time to see the attractions?'

The frosty old lady at the entrance didn't seem particularly keen to have our custom. She pointed to a sign that indicated we had only thirty minutes left until the place would close for lunch. Our visit coincided with an outing of children from what we presumed was a local primary school. There must have been about thirty boys and girls bustling around the several rooms in their neat little uniforms.

Most of what was on display was military memorabilia from the various stages of colonial occupation. There was a sword that had belonged to a German army officer, a rifle made in Berlin, an artillery piece made by Krupp's munitions factory and some helmets and revolvers.

In acknowledgement of Namibia's indigenous population there was a small alcove where amid a collection of spears, drums and tired looking animal skins we discovered a life-sized figure made of papier-mâché. Both Paul and I stared in horror at the grotesque, almost Neanderthal features that had been carved out of the material. There was an inscription that read, 'This model depicts a typical African native at the turn of the century.'

A few meters away there was another replica, this time of a German army officer of the same period. Neatly dressed in uniform, handsomely mustached and looking chivalrous and gallant, the contrast couldn't have been starker, nor could the underlying message. Here was the struggle between 'civilisation' and 'barbarity' represented in the difference between these two figures, one huddled beside an open fire with some primitive stone tools scattered around him while the other held a bible and a sword to help rescue the native from his desperate situation. Finding that distortion of history in a place that was supposed to represent it objectively, and in front of a group of impressionable school children too, surprised and shocked us.

'How can you display these things?' I said to the old lady at the entrance to the museum.

'What things?' she asked, sounding surprised.

'Those figures over there! Look at the one of the African native. You've turned him into a monkey. I thought museums were supposed to present the facts, not distort them.'

She seemed offended. 'Excuse me,' she said with considerable condescension, 'but when my grandfathers came to this country in the last century that's how they found them.' Her voice was raised so that the children stopped what they were doing to look towards us. 'Do you know that this museum is listed in guidebooks? Our town is proud of what we have here. If you don't like it, I suggest you leave.'

Her tone and manner irritated me, as if I were some naïve outsider in need of a history lesson. The children had by now stopped their chatter, guessing that our argument was not yet over. 'I don't know about these kids but if any adult comes away from here thinking that this place gives an accurate reflection of history then they must be blind. The only people that could ever enjoy this spectacle must be racists like you. Quite frankly you should be part of these appalling exhibits.'

She gave a gasp and put her hand to her mouth. The children gasped too and one of their teachers placed herself in front of them. Paul was tugging at my arm, ushering me out of the door. 'It's time to leave. They might call the police.'

Back in the car he did not argue when I told him that his guidebook was hardly worth the paper it was written on. 'How one earth could it have recommended that place? I suspect the author of that chapter has never even been there.'

He was silent for a while as we drove away. 'Does this mean there are no more history museums on the itinerary?' he asked, when we were out of town. It was some time before I deigned to respond.

It was dark by the time we pulled into Etosha National park. Visiting there had been my idea. Paul had been less keen, remarking that in Zimbabwe we were spoiled for such places to visit. But Etosha was billed as a special location because of its semi-desert environment and unique wildlife.

Since it was on our way to the sea too, we could stay for a few nights before proceeding to the coast and a place called Swakopmund.

Partly to keep me awake and partly for his own edification, Paul read me a description of the facilities we could expect at the rest camp to which we were headed. There was a swimming pool, a good restaurant and private chalets with air conditioning and soft beds. The further I drove the more appealing this all sounded. We were hungry too since we had eaten nothing since breakfast. I had been in such a hurry to leave Grootfontein that I had driven past the café where we had planned to buy sandwiches. Invariably the conversation turned to what would be on the menu. We had pretty much agreed on the three course dinner we would have by the time we arrived.

In the small office at the front gate of the park an official told us that we were too late for the restaurant. It had closed thirty minutes beforehand. He shook his head when we asked him for directions to the chalets. They had been booked out 'months in advance.' The only facility he could offer us was a campsite in another location, thirty minutes from where we now were.

'But we don't have a tent!' I said, my dreams of a comfortable evening on a full stomach rapidly receding.

'Don't worry. You can rent one.'

'What about food?' Paul asked. 'Is there another restaurant where we can eat?'

'There are barbecue stands at the campsite. You'll have to cook your own.'

When I asked him if there was a store nearby where we could buy some provisions he grinned. I could see we were becoming a subject of amusement.

'The nearest town is miles away. That's one reason why people come here,' he added, in a tone I took exception to.

He pointed to a poster in his office advertising the remoteness of the park and the experience it offered of Wild Namibia. The implication was that we should have done our homework before driving hundreds of miles to get here, and the fact that he was right only irritated me the more.

Paul, who could sense my growing frustration, jumped into the conversation. No doubt he was concerned that we were about to have another altercation. He thanked the official for his advice, agreed to pay for a tent and asked for directions.

Before we left he also managed to establish that the restaurant would be open early the following morning. 'By the time we wake up tomorrow, fried eggs, sausages and bacon will only be a few minutes away,' he said. The problem was we still had another twelve hours to get through.

The campsite was remote and we had difficulty following the rough track that led there. When we finally arrived we had to lift the barrier that blocked the entrance since no one was there to do it for us. As we drove through we could see a large open space ahead of us, with a few barbecue stands to cook food, a tap connected to a water tank and some rustic latrines. Compared to what we had expected on the drive to the park it was a major letdown. This time it was my turn to apologise for the choice of destination.

Paul, who had graciously volunteered to put up the tent, pointed out that there was no fence that he could see.

I reassured him that it must exist, probably hidden to foster an illusion of the wilderness the poster back at the front gate had enthused about. 'Otherwise how would they manage to keep out the wild animals?'

Thankfully there was another group when we arrived. They waved a greeting when we pulled into a space beside them. It was immediately obvious that they belonged to a different class of traveller. They had a small generator that provided electricity for the lights they had strung up around their several large and spacious tents. From the fire that was glowing in the middle of their camp we could catch the smell of frying meat.

'Is it wise to be this close?' I asked Paul, when we heard the sound of popping beer cans. 'How will we manage to fall asleep on empty stomachs if our neighbours are gorging themselves at the same time?'

Whatever proficiency Paul might have had as a navigator or changing a tire, putting up a tent was not one of his skills. Nor was it one of mine. We muddled around for about thirty minutes with various poles and bits of rope, our exasperation only kept in check because of not wanting to show ourselves up in front of our audience. Judging by the time they were taking to cook their food they were set to have a considerable feast. It was our antics that were providing them with some pre-dinner entertainment.

Eventually we managed to put up something that looked like a tent, an achievement which occasioned some good natured applause and cheering. 'I wish they would throw us a leg of chicken instead. Even a few cold beers would do,' Paul said to me, as we nodded towards them as graciously as we could.

Maybe they heard us. Maybe they took pity. Whatever the reason, one of them came over and handed each of us a can of beer. After introducing himself he pointed to where his companions were sitting. 'Excuse me for saying so, but you don't seem that well prepared. Why don't you come and join us for something to eat?'

I tried not to seem overeager in accepting. 'Are you sure? We don't want to intrude.'

Thankfully he was insistent. 'Look, man, we always cook more than we need. It will only get thrown away if you don't help out.'

There were five in the party, all men and all built like rugby players. I tried to avoid their handshakes as diplomatically as I could, since after the first one I was already nursing some bruised knuckles. Dirk, the person who had come over, was right. They had cooked enough food for twice their number. They were generous to a fault and constantly plied us with more steak and chips.

'At this rate we won't need breakfast tomorrow,' I whispered to Paul after another refill.

'At this rate we'll have hangovers,' he replied, as one of our hosts handed him another beer.

Their accents sounded South African but it turned out they came from Namibia, from the capital of Windhoek a day's drive away. Their visit to Etosha was an annual pilgrimage, one of them said, that dated back to the time they had gone to college together. To keep in touch and to escape from their wives and various jobs they came for a week every year to see the animals, to reminisce about old times and to drink copious amounts of alcohol. Every few minutes another can was pulled out of a large cooler box and the contents consumed in a few quick gulps.

Between mouthfuls of food we ended up talking about rugby, a subject that Paul knew considerably more about than I. I was happy enough, though, for the conversation to be steered in that direction. Truth to tell I was concerned that we might end up in controversial territory: the merits or otherwise of Namibian independence or what we were doing in Zimbabwe helping a Government that had defeated the whites in a recent war. After a long day behind us and my earlier outburst at the museum I was not ready for another argument about politics and the fraught racial history of the region.

Several beers later, Paul asked them why they preferred this location to the much more comfortable guest houses we had read about earlier. 'What's so special about this place, that you keep coming back every year?'

According to one of them, the park beside the chalets was too regulated. 'There are officials there telling you all the time what you can and can't do. What's the point in visiting wild Africa if someone is breathing down your neck the whole time telling you how to behave? Otherwise you might as well visit a zoo.'

I remembered the long list of prohibitions displayed at the office we had passed through earlier: Don't get out of your car to get close to the animals; Don't sound your horn unless you have to; Don't leave litter behind; Don't light fires outside designated areas. It sounded pretty regulated to me, so what had he meant when he said there was no one around to tell you what to do.

Dirk shone his torch into the darkness that surrounded our camp, a beam of light that picked out nothing apart from some distant trees and more darkness behind them. 'Chris, take a look around. Can you see anyone here enforcing the rules? Did you meet anyone at the gate handing you instructions? Can you see a fence with regulations stuck to them? We're on our own here. There's nothing but us and the rest of Africa.'

I shifted uncomfortably. No fence. No one in authority. Nothing to protect us against the resident wildlife. I had experienced that once before when I had been stranded overnight on the road to Siakobvu after an accident. I had sworn then never to put myself in such a situation again, but it seemed that I was about to repeat the experience. Free steaks and free booze notwithstanding, it seemed we had ended up in the wrong place.

I could see that Paul shared my concern. 'Aren't the animals here dangerous?' he stuttered. 'What do we have for protection?'

'This,' Dirk replied, and pulled out a handgun from somewhere beneath the seat he was sitting on. His colleagues did the same, proudly showing off their various revolvers and even asking if we wanted to handle them. Their display of weaponry, however, did nothing to allay my fears. Why did they need guns in the first place? What were they planning to shoot?

'Didn't they warn you at the front gate?' Dirk replied, as I handed him back his revolver. 'This campsite is notorious. A few months ago someone was attacked by a hyena and had part of his face bitten off.'

As if on cue and at the edge of where our lights penetrated the darkness, there was a high pitched cackling sound that forced Paul and I to grab one another. I could just about see the dim shape of what looked like a large dog prowling among the trees. I had read that hyenas were shy and kept away from humans, but Dirk claimed that the ones in Etosha were bold and aggressive. It was unlikely that we would get through the night without the campsite being raided. 'Make sure you keep the entrance to your tent fastened, otherwise they'll poke their heads in and have you for supper. Do you want another beer?'

Back in the tent some time later Paul and I had a heated discussion. It was stiflingly hot but Paul wanted to keep the flaps firmly closed. 'I'd rather be clawed to death than suffocate,' I replied.

In the end we agreed on a compromise. The flaps would be kept half open but we would pile up our luggage at the entrance to the tent to prevent anything from getting in. 'It's all a joke anyway,' I said, as much to reassure myself as my nervous companion. 'Our friends are probably exaggerating. In return for providing us with dinner they wanted some entertainment. I bet you they're having a good laugh at having spooked us. In any case, don't you think the official at the front gate would have warned us if this place were so dangerous?'

We both woke up when the shooting started, loud cracks of noise that were punctuated in between by the whoops and yells of our neighbours. The lights from their campsite had been switched off but the beams of several torches penetrated the darkness, throwing eerie shapes on the walls of our tent. Despite Paul shouting to me to keep my head down I crawled over to the entrance to look outside. I could see Dirk and his friends firing away and at the edge of where the darkness began the retreating forms of large, loping animals.

'You can come outside if you want to now,' someone said a few minutes later, tapping on the tent. 'They've gone.'

Evidence of the hyenas' visit had been left behind. Empty beer cans were scattered around as if they had become impatient with not finding anything edible. Dirk held up a thermos flask that had been left outside, the hard metal clearly indented where it had been bitten. 'That's what these animals can do if they get hold of you. Imagine if it was your head they were chewing. It would pop like an orange.'

Although we declined the celebratory whisky that was being passed around we stayed for a while longer, neither of us anxious to return to the tent. Our companions were animated, clearly enjoying the moment. I wondered then if they were really here to observe the wildlife, or to take pot shots in their direction.

'I think I winged one of the bastards,' one of them said.

'They won't be back any time soon,' commented another, as if he were referring to ill-mannered hooligans in need of correction rather than dumb creatures scavenging for food.

'What's the plan for tomorrow?' Paul asked as we walked back to the car. We had decided to swap the relative comfort of our sleeping bags and mattresses in the tent for the discomfort of hard seats in the back of our vehicle. But it had metal and solid windows instead of flimsy canvas to protect us. We had both realised too that after what had happened it was unlikely we would get much sleep in the few hours of darkness still remaining.

It was a rhetorical question. We had already made up our minds. Despite free beer, free steaks and a front row view of Etosha's wildlife we did not want to spend any more time in this place. Dirk had said they were there for the rest of the week. We were welcome to share their food and provisions. But the thought of another night of gunshots, hungry hyenas and hunting stories did not appeal to us. It was time to cut our losses and drive to the coast.

11

Diamond Road

Grootfontein had reminded me of a small Bavarian town. Swakopmund was like its coastal counterpart, a resort perched on the same Atlantic Ocean that washed the shores of Germany thousands of kilometers away. It was only in the spaces between towns and villages that I had a sense of Namibia's distinctiveness. In the dry, dusty desert we had driven through to get to the coast we had seen strange looking cactus plants and exotic trees that were found nowhere else on the continent. The moment we entered an urban area it was as if the original European inhabitants, and their more recent descendants, had tried to create replicas of what they had left back home. 'Why did they come all this way,' Paul said, 'if they were so determined to remind themselves of what they left behind?'

There had been something similar in Zimbabwe in terms of the architecture in parts of its capital city and major towns. Many of the commercial farms had given themselves names that would have been found in Somerset and Kent, but there was nothing quite so determined as what we encountered in Namibia.

'Maybe it's because they are still so close to independence that so little has changed,' Paul observed after we had exited the history museum in Swakopmund. Despite my outburst of the previous day he had convinced me to visit another one, to see if what we had found in Grootfontein was an aberration.

Thankfully there were no papier-mâché models of grotesquely featured Africans to prompt another exit, but while the grainy photographs of Namibia in the early part of the 20th century gave a fascinating insight into the lives and customs of the early German settlers, there was the same invisibility of the local population. Apart from a few token images of subjugated and bewildered looking tribesmen, the way in which the indigenous inhabitants featured so little in the photographic record of those years provided enough of an indication of the way they were perceived, or not perceived, by the newcomers to the country.

Swakopmund itself was quiet and intriguing in a touristy kind of way. It had cafes and restaurants and winding streets with names like Bismarck Strasse and Kaiser Wilhelm Avenue. The souvenir shops sold German beer mugs, works of literature by such worthies as Goethe and Schiller and in one or two of them a collection of medals and memorabilia from the First and Second World Wars. The father of Luftwaffe commander Hermann Goering, second in command in Nazi Germany, had been a one-time colonial governor of Namibia. In the centre of town there was a street named after him.

'Nothing has changed here,' Paul remarked. 'It's as if this place has been preserved in a protective bubble, as if what has just happened to the country has passed it by.' We were walking along the pier, a long jetty fronting the ocean that would occasionally send waves crashing over it. There were old ladies dressed in raincoats and walking their poodles, some couples sitting on benches and speaking German, and apart from an occasional face that stood out by contrast, hardly an African among the population that was enjoying the view.

Accommodation had been easy to find despite the warning in Paul's guidebook that it was often impossible to locate a place to stay. Luckily for us we had arrived in the off season, the cooler part of the year. But between December and April, when the interior of the country baked in temperatures of over 40 degrees centigrade, Swakopmund was the location of choice for those who could afford to escape to the sea breezes and fresh winds that blew off the Atlantic.

In the bar of the Strand Hotel we met Oliver, a marine biologist who had been posted from a University in Germany to a research institute in Swakopmund. He had been here a year and would be leaving in a few months time. Although he had enjoyed his work and appreciated the fact that the local beer was as good as anything he could find back home, he had felt that his original desire to work for a time in Africa had not been realised. 'You're right,' he replied, when we said that Swakopmund seemed a pleasant enough location but had little to do with the rest of the continent behind it. 'I'm going to Tanzania next year. Let's hope I can meet more Africans there.'

'What's so special about the marine environment near Swakopmund?' I asked him, wondering why it merited a research institute of its own.

He replied that Namibia's coastal waters, to a distance of about fifty kilometers, boasted some of the world's richest fishing grounds. This was because of the Benguela current, a cool body of water that flowed northwards from the Antarctic. While it was partly responsible for creating the desert further inland, since it provided no moisture for rain, it also carried a large amount of plankton and other micro-organisms. 'We estimate there are enough white fish here to feed most of southern Africa,' Oliver said, now getting into his stride, 'but that depends if stocks are well managed and if arse-holes like the Spanish and Portuguese keep away.'

Both Paul and I were taken aback. With his thick framed

229

glasses and boyish expression Oliver didn't look as if he knew any swear words, let alone was prepared to use them. But he was clearly indignant about something and when I asked him what it was he pointed to the harbour and a large fishing boat that had been anchored off shore. It had some Spanish name, like *Bella Margarita*, painted on the side and when I commented that it seemed a very long way for a vessel to come and catch some fish he replied that such was the abundance of stocks in these waters that it could fill its sizeable hold in a matter of days.

It seemed that the fishing grounds in this part of Africa had attracted in recent years a fleet of what he called 'predatory trawlers,' principally from Portugal and Spain. They had ignored restrictions on quotas and net sizes, and had plundered waters close inshore which was where the younger fish matured and grew to size. 'If this continues the sea around here will become the equivalent of the desert it has created inland. There will be no fish to speak of, and it's not just happening in Namibia. Other countries along the coast of Africa are having their fishing grounds robbed too. The problem is that these countries have little or no means of policing their shores.'

Oliver likened the crews and owners of these boats to the modern day equivalent of former pirates, which led me to wonder why they had anchored in Swakopmund in full view of the authorities. 'Are they having a few beers in one of the local pubs?' I asked. 'Isn't that a bit like adding insult to injury?'

It turned out that they were not drinking beer anywhere. They had been incarcerated in the local prison after their vessel had been seized. They were not alone either. Over the past few months some six or seven vessels had been appre-hended, escorted to various harbours along the coast and their crews detained. It was the South African navy that had intervened to help their Namibian counterparts, a gesture prompted not so much by solidarity but by self-interest. According to Oliver, South Africa's coastal waters were at risk too and it wanted to send a clear message that this state of affairs could no longer continue.

'One difference with previous pirates is that these ones seem to have the open backing of their national Governments.' The seizure of the vessels, each one worth several million dollars, had not gone down well in the capitals of Spain and Portugal. Both countries had launched formal protests at what had occurred and were pressing for the boats and their crews to be immediately released.

This diplomatic crisis, claimed Oliver, was fraught with hypocrisy. The principal reason why Spanish and Portuguese boats sailed southwards to Africa was because of regulations that protected declining stocks of fish around their own coasts. Effectively prohibited from fishing in European waters for large parts of the year, those fleets were trying to take advantage of poor regulations and limited enforcement in other countries. 'It's nothing short of sanctioned plunder,' Oliver fumed. 'They're trying to ensure that people in Europe have fish and chips on their tables whenever they feel like it, while many Africans would be lucky to have such a meal at all.'

Oliver's commitment was impressive. He had written to his own university about what was happening, had sent articles to newspapers in his home city and written letters of protest to the embassies of Spain and Portugal. He admitted that before he came to Namibia he would probably have classified himself as a 'typical' scientist: somewhat conservative, disinterested in politics, more dispassionate than engaged. But what he had seen had irked him immensely and it was clear from the way he spoke just how angry he had become.

'First it was diamonds. Then it was land. Today it's fish. We robbed these people then and we're robbing them now. I'm supposed to concentrate on researching the life cycle of phytoplankton in the coastal waters of Namibia, but I've come to see the importance of the bigger picture. Maybe Swakopmund, as you say, is not typical of the rest of the continent but if it's given me an opportunity to open my eyes then I can't say I'm sorry I came.'

'Hey mister. Would you like to buy some glass?'

We were filling the car with fuel at a garage in Keetmanshoop, a small town in the far south of Namibia. On my travels in the continent I had been offered stone carvings, walking sticks, ornamental drums, colorful bits of cloth and amulets and charms for nasty diseases. But this was the first time I had ever been offered glass, something I was not aware had a distinctive African identity. I was curious.

'Well, where is it? I can't see anything you're selling,' I said to the young man who had sidled up to me.

'I can't show it to you here,' he replied, pointing to a policeman on the other side of the road who was still some distance away. 'Let's go to the toilet. You can see it there.'

'Sorry but I'm not going to a toilet with a complete stranger. If you've something to sell I want to see it in the open. Besides, what's so secretive about a bit of glass?

He looked at me as if I was either naïve or stupid but pulled out a piece of paper from a pocket in his trousers and hurriedly unwrapped it. Buried in its folds was something that looked like a fragment of broken window, mine for the princely sum of one thousand dollars, 'not Namibian but American,' he added, just in case I had misunderstood the price.

It clicked. This must be an uncut diamond, one of the commodities that the country was famous for. It looked unimpressive and if someone had asked me to spot the difference between what was there and the sliver of glass I had originally thought it was, I would have been unable to do so. What I did know, however, was that the penalty for selling illicit diamonds in Namibia was harsh and the penalty for purchasing them just as severe.

'Clear off,' I said, pretending more indignation than I actually felt. I had read about unsuspecting tourists being set up. 'If I purchase a diamond I'll make sure to buy one at an official outlet,' I added, just to emphasise how principled I was. The young man scurried off down the street, anxiously looking back to make sure that I had not alerted the policeman who by now was much closer.

Arriving too late the previous evening to continue driving, we had stayed the night in Keetmanshoop. Further west towards the coast was the town of Luderitz where we were headed, a port established by the Germans in the latter part of the 19th century.

Our visit to the extreme southern part of the country was prompted this time by a request from my head office to investigate a local cooperative. One of the Ministries we wanted to engage with had forwarded the details to London. The members of the group required help with accountancy and marketing and we had been asked if they could have one of our workers for a year to develop their skills in these areas.

'It's miles from anywhere,' Paul remarked, well over a day's drive into our journey from Windhoek. There was still another day ahead of us and apart from Keetmanshoop and one other town further north, we had seen nothing but empty tracts of land, occasional ranches, and road signs indicating that Luderitz was still hundreds of kilometres away. I had known that Namibia was sparsely inhabited, the second least densely populated state in the world. But I had not been prepared for quite how devoid of people this part of the country really was, and wondered where the bulk of the 3 million population resided.

Signs warning trespassers to keep out had occasionally appeared near the farms we had passed earlier. But they became more frequent the further west towards the coast we proceeded, something that confused me. The land stretching for miles behind and in front of us had transformed into classical desert, incapable of supporting agriculture or cattle ranching of any kind. Why then these miles of fence along the road, the occasional police patrols we encountered and on one occasion a helicopter that hovered noisily overhead before swooping off and disappearing into the distance?

'Because we've now entered Namibia's biggest diamond producing area,' Paul said, reading from his guidebook, 'and prospecting for diamonds is strictly prohibited.'

'But why a fence? Don't you have to dig a large hole to find them? You'd be spotted miles away. They can't just be lying scattered around waiting for someone to jump out of their car and grab some.'

'Well according to this book that's exactly what you could do, if you were allowed. It says that Namibia's diamonds are largely alluvial, that over the course of thousands of years they were washed out by rivers from deep underground. They're now scattered on the surface of this desert for hundreds of miles, which was how they were first discovered.'

Paul read further. As in other locations when precious stones had first been found there had been a mad scramble of prospectors and adventurers rushing in to make a quick fortune. In later years, however, the industry had become much more regulated. The reason for this was simple. If there were too many diamonds on the market at any one time their value would drop to a point where they would become worthless.

'The value of precious stones is entirely dependent on their scarcity,' Paul explained. 'Who would pay thousands of dollars for a piece of jewelry if diamonds were as common as glass? That's why De Beers was set up to regulate the market. It buys up all the diamonds and then every year releases enough to meet demand, but not so much that it would undercut the price. As part of the deal, countries like Namibia agree to police their territory, so that so called 'illegal' diamonds don't undermine this arrangement. That's why there is all this security and why you can't get out of your car even if you wanted to have a pee on the side of this road.'

On the outskirts of Luderitz there was a sign pointing to an abandoned town that according to Paul was once the diamond capital of South-West Africa. It was only a few kilometres away and so we decided to take a detour. Kolmankoop had now been infiltrated by encroaching sand dunes, which gave the place a ghostly, bereft appearance. In a small museum that was attended by a surly official, we read that in twenty to thirty years' time the town would probably disappear completely, that visitors to the area far from being able to stroll through its streets would have to walk on top of the sand that buried them.

In keeping with the other museums we had visited, the history of Kolmankoop and its nearby port of Luderitz, focused mostly on the endeavors of its original German settlers. There were photographs of the army officer credited with 'discovering' Namibia's first diamonds. On a stroll one evening with his dog he had seen bits of glass glittering in the moonlight and had picked some up. More out of curiosity than expectation he had sent them back with a friend to Berlin to have them looked at. A few months later he had received word that they were high grade diamonds worth a small fortune.

Over the next few years the town had expanded and developed into Germany's prize colonial possession, able to import the costliest luxuries from the homeland in return for keeping the aristocracy there supplied with precious stones. It had boasted a hospital, a power station, a theatre, a casino and a railway station. It had the continent's first tram. Now half buried in sand, its chimney poking above the dunes, was the remains of an ice factory. According to the blurb beneath a photograph of its original construction, the need for ice was to keep the imported beers and wines from Germany at just the right temperature for its spoiled inhabitants.

For several years the principal method of finding diamonds was the same one that had led to their initial discovery. On moonlit evenings long lines of men, women and children would crawl for hours on their hands and knees across the territory. Behind them they trailed pouches which they filled with the stones they found. Not surprisingly they were African, seized from the surrounding area or imported from further afield. In the few photographs of 'native life' that were on display they looked miserable and abject. Their supervisors, there to make sure they kept in a straight line or didn't escape, looked more than willing to use the whips they carried at their sides.

The next day we met Andreas, the chairperson of the organisation we had travelled to meet. I had mentioned our visit to the abandoned settlement on the outskirts of Luder-itz and he had told us that before joining the fishing cooperative he had worked for several years in a mine in the southern desert. Finding diamonds by then, he said, had developed into something much more sophisticated than crawling over the ground. There were mechanical diggers to collect the sand, machines to sift it and a factory where the stones were washed and graded. Like the other workers,

Andreas lived in an isolated compound for weeks on end. Whenever it was time to go home they had been rigorously searched to make sure they were not smuggling anything out with them.

'Would you believe they even checked our teeth? It seemed that someone once had his dentist drill a hole in his molars so he could conceal diamonds inside his mouth. After he was discovered they checked there too, and in all the other places on our bodies where we might hide them.'

Andreas was little more than five feet tall, was lighter skinned than most of the local Namibians we had so far seen and had slanting, almost oriental eyes. These were characteristics, he said when I asked him, that marked him out as a member of the Nama, an ethnic group related to the original Bushmen of southern Africa. I had read that like the Herero they had been pastoralists, and that attempts by the colonial authorities to restrict their movements had led to conflict. Under the leadership of their charismatic leader, Henrik Witbooi, recently elevated to the status of national hero, they had raided and harassed the German army for several years from their base in a range of inhospitable mountains in the south of the country.

Like the other tribes which had opposed German rule, the Nama fared badly in the repression that followed. Half the original population was said to have been wiped out. 'There are only a small number of us left now,' Andreas declared, 'no more than forty to fifty thousand at most.'

As we walked along the sea front to find some other members of the cooperative that he wanted us to meet, we continued our history lesson. Just off the coast of Luderitz, on a small island linked by a causeway at one end of the bay, was a camp where many Nama had been imprisoned after their defeat by the German army.

Aptly named 'Devil's Island,' it was apparently a precursor of the concentration camps that had been established by the Nazis some forty years later in different parts of Europe. Paul and I shuddered when Andreas described what had gone on there, including the medical experiments conducted on his people. In the light of day and amid the blue sea that sparkled around it, the island looked idyllic and peaceful, an impossible location for the atrocities that had gone on. We wondered too why it was that the kinds of memorials erected in Auschwitz and Dachau, so people would not forget the terrible things that had happened there, had not been built here too in one of the places where they had first occurred.

Andreas told us that his involvement in the fishing cooperative, and his determination to see it succeed, was inseparable from his own history and from a desire to escape the tortured past of his people. 'I realised one day when I was being searched by a security guard back at the mine where I worked, how much of a stranger I still was in my own country. This was our land, a place where my ancestors had lived for centuries. Yet because of diamonds, which in our own culture had no special value, foreigners had come and turned us into slaves. They told us where we could and couldn't walk. They said we could live here and not there. Do you know that if you were caught with one of their precious stones, even if you had found it while walking on the beach, you would be flogged or imprisoned? I decided that I could no longer work for an industry which was still owned by outsiders. So I turned to fishing instead.'

Over the few years the cooperative had been in operation it had registered considerable success. But their sale of lobsters, crayfish and crabs to the South African market was still mediated by middlemen who they believed were ripping them off. They wanted to deal directly with the buyers themselves but for that they needed a better marketing strategy and an administrative and accounting system that could support them to grow and expand. Which is where we came in.

In the time we spent with them, Paul and I were struck by what they had so far achieved and their ambitions for the future. No doubt with the proper skills and support they could do considerably more. I had confessed an original skepticism to Andreas when we had first met him, since my observation of cooperatives in other countries had been that they were often the creation of well-meaning development practitioners, rather than homegrown entities that enjoyed the full enthusiasm and commitment of its members. This time I had been more impressed, and in particular by something that Andreas had said when I had asked him specifically what it was they were looking for from my organisation.

'We're not asking for a handout. We don't want to be one of your development projects. Our desire is to stand on our feet and become a successful business. It's not just so that we can meet our own needs, to feed our families and send our children to school. It's to set an example to the rest of my people of what we can do if we become our own masters, if we refuse to be the servants of others. We want knowledge, not charity. Please see what you can do.'

My sympathy for the needs of Andreas and his cooperative notwithstanding, there was something that continued to bug me as we returned to Windhoek the following day. Where were the poor people of this country? I accepted that during our visits to Rundu, Grootfontein, Swakopmund, Keetmanshoop and Luderitz we had barely encountered any local communities, but the Africans I had seen when we came across them seemed much better off than their counterparts in Zimbabwe, Malawi and Mozambique. Their houses were better constructed. They had running water. A school we visited in Luderitz had enough books for all the pupils. Did Namibia really merit the assistance of my organisation? Weren't there other places that were more of a priority?

This perception was widely shared among the donors we visited in the capital, when we went looking for money to support a potential programme. 'Quite simply, Namibia is not poor enough to merit a major investment of aid,' claimed one individual, who was probably being more honest than other officials we had visited who had fobbed us off with vague promises of support. 'It has one of the highest per capita incomes in the region, more than what we see in countries like the one you're working in. Yes, there is some sympathy because it has just won its independence but with diamonds, uranium, tourism, fishing, merino wool and a population of less than three million, I don't think you'll have much success in finding money for your projects.'

A couple of days in the capital and I was increasingly inclined to the same judgment. We had driven around much of the city and despite my detours through back roads in search of more neglected suburbs, I had seen nothing of the slums and shanty towns I had witnessed in other places on the continent. I knew that in Harare many of its poorer neighbourhoods were concealed, but a few turns off the main road and you could always find them. Windhoek, however, had nothing like Dzivarasekwa and Porta Farm squatter camps and while clearly there was a distinction between the richer and poorer parts of the metropolis, the poverty I was looking for remained elusive. I had promised to write a report to head office with my recommendations.

The gist of what I was thinking so far was that our assistance would be better directed elsewhere.

It was a colleague from another charity who listened to my arguments but shook his head when I had concluded. The issue of GDP and per capita income, he said, was spurious. Sure, Namibia had a small population but the fact that a few thousand whites and a few wealthy blacks had acquired extravagant wealth did not mean that everyone was well fed, well housed and well watered. I needed to remember the history of the country. It had endured an apartheid style system of government for decades, which meant that privileged cities like Windhoek and Swakopmund had prospered while poverty had been located elsewhere so as not to spoil the view.

'This is a country of extremes. Don't be fooled by the pretence of modernity and progress. The places you have seen so far are not representative of the whole. You need to go further north to find the people you are looking for. If you come back and say that you still wouldn't recommend your organisation to come and work here, then in my view you don't deserve to work for a charity.'

We had driven from Windhoek the following day and at some point, as our colleague had said, had crossed over into a different country. Beyond the town of Ottwajaronga it was as if the rest of Africa had suddenly begun. The towns and villages had thickened considerably. The commercial estates had been replaced by the meagre fields and impoverished dwellings that were familiar from Zimbabwe's communal lands. The roads had changed too, not in terms of their condition but because we now had to compete with overcrowded buses we had never encountered on our journey so far. 'You asked where the rest of the population was hiding,' Paul said as we progressed further into Ovamboland. 'Looks as if they were here all along.'

Pastor Cornelius was a large, imposing gentleman with a shock of grey hair and white bushy eyebrows. We had received his contact details from the same person who had pointed us northwards and in the office of his church he seemed happy enough to answer our questions about the history and profile of his province. Echoing much of what we had heard the previous day, he said that the system of government in the country before independence had meant that the State had effectively abandoned areas designated for the African population to struggle on their own.

'Only the roads were maintained, so that the army could move around more effectively. You'll have seen the barracks in every town too, to make sure the population never became too troublesome. But as for education, health care, housing and employment, that was left to a local administration that was given little money to invest in these things.'

He went on to say that this system was only a more modern equivalent of the 'native reserves' policy adopted by colonial administrations throughout the southern African region. 'It didn't suit their economic interests for these areas to become self-sufficient. They wanted to maintain them in a state of dependency, where people would be desperate enough to accept the wages that were offered in other parts of the country that needed workers.'

Effectively the 'Bantustans,' as he called them, were labour reserves, justified under a rhetoric of preserving the separate identity and cultural autonomy of the different races. The migrant workers that the northern parts of the country exported to the mines and farms in the centre and south had no rights of residence in their new locations. They could be, and frequently were, fired at a moment's notice. Without the necessary permit to be there they had to return to their home areas, back to the poverty they had tried to escape from.

In the absence of state structures to support the population, Pastor Cornelius claimed that it was churches like his own that had become the principal providers of education, health care and social services. 'Religious affiliation for people here is not just a matter of meeting their spiritual needs. The churches were the safety nets that prevented people from falling through the cracks.'

'Does someone have to become a member of your church to access your charity?' I asked.

My question was prompted by a common enough criticism that faith based institutions demanded an ideological return on their humanitarian interventions. In communities I had visited in Zimbabwe, people had wondered, because of the name of my organisation, whether they had to be Catholics in order to benefit from our programmes. Many claimed that in order to get assistance from some religious organisations, they had to wear their uniforms, sing their hymns and attend their services on Sunday.

'You can't generalise,' Pastor Cornelius responded. 'Some churches demand their pound of flesh, that's true. In my own establishment it was never a condition. My view is that if you convert someone through bribing them with food and other handouts, they will lapse in time and join the next church that comes along offering them something more attractive. I hope that answers your query.'

He went on to say that the members of his community he was most concerned about today were an increasingly disgruntled, angry and bored group of youths. We had seen many of them on the drive north, camped outside the beer halls that Pastor Cornelius said he was in serious competition with for their hearts and minds. 'Idleness is a tool of the devil,' he said in biblical tones, claiming that if teenagers had nothing to occupy their time then alcohol, drugs, crime and sexual promiscuity were understandable, though hardly praiseworthy, alternatives.

While poor employment prospects and 'an absence of things to do' in the communities of northern Namibia had been prevalent for many decades, the contemporary reality was complicated by another factor. 'This is a different generation. Children today are more informed, better educated and more exposed to outside influences. If you are ignorant about the world outside your own, you are more inclined to accept what you have been given. But the big challenge for the new government is how we meet the demands of a generation that has other ambitions, which will demand a lot more than their parents from the people who govern them.'

His church had several projects, aimed at providing vocational training and practical skills to children who had left school with academic qualifications but no opportunity to use them. There was a community radio programme as well, to provide young people with something 'more wholesome' than the music that was blaring out of the establishment on the other side of the road. He acknowledged that it was a limited and piecemeal attempt to do something for his parishioners. A more comprehensive solution required a much more generous commitment by the Government to invest in a part of the country that up till then had been seriously neglected.

'Is this happening? Will it be a priority for your new rulers?' I asked.

He seemed cautious in answering. 'We don't have diamonds here. We don't have uranium either. The land is exhausted and there are no wild animals to attract tourists. All we have are lots of poor people. We know that part of the peace deal that was signed stated that the economic status quo should be maintained. So will the government

244

want to invest in a part of the country that has little to offer in return? I suppose it depends on whether our leaders remember the communities they once came from or whether they listen to the people who are comfortable with the way things are.'

12

The Mountains of the Moon

'Did you know that Lesotho has the highest incidence of lightning strikes in the world?' the passenger beside me on the flight from Johannesburg to Maseru told me. Apparently, there are numerous fatalities a year. As he proceeded to provide a detailed description of the climatic factors responsible for this state of affairs the pilot announced that we were entering an area of turbulence and would have a bumpy ride all the way there.

Something of a nervous flyer, I tried to steer the conversation in a different direction. 'What else is Lesotho famous for?'

'Traffic accidents. The locals drive like crazy and on these mountain roads all you need is a nudge and you're over the edge.'

Thankfully the clouds cleared. As we descended towards Maseru I could see nothing but mountains below and on more than a few of them a thin glaze of snow, like icing on a cake. The other thing I noticed from the air, confirmed as we descended, was an almost complete absence of trees. I would have expected miles of forest but Kurt, the Swedish engineer sitting beside me who was a regular visitor to Lesotho where he was involved in planning its biggest dam, told me they had all been cut down.

The highest accident rate in southern Africa. The most extensive environmental degradation. The most lighting strikes in the world. Was there anything positive, I won-

246

dered, as we clambered out of the small aeroplane and made our way to the arrivals terminal.

'Welcome to the mountain kingdom of Lesotho, Africa's most beautiful country,' the billboard behind the Custom's counter declared. Maybe I had my answer.

Once again I had managed to organise a visit to another country by combining business with my desire to explore. My organisation had decided that after several years of working for them in Zimbabwe, I merited some training. I had seen an advert in the newspaper from a 'prestigious' training institute in Lesotho that offered a range of courses for development professionals and staff of non-governmental organisations. *Principles and practice of promoting community development* appealed to me.

I had made a telephone call and had spoken to someone called Charles, the head of the institution. They had people from all over the continent attending their courses, he said. They had top class trainers, himself included, and made sure that theory was complemented by solid, practical exposure since their intention was to promote effective aid workers rather than bureaucrats. This was music to my ears and when he told me they had an upcoming course on the subject, I told him to book me immediately.

'I'd like to see some of the country too,' I added. 'Where would be good to visit?'

'There's a pony trekking place a few hours outside the capital. You hire a guide, ride off into the mountains, stay overnight in a village and come back a few days later. I haven't done it myself but it comes highly recommended. Do you want a telephone number?'

Over another crackly line the following morning, I managed to confirm a one week trek, commencing the day after my training was completed. Although I dissembled about having substantial previous experience, a requirement for a trip of longer than a couple of days, I felt that my rambles around the north of Sudan on the back of a donkey would more than qualify me.

I was flattered by the fact that Charles himself was there at the airport to greet me, standing behind a piece of cardboard with my name on it. I would have expected a prestigious training institute like his own to have sent a driver to pick me up, or organised a taxi, but here was the head honcho in person welcoming me to the country.

I wondered a little about his unorthodox appearance: baggy jeans, a floral shirt, a ponytail, and a hat set at a tilt on his head, but my surprise was offset by his effusive manner. Probably noticing my initial hesitation he said that the aid establishment needed an occasional maverick to shake it out of its complacency. 'There's nothing wrong with trying to look a little bit more like the people we're supposed to be helping, is there?' he asked, placing a friendly hand on my shoulder.

'Is there anyone else we have to pick up?' I had thought that maybe a few of the other international participants had also boarded the flight that day from Johannesburg.

'No, you're the only one. About those other international participants,' he added, as we exited the airport, 'we can speak later.'

Our transport into town was Charles' private mini-bus, a rickety affair that looked exactly like the other dilapidated taxis that plied the route between the airport and the capital. 'Forget the seat belt,' he said, as I tried to fasten myself in. 'That hasn't worked for a long time.'

As we rattled our way into town, Charles would frequently take a hand off the steering wheel to point to some landmark on the outskirts of Maseru. Every time he did so I was reminded of Kurt's words of warning. 'Is it true that Lesotho has the highest incidence of traffic accidents in southern Africa?' I asked, hoping that this question might prompt him to drive more carefully.

'Probably, I've had several, but no one has managed to kill me. Otherwise I would be a ghost driving you from the airport,' he laughed, a remark which did nothing to convince me I was in safe hands.

Charles could certainly talk, at a gallop mostly, and by the time we reached the centre of town I had pretty much heard his life story. Originally from South Africa, he had belonged to a wealthy family but the excesses of apartheid, the influence of rock music and an Asian girlfriend had led him into exile.

He had worked in a number of countries and had turned his hand to a variety of professions: teacher, barman, tour guide, house painter. He had even been a shark fisherman in eastern Australia. The heady years of independence in a number of African countries had brought him back to the continent, but not to the land of his birth which he rarely visited, despite the fact that he could see it every day from the hill in Maseru where he lived. 'Not until they free Nelson Mandela,' he said

It was charitable work that had first brought him to Lesotho, as part of a feeding programme set up by an international agency to respond to several years of drought and poor harvests. He had toured most of the country and fallen in love with its dramatic scenery and the friendliness and openness of the people.

'The Basotho in South Africa are pretty much treated as third class citizens. For years the men have worked in our gold mines and the women as servants in our homes, cleaning the arses of spoilt babies. Once they reach their sell by date they are declared *persona non grata* and are sent back where they came from, often with nothing to show for their years of hard labour and service. Yet even as a Boer I never faced any resentment or antagonism when I visited local communities. That was one of the things that most surprised me and made me want to stay.'

Charles had married a Basotho woman, had several children and a large extended family. 'I've asked my wife on several occasions to provide a guidebook so I can keep up with all her relatives. It's the family more than the state that provides the social safety net in this part of the world. You know that if something bad happens to you there will always be an uncle, a cousin, or a distant nephew ready to help you.'

I had expected Charles to drive straight to the hotel which he had booked, but he had other plans. 'It's your first night in Lesotho. I didn't think you'd want to stay in your room staring at the walls. Let's have some refreshments before I take you there.'

Judging by the greetings that accompanied our entrance it seemed that he knew most of the patrons of the bar. Popular, crowded, noisy and smoky we pushed our way through to what turned out to be his 'usual' table, where drinks arrived without us placing an order.

'The first lesson on the principles of community development,' he declared, raising his bottle and clinking my own, 'is that if you want to get to know the people you are trying to help, then first drink their beer.'

Charles talked a lot about many things but very little about the course I was scheduled to begin the following morning. He handed me no timetable, no background materials, no outline of what I could expect over the next few days. Wondering if my evening would be better spent preparing for my course rather than getting drunk with one of the trainers, I asked him if there was something I should read beforehand.

'Don't worry,' he said, pouring me another beer. 'This is

all part of your training. All that theoretical stuff, we can deal with tomorrow.'

Sometime over the course of the next few hours I came the closest to finding out Charles' philosophy of development. I had asked him what had prompted him to become a teacher rather than a field worker, since he had talked with considerable passion about his love of being out in the communities.

'I hope you don't take this personally, but most development workers are in serious need of rehabilitation. That's why I set up my school. The problem is that you don't know how to interact with poor people or how to function at their level. Too convinced of what you have to offer, you are not open enough to what you could learn.'

He went on to say that when people were faced with outsiders who saw only their helplessness and inability, these became the characteristics they deliberately displayed. 'They know it prompts more pity and they know that more pity means more aid. I remember during a cholera outbreak in a village near Maseru that the people there refused to dig the latrines that would save their lives. "Go and do it for us," the headman said, "since you've done everything else for us over the last few years." That statement made me realise that aid can end up doing more harm than good.'

According to Charles, all the technical skills in the world counted for much less than the ability to foster relationships, and interact with people from different cultural, social and economic backgrounds. 'I've met some aid workers who have doctorates in development studies yet they can't hold a simple conversation with a peasant farmer who has fallen on hard times. If you can't relate to someone as an equal then choose a different profession, is what I say.'

It didn't surprise me the following morning to learn that there were no other participants from outside the country on the training course. There was a Swedish lady based in Lesotho who had signed up for *Logistics Management*. In addition there were two recent graduates from the University of Maseru, keen and eager young men who were intent on a career in the aid fraternity. Our small group of four was all there was.

Nor did it surprise me when Charles handed out a time-table that indicated he was the only trainer. Despite having drunk a considerable amount the previous evening, I was clear minded enough to realise that he was a one man show. He had answered the phone when I had called from Zimbabwe. He had picked me up at the airport. He had driven me to a bar and provided my first evening's entertainment. When he had written out a receipt for the money I handed over for the course, I knew that he was the accountant too. The prestigious training institute he presided over was himself. 'It's the people who will teach you,' he replied when I asked him if the course wouldn't be better served by our having to listen to a few voices other than his own over the next few days.

I had two options. I could scream and shout and raise a fuss about having been duped into travelling several thousand kilometres to come to Lesotho. I could demand my money back and threaten to contact all my colleagues in the aid sector to warn them about the bogus school that Charles had set up in Maseru.

The other option was to go with the flow. Charles had a view of development much of which resonated with my own. He seemed to have had considerable experience too. He was very knowledgeable about the region and could certainly tell a good story. If nothing else the next few days would be entertaining. In the end, I expressed some surprise at having been 'misinformed' but decided to remain.

The lady from Sweden, however, needed more placating.

What Charles was proposing in his timetable was way off the subject she had signed up for. Finally, and for a part refund of what she had already paid, she agreed to stay on but on condition that she could have all her money back if she felt that she was not learning anything useful. Relieved that they would not be on their own, the two youths from Lesotho gave a cheer when we announced our intention to continue. 'Let's get down to our first day,' Charles said, rubbing his hands. 'We're in for some fun.'

As I had guessed, there was no theory, no written documents, and no lectures on the philosophy of development. Our first practical exercise was to drive to one of the largest open air markets in Maseru where Charles deposited us with a simple instruction. 'You all know the famous Lesotho blankets, don't you? It's what the people here wrap around themselves to keep out the cold. There are several stalls here all selling different makes and colours. I want you to negotiate the best deal that you can.

I'll pick you up at this very spot in about two hours,' he announced. Then he drove away.

'I think I want my refund already,' the Swedish lady said, before marching off through the crowd of people into the centre of the market.

The two young men followed her too, looking smug and confident. 'I bought a blanket for my father a few months ago,' one of them said, 'so I know what the asking price should be. We'll finish this task in a few minutes.'

In the first few stalls I visited, the price of the blankets was not negotiable. The cost of each one was indicated on a small piece of paper fastened by a staple to some part of it. When I tried to discuss the cost, I was told that these were the best prices on offer and that in any case a foreigner like me was well able to afford what they were asking.

I fared better in a few of the other stalls. My experience of

253

haggling in markets in Sudan and Algeria had taught me that the best way to get a good price was to pretend disinterest. Only when one was about to leave should one ask, as casually and as nonchalantly as one could, about the price of a selected item. Then you began the process of negotiation, interrupting the conversation with remarks about unrelated subjects such as the weather, the state of the roads, the President's latest policy, to generate an impression that the purchase of whatever was under discussion was of little consequence. Convinced that you were not desperate enough to pay the initial asking price, the trader would eventually settle for less.

'Where are you from?' asked an old gentleman, as I ambled my way through another section of the market.

When I told him I came from Scotland he pointed to an empty seat beside him and asked if I would like to join him for tea. 'Did you know that the first Basotho blankets came from Scotland?' he said, as I accepted his invitation. 'It was only a number of years ago that they started making them in South Africa.'

As we sipped our tea he told me something of the history of Lesotho's most famous garment, and its contemporary significance in their society. Over a century ago it had replaced the skin coverings worn by local people, partly because the missionaries had made such a fuss about traditional clothing being unchristian and uncivilised. When the then king of Lesotho, Moshoeshe the first, was presented with a blanket by a Scots merchant called Fraser, he had granted him a royal charter to provide all of the blankets to be worn in his kingdom. The king had also insisted on various motifs to be woven into their design. Many of these had continued to the present day.

Originally imposed on them, the Basotho has subsequently embraced the wearing of imported blankets not just as a practical measure against the extreme cold of their climate, but as a sign of their national identity and culture. Every Basotho man and woman, claimed the old man, had several blankets in their possession which were brought out for special occasions.

'When a boy becomes a man he gets a particular blanket. When he marries, his family buys him another one. When he has his first child he buys a special blanket for his wife. There are blankets for all occasions. Let me tell you something. If you wear the wrong blanket to an event, people in my country get very upset. That's why you have to be sure to pick the right one.'

'Have you always been a blanket seller?' I asked. 'Is this something that runs in your family?'

He shook his head and told me that he originally came from a village somewhere in the mountains of central Lesotho. It was an area that was remote, inhospitable and barely able to support the people who lived there. Like other young men in his village he had made the trek to the gold mines of South Africa and that was where he had spent most of his working life.

His description of his experience across the border was much like the one I had heard from Sekuru Francis. It was the same story of neglected compounds, difficult working conditions and overseers who frequently beat them if they did not work hard enough. There was the same boozing and fighting to keep them entertained when they had a few spare hours to relax.

'Once a year we were allowed to go back to Lesotho to see our families. Our children would look at us as if we were strangers. Unless there was a death in the family we weren't allowed to come back at any other point in the year.'

Failing health had prompted him to leave, and the fact that he had managed to accumulate enough savings to set up a store. His business was too small to be really prosperous but it was enough to get by. 'With what I had saved I also managed to put my children through school and college. I doubt they'll want to stay in Lesotho. There aren't opportunities for them here, but at least with an education they can do something different. I hope their future is not like my past.'

The two hours went by and when I glanced at my watch I realised it was time for Charles to pick us up. 'Look,' I said, 'I'm going to buy a blanket from your store, partly because it's one of our tasks on this training course I'm on, but also because I want to. It will be a reminder of this meeting and our conversation. Choose something for me that would be appropriate, so I don't offend anyone and at a price you think is fair. I'll be happy with that.'

Back at our meeting place, Charles asked us to present what we had purchased, to indicate the price we had paid and to say something of what we had learned that morning. Even the Swedish lady seemed more relaxed. She had spent an hour or so with a Basotho woman and, like myself, had found out not only about blankets but also about the history and circumstances of the trader.

The two students had finished the exercise, as they had originally boasted, within a few minutes. While they had purchased blankets at a price somewhat less than what we had paid, they admitted they had learnt nothing that morning about an important aspect of their own culture, nor about the individual who had sold them what they had asked for.

'I want you all to reflect on something,' Charles said at the end of our different accounts. 'Development is not just about delivering a well, a clinic, a school, food or a tractor to an impoverished village. It's about interacting with the people. If you want their labour, their contribution, their support and trust then you have to show some interest in who they are. You can't do that if you are only fixated on giving them something. Showing an interest in other people not only means that you will run a better project, it might make you a better person too.'

The rest of our 'rehabilitation' passed in much the same fashion. Charles would take us to various locations, introduce us to the people and deliver an instruction before driving off. He would return a few hours later to analyse what, if anything, we had learned.

An agricultural project that had barely produced a vegetable after three years highlighted his message that unless you knew the people you were helping, expecting them to contribute their time and labour would be a waste of time. It was the same with a woman's cooperative on the outskirts of Maseru. They produced crafts to a high standard but their husbands drank any money they earned. Their own children were neglected because of the extra demands of work on their already challenging schedules. These concerns had been shared with the organisation that supported them. 'But they were too busy to listen,' said one woman, a refrain we heard throughout our visits.

Although much of what I observed was familiar from my own work in Zimbabwe, I appreciated the time and space to reflect on the value of Charles' provocative observations and the insights and views of my colleagues on the course. 'You can keep the rest of my money,' the Swedish lady announced on the final evening, when we had gathered at Charles' favorite restaurant. 'This turned out better than I had expected,' she said, echoing the conclusion we had all come to.

At another market early the following day Charles dropped me off at a place where I could catch a mini-bus to the village where I would start my trek. In a small café where we had a farewell breakfast, he spoke to some customers who were also travelling in my direction. 'Tell the driver to be careful,' he said. 'That road can be dangerous.'

The journey from Maseru would probably have been described as spectacular by anyone with the luxury of observing the scenery. I was too preoccupied with my own safety to notice. Squeezed between two large women, I could barely move, although there was some consolation in the fact that the bumping and shaking were cushioned by their considerable bulk . Despite what the passengers had said beforehand, the driver was reckless, darting in and out of the traffic and getting perilously close to the edge of the road and its alarming drop. Shouts of 'slow down' by someone in the back were met with his curt reply that if anyone was unhappy they could get out and walk.

At a stop midway I toyed with the idea of taking my bag and finding another lift. But one of the other passengers shrugged his shoulders and told me that it would be much the same in any other taxi. 'Your chances of an accident are not much different whatever driver you choose. Just pray like we do and hope that God calls you another day.'

Three hours later, somewhat shaken but still alive, I was deposited in front of the Basotho Pony Trekking Centre. Charles had told me beforehand that the Centre had been established as part of an Irish aid program. 'The Irish have adopted Lesotho,' he said, adding that they were one of the country's biggest donors. When I asked him why, he said that it was probably because the Basotho loved horses, a passion shared by every Irishman too.

Given his generally critical outlook I was struck by his positive assessment of Irish aid, and in particular its role in helping to save the Basotho pony. This small horse had been bred for centuries. In this wild and inhospitable terrain it was the best means of transport. It was hardy, could withstand the plummeting temperatures of cold winters and was completely unperturbed when confronted by the perilous slopes on the mountains.

But vetinarians had noticed that the stock was deteriorating and, unless some new genes were introduced, the characteristics for which it was valued could soon disappear. 'Who better than the Irish to provide horses?'

Several stud farms had been set up in various parts of the country. For a small fee the inhabitants would bring their mares to be serviced. According to the same veterinarians, the project had already registered considerable success with a healthier, sturdier and more genetically stable Basotho – Irish pony as a result. Capitalising on the infrastructure that had been set up as part of the breeding programme, a pony-trekking industry had also been established to help attract tourists into the country. This provided employment for the locals and some revenues for the villages where the visitors would stay.

'So, you're not just paying for an interesting trek in the mountains but contributing to sustainable development too,' Charles had concluded.

At reception I was told that the person I had to see was in one of the nearby fields. I could either wait or walk down to find him. There was no difficulty in locating him, since a small crowd of people had gathered. Wrapped in their thick blankets and strange conical hats, they seemed animated by what was taking place beside them. It turned out that the breeding programme was also a public spectacle. What they were observing was one of their animals being mounted by a large Irish pony. Neither of the horses seemed embarrassed that their every move was being eagerly scrutinised and commented upon. When the elongated member of the stallion was manipulated by a helper into the flanks of the mare, the onlookers erupted in cheering. When he jerked and shuddered a few minutes later they clapped and whistled as if he had completed an inspired performance.

'So, you're the person who booked for an entire week,' the supervisor of the pony trekking excursions said when I finally introduced myself. He looked me critically up and down as if making a judgment as to whether I was up to it. 'Let's go to reception to finish the paperwork and introduce you to your guide.'

Inside his office was a small group of Americans who had just returned from their tour in the mountains. The two men and two women were noisy and argumentative and were bitterly complaining about their recent excursion. 'It's those fucking saddles,' one of them explained when he was asked what had gone wrong.

When one of the women hoisted up her skirt I tried not to stare at the red welts on the inside of her legs. According to her a bottle of lotion was more important than the eating utensils, sleeping bag, bottles of water and warm clothes they had been instructed to bring beforehand. 'Were you told to bring some?' she asked, turning towards me. When I replied that I hadn't been she announced that the centre should be prosecuted for gross negligence.

I was further alarmed when I found out that their trek had lasted no more than a few days. I tried to ignore their looks of pity when I confessed that I had booked for an entire week. I had ridden ponies before, I said, and was a good walker too. 'When it gets too sore I'll just hop off and walk for a few miles.'

'On those paths, you must be joking,' one of the young men snorted dismissively. 'The best place on these slopes is on the back of your horse. Remember that they have four legs while you only have two.'

My concern that I might have signed up for something

more than I could handle worsened when I was asked to complete one of the forms that was handed to me. It requested information such as my next of kin, people to be contacted in case of an emergency, and my medical insurance details in case I needed to be helicoptered out of the mountains. I was also asked to sign a disclaimer that if anything nasty happened the centre would not be held liable. 'It's only a formality,' the supervisor said. 'We've had no fatalities as yet.'

Outside reception the same crowd had gathered again. When I asked the supervisor whether they were there to see another mating performance he told me that this time I was the object of their attention. 'It's not every day we have someone going on a trek for a whole week. They've come to see you off. The Basotho appreciate a good horseman.'

What was I supposed to do? I tried to recall my donkey riding days in Sudan and whether it had demanded any particular skill. All I could remember was getting on the saddle and the donkey taking off in whatever direction he had happened to be facing. All I had done was hitch a lift. Were Basotho ponies any different?

In the middle of the crowd, I was introduced to my guide and the three ponies he was holding. The supervisor had told me in his office that the guide was one of the best they had. He knew the mountains like the back of his hand, could speak tolerable English and was popular among all the trekkers he had so far accompanied. Moses came forward to shake my hand and then pointed to the animals in front of us. 'Which one would you like to ride?' he asked.

I was sure this was some kind of test, that having claimed to have had experience before I was now being asked to prove that I knew something about horses. The problem was that all of them looked exactly the same. I felt it was prudent to pretend that I could spot some differences and so

I walked around, patting this one on the back, prodding the knee of another, trying to look like the cowboys I remembered from films I had seen as a child. Meanwhile the onlookers, with the same open curiosity they had earlier displayed in front of their cavorting animals, commented among themselves as I took my time.

I settled on a slightly fatter one in the end, for no other reason than that the saddle seemed to fit better on his back. There were murmurs of approval from the audience, but whether this was because I had made a good choice or because I had made something of a show was difficult to say.

I declined an offer of help to mount the pony I had chosen, knowing that if I could not get on by myself, this would compromise whatever positive image of horsemanship I had managed to cultivate. In any case, the animal was placid enough and generally unperturbed by the gawking onlookers. He was more preoccupied with a few last mouthfuls of grass. When the crowd parted to let us pass I gave him a gentle dig in the flanks, enough to propel him forward. Taking up a position behind Moses and his other pony we trotted out of the centre. I did not even bother to look back at the people who waved us off. 'See you in a week,' the supervisor shouted as we exited the gate. Though I did not say it loud enough so he could hear, I muttered 'I hope so' under my breath.

I had worried about how I would get on with my guide. A week touring the remote mountains of Lesotho with the same individual could turn unpleasant if we didn't get along. But it became clear soon enough why Moses was so popular. He was affable and pleasant. Most importantly for a guide he seemed happy to share his knowledge of the country and remained unruffled by my constant questions.

Unlike his brothers, cousins and nephews he had not made the trek to South Africa. He said that he knew enough about what life was like in the mines to dissuade him from trying. He had been a farmer for a while but when the pony trekking centre was established he had found regular employment. 'No, I don't get tired of covering the same territory week in and week out. The mountains change. One day they are soft and gentle. The next day they are hard and angry. It's like meeting a new person every day.'

As for the trekkers, his experience had generally been positive. Sometimes he would have someone who complained: about the pony, about the food, about the villages where they stayed, about the tea that Moses regularly supplied every couple of hours. But most were appreciative and curious too, and he enjoyed interacting with people who showed an interest in his country.

The first few hours of riding were comfortable enough and I began to wonder what the Americans had been making all the fuss about. The saddle seemed fine and Moses had shown me how to place my legs in the stirrups so they did not rub quite so hard. He had asked me how much experience I really had and when I told him that I had only ever ridden a donkey some years previously in Sudan he laughed and said that he had guessed as much. 'Don't worry,' he reassured me. 'It's not that difficult. Trust your pony. That's the most important thing you need to know.'

After a while it became clear that the pony not only knew a lot more about where we were going than I did, but also how best to get there. On several occasions he would ignore my attempts to steer him. He would choose a path that invariably turned out better than the one I had wanted him to take. When he stopped and refused to budge Moses told me that the pony needed a rest. 'Hop off his back and walk for a while. He'll let you on again when he's ready.'

Relieved of the effort of having to think for myself, I had time to sit back and contemplate the scenery. Despite the dramatic slopes and the stark backdrop of the mountains, there were more frequent signs of cultivation than I would have expected. The staple crop in the area was a kind of hardy millet that was one of the few things that grew this high up. Much like the sadza in Zimbabwe, millet porridge was eaten with vegetables or a popular stew made from goat meat. I had seen very few cattle since we had left the town, and Moses confirmed that the grazing was generally too poor in upland Lesotho for the size of herds that were common elsewhere. But goats were numerous and on several occasions we came across large herds of them, scrambling across the hillsides in search of whatever fodder they could find.

It was their grazing, combined with the pressures of population on scarce resources, which had left much of Lesotho treeless. I had read that if deforestation continued at the same rate, the country would have no trees left within a period of twenty years. I had travelled enough in Africa to know that local forests were at the heart of many rural economies, providing wood for construction and fuel for cooking and heat. What was the substitute in Lesotho?

In the mountains, where temperatures frequently fell below zero, earth and stone were the materials used for building. Moses pointed to a kind of thorny scrub that covered several of the slopes and said that this was sometimes cut too and inserted between the stones to keep out the cold wind that blew in winter. Most families now had kerosene stoves for cooking but where villages were too remote for a regular supply, people resorted to the use of dried dung from their ponies. 'When it's not being used for cooking, it's the only fertiliser we have for our fields. You won't see any pony shit lying around this part of the world. All of it gets used for something or other.'

Sitting on the back of a sanguine pony and being rocked to an agreeable rhythm, I lost track of time until Moses stopped a few hours later and said that it would soon get dark. 'We need to press on more quickly,' he said, looking worried. 'I don't like the look of the weather over there.' He pointed to where some heavy clouds were gathering behind the mountains.

'I brought an anorak with me,' I replied, adding that in the country I came from we were used to rain.

Moses told me that it wasn't the rain he was worried about. 'These clouds bring lightning. I don't want to be caught out in the open when the storm arrives.'

The ponies seemed to sense what was happening and without any prompting picked up their pace. I recalled Kurt's first words that he had spoken to me on the aeroplane, that Lesotho had the highest fatality rate for lightning strikes in the world. As the clouds thickened and the peels of thunder moved closer I knew that I was about to have a grand-stand view of what he had been talking about.

The lightning started just as we entered the village. 'Leave your things,' Moses shouted and pushed me through the door of the first house we came to. Inside was a group of women and children clustered around a small stove. Though they nodded a peremptory greeting, I could see that they were scared.

Although the storm was close it seemed to hover around some neighbouring mountains. Through the curtain of rain that began to fall, I watched in fascination as the forks of lightning flashed between the sky and the ground. It reminded me of a fireworks display, but one that was out of control. In the semi-dark of the room the small stove barely illuminated the faces of the people around us, but whenever the lightning flashed it was as if a bulb had suddenly been turned on – illuminating everything.

I checked my shoes, unable to recall whether rubber soles conducted electricity safely or simply exaggerated the shock. Noticing what I was doing Moses turned towards me and gave a thumbs up, which I presumed meant that I had the correct foot wear.

A few feet outside the door, the ponies huddled together, their noses touching as if in reassurance. I could see what Charles had meant when he had said they were renowned for their equanimity. They barely flinched when the noise and rain intensified, and seemed much calmer than the nervous inhabitants of the house.

On average, scores of people each year were struck and killed by lightning in the mountains of Lesotho. A combination of altitude, weather and lack of tree cover accounted for the fatalities. At the same time, local people continued to refuse the advice of scientists to install conductors on the roofs of their homes. Charles had explained why:

'There are intense cultural beliefs around this issue. Most people believe that if you are struck by lightning it is because you have offended a neighbour or done something to make them jealous. Sticking a metal rod with a wire to the outside of your hut is not going to convince people, who have a different concept of the world, that it will protect them.'

Half an hour later, Moses announced that the storm was moving away. Soon enough the pauses between the thunder grew longer and the flashes of lightning more distant. The rain still poured down in a solid sheet, however, and once or twice when the sky was illuminated I could see that the main route through the village had transformed into a small river flowing down the mountain.

The family turned out to be distant relatives of Moses. We were to stay the night with them. They had a room in the back with mattresses for visitors. Once the rain eased off they would prepare a meal of sadza and goat meat, if I had no objection to trying local food.

'I could eat a horse,' I replied. Moses laughed, adding that we had to ride our ponies rather than consume them but that sometime over the next few days he would organise a meal of dried horse flesh, a delicacy in these parts offered only to the most prestigious visitors.

I would have been happy to offer more than the few dollars that Moses suggested, but he insisted that this amount had been agreed among all the villages, and that it was best to stick to the rate. If I had a few spare pens and some paper that I wanted to share with the children before I left, then that was up to me.

The oldest boy acted as the translator for the family, who had overcome their initial reserve and were eager to ask questions. He had learned his English in secondary school, back in the town we had come from earlier that day. Now he was on holiday and would only return a few months later to complete his final exams.

'Of course I won't come back here when I finish school,' he said with some surprise when I asked him if he would return to his village. 'My family didn't give me an education so I could become a farmer. Maybe I'll get a job in Maseru or one of the other towns, but most probably I'll go to South Africa. That's where my father, uncles and cousins are working. That's where all the men from our village end up.'

That statement seemed to be backed up by the profile of the family around us. The boy we were speaking to was the oldest male in the household at only fourteen years of age. There was a grandmother, an aunt, his own mother and five children including himself. Out of a population of several hundred in the village, they reckoned that there were no more than four or five men who had stayed behind. The rest were women, children and a few grandfathers who had done their stint in the mines and had only come back when their working lives were over.

The children wanted to know where I was from, what I thought of their country and what my own wife and children were doing back wherever it was I had left them. Not for the first time in Africa the fact that I was not married seemed to surprise them. I remembered in Sudan the solicitous attention of my colleagues at school, even though I was only twenty-two years old at the time. Did I have some medical ailment that accounted for my single status?

The grandmother who had joined us around the fire pointed to the boys and girls who were questioning me and announced with considerable pride that she had more grandchildren than she could count. What was wrong with me? Why was I waiting?

'I travel a lot. I'm never at home. What kind of woman would want a marriage like that?' I replied.

Even as I said it, I knew that this argument would carry little weight in a country where most husbands were absent for more than eleven months in the year and where children grew up without the presence of their fathers. Marriage and having children were about securing your future, and having someone to remember you when you passed on. It gave you the stability of having somewhere you could call home, even if you rarely had the opportunity to enjoy it.

Although I was happy enough with my own reasons for not having settled down, I had never had a discussion with friends, colleagues and even complete strangers in Africa that had satisfied them on this point. Sekuru had been the most persistent and, as my self-appointed father, continually reminded me that time was running out. By now I should have had at least three or four offspring, rather than the zero I could claim. I had declined his offer to visit a local doctor who specialised in 'male problems,' reassuring him that on that front, I was perfectly fine.

I woke up the next morning with the children clustered around me, poking and nudging me to get up for breakfast. By the time I had washed, thankful for the bucket of warm water the family provided, Moses had already saddled the horses and loaded our bags.

Over the generous helping of eggs, potatoes and goat meat that filled our plates he pointed to what seemed an impossibly steep ascent up the mountains behind us. That was where we were headed. By the end of the day we would reach an upland plateau where the ground was more level and the walking easier. But first we had to get there and as he urged me to eat as much as I could, since the next meal would only be that evening in the next village, I knew that we were in for a tough climb.

Although the rain had stopped, evidence of the heavy downpour of the previous evening was all around. The ground was wet and soggy and we had to cross numerous small streams and rivers as we made our way upwards. According to Moses, water was one of Lesotho's principal exports. South African farmers needed vast quantities to irrigate their fields and in order to better regulate the flow, and maximise its profits too, Lesotho had recently embarked on the construction of several large dams. The biggest was the one that Kurt had been working on for the last few years.

'People are divided,' Moses responded when I asked him if this programme had popular support. The dams would displace a lot of people. There would be a loss of precious farmland too when areas became flooded, and since the country had so little in the first place, there were worries that Lesotho would become even more dependent on food imports. But on the plus side the revenues from the sale of water would be regular and substantial. Some of the dams would produce electricity too. Having an alternative source of energy could help save trees and avert the country's impending environmental catastrophe.

Moses himself was cautious in making a judgment. 'It all depends on who benefits. Will the Government help the people who lose their homes? Will they provide electricity to villages like the one we have just left? Will money go to the people who need it the most?' As he was speaking I reflected on what I had seen in Nyaminyami and how the Tonga who had been displaced from their homes by Kariba dam were still suffering thirty years later.

Trusting in your pony was easy enough when you were on a relatively flat piece of ground, and a fall meant nothing more than a few light bruises or a sore backside, but on the steep slopes of the mountain it became much more difficult to follow that instruction. My gaze constantly reverted to the considerable drop that awaited any small slip or error and though Moses advised me to look ahead, I became increasingly nervous the higher up we proceeded.

Eventually I dismounted. 'If I fall then I'd prefer that it's because of my own mistake rather than anyone else's,' I replied, when Moses reminded me again how reliable our animals were. I could see that he was slightly miffed by my decision but he was too professional and polite to say so. When he saw me struggling up the steep path we were on he told me to catch hold of the tail of his pony, and allow myself to be dragged up that way.

It was during one of our frequent stops that Moses pointed to a small group of men a few hundred yards away who were descending towards us. Protruding above the bags they were carrying on their backs were the barrels of what looked like rifles. 'Don't worry. It's only the national army,' Moses reassured me when he saw my look of concern. 'We'll meet several more of these patrols by the time we're finished.'

They were not on a simple training exercise as I had first assumed. 'We want to check your bags,' they said, politely but firmly when they reached us. Moses signaled them to go ahead and after they had satisfied themselves that we were not carrying whatever it was they were looking for, they saluted and trotted off down the path we had just ascended.

'They're looking for drugs,' Moses said, when I asked him what the search had been about.

'What kind of drugs?' I replied, wondering if I had been suddenly transported from the uplands of southern Africa to the mountains of Afghanistan. As far as I knew the country exported nothing more controversial than water, horses and mine workers.

It turned out that apart from millet, Lesotho also produced high quality cannabis, a commodity much appreciated in the towns and cities across its border. While not on the scale of drug exports from other parts of the world, it was enough to prompt the concern of the South Africa authorities, who in turn prodded the Lesotho Government to do something about it. Moses was skeptical as to whether the army patrols had registered any success in curbing the traffic. 'You can see the soldiers from miles away in this part of the country. By the time they get to a village, whatever drugs might have been there will have long disappeared. I think it's more of a show for the South Africans.'

Once again we reached the next village as it was getting dark, although this time there was no storm pursuing us. The last few miles had been a lot easier over the flat ground that Moses had promised, but on an empty stomach and with my legs beginning to ache, I could feel myself flagging. I found it difficult not to collapse in a heap in the hut we were shown to. Moses had to remind me that there was still some food to eat and a cup of his strong tea to help keep me awake.

As we were eating our meal there was a light tapping on the door. A woman entered and after greeting the family spoke to Moses, pointing towards me at the same time. Her son had had an accident while working in their fields earlier that day. He had apparently cut his arm with the machete he had been using. The nearest clinic was back in the village we had left that morning. They had heard that there was a European visiting the village and wanted to know if I could come and look at him.

One of the things we had been instructed to carry with us whenever we travelled was a first aid kit. It was a simple affair, with nothing more elaborate than some bandages, plasters, antiseptic, cotton wool and aspirin. I had also attended a one-day course on dealing with minor medical emergencies but that had been several years ago and I was unsure how much I could remember. When I told Moses to tell the woman that I was no doctor and that all I had were a few bandages and some aspirins, he replied that this was more than what they had themselves. 'At worst you can do no harm.'

Word seemed to have spread, even before we got there. By the time we reached the household on the other side of the village, a crowd had gathered around a young boy who seemed indifferent to all the fuss and commotion about him. The cut itself was not as deep or as serious as I had feared, although I told the family that they would have to travel to the clinic the following day to check whether he needed stitches.

I washed the wound as best I could with hot water and dettol, placed some gauze on top of it and then wrapped it up in a neat bandage. Then I gave him some aspirin, not because it was necessary but because I knew from experience that no medical consultation in Africa was ever complete without the prescription of a tablet. When the boy, who had barely flinched throughout, waved his bandaged arm in the air the audience erupted in cheering. People came up to shake my hand and to clap me on the back as if I had completed some elaborate surgery.

I refused the money that the woman tried to press into my hand as we exited the house. I told her that she should keep this for the following day in case there was any charge at the clinic. Although Moses patted me on the back too as we returned to where we would sleep he seemed concerned. 'We need to leave this village earlier than I thought,' he said, 'even though I promised you a late start tomorrow.'

'Why?' I asked, reminding him that today had been difficult and that I had been looking forward to a leisurely breakfast and relaxed departure.

'Because word will get around that there is a visiting doctor. Unless you want to spend the whole day attending to patients, I think it best to leave as soon as we can. Let's just hope that word doesn't reach the rest of the district as well.'

Five days later, my first aid kit now empty, we arrived in a village from where we could see the pony trekking centre some distance below us. We would be there the following day. I was not unhappy to be returning but I had also grown used to the routines that Moses had established; our early departures when the mountains were at their most dramatic, an easy pace to get to the next village by late afternoon, the camaraderie of being huddled around a fire at night exchanging pleasantries with the families that hosted us.

As Moses reminded me on several occasions, I had not only eaten all the varieties of local food on offer but had sampled Lesotho's prohibited export too. I had woken up one night feeling lightheaded and dizzy. The sensation was not entirely unpleasant but I had nudged Moses awake, just in case I had contracted an illness. He had laughed and told me that in the storeroom next door were several sacks of home grown cannabis. That accounted for the feeling of being disembodied and floating in the air. 'You didn't even pay for it,' he joked over the next few days, adding that I should have given something to the family for their extra hospitality.

That last evening I had asked him if he had ever felt inclined to exchange his life in the mountains for the bright lights of Maseru, or the cities in South Africa where many of his compatriots now resided. Over the previous few days we had passed through impoverished places with no electricity, running water, clinics or other amenities.

He had shaken his head. 'If life is so good elsewhere then why do so many people return? You've seen the old men in the villages. Most of them worked in the cities and could have stayed. Instead they came back.'

'So, what brings them home?'

'Precisely because it is home and because you are not treated like a stranger. I know our villages are poor. I've seen what life is like in cities, but everyone in the end wants to return to the place where they feel most comfortable, where they can best be themselves.'

After he had answered, he pointed towards me. 'What about you, Mr. Chris? Where do you feel most at home?'

I knew that he would not have asked that question unless we had become friends and that I would not have answered as I did unless I felt comfortable admitting to him that the life of an expatriate worker living in different countries and belonging to none, had its downside too. As we shared our meal that final evening I mentioned too that I felt envious of someone who seemed so rooted in the place they came from, and so at ease with the circumstances around them.

'Watch that you don't end up like those nomads you keep on talking about,' my friend Peter back in Ireland had warned me several years ago. That was exactly what had happened, I thought to myself, and wondered when and if it would ever change.

13

'Mukwasha'

'So what's wrong with girls from Scotland?' my father had asked, when I told him I was seeing someone from Zimbabwe.

'I might ask you the same question,' I replied, reminding him that my mother was German.

'That's hardly the same thing as marrying someone from the other side of the globe.'

'Why are we discussing marriage? I only mentioned I was seeing someone.'

'You've hardly ever talked about any of your girlfriends before. So telling me now means you must be serious.'

'Even if we did get married, and I'm not saying we would, what would be the problem? Your own family wasn't too keen on you marrying Mum. Yet you ignored them and went ahead. Did you regret that decision?'

'Of course not, but in a mixed race marriage there are cultural issues to consider, your different ways of perceiving the world. There is the prejudice of others; the way they would stare, the remarks they might make about your children. All I'm saying is look before you leap and if you make such a decision then be prepared for what might follow.'

I shrugged my shoulders. My father was a practical, considered man, or at least that was the persona he had always presented to us, and so these kinds of discussions about measuring the consequences of your decisions before you made them had been common enough in our family for as long as I could remember. For as long as I could think for myself I had largely ignored him, convinced that if you never took a risk then life would pass you by and leave you stranded in later years contemplating a past that had little worth remembering.

But as he had said, a leap of some sort would be involved and as I sat in a church in Harare with my about-to-be wife almost a year after our discussion, I was still unsure about where I would land. Marriage, a home, children, stability, had never been my thing. Yet here I was, five years after arriving in Zimbabwe, about to exchange my independence, freedom and past for a life with another person. I had no regrets about being there but as I shouted, 'Yes, I do,' above the noise and commotion when we reached the most important part of the ceremony, I took a deep breath too in anticipation of my future.

Kwadzi looked radiant, her face framed in a white tiara, her manner as calm and assured as it always was. Once or twice she winked in my direction and I remembered her words of the previous evening, her final advice before the big day. I was not to feel intimidated when I saw the crowd. She had a huge family, hundreds of relatives many of whom she barely knew. They would all be there, as custom demanded. There would be scores of friends too, because she was popular, and colleagues from work, because she was their boss. 'Weddings here are about community and family more than about two individuals deciding to live together. My ancestors will probably be looking on, but don't worry. If they didn't approve of you, you would never have got this far.'

Amid the clapping and cheering I could hear the voice of Sekuru Francis, louder than all the others. For a few days in the run up to the wedding he had fussed around me. The suit

I was to wear was not quite right. My beard needed a trim. My hair was too long for what propriety demanded on such an occasion. Just before I stepped into the car that would take me to the church he had sprinkled the contents of a small bottle over me, some *muti* he had acquired from the traditional market in Mbare to make sure I performed my conjugal duties that evening.

As he waved his stick in the air and displayed his various moves I was glad he was there. Beside him were my twin sister and my favorite aunt, both called Gisela. Apart from them, a handful of friends and Fortunate from work, every-one else belonged to Kwadzi's camp.

I was concerned that my side was under-represented. I had dissuaded my parents from coming. My mother was a poor traveller and I had worried that the novelty of a new environment and the unfamiliarity of a very different culture would have unnerved her. I didn't want her tetchiness to be interpreted by Kwadzi and her family as a sign of disap-proval, of opposition to our marriage, but my sister had told me when she arrived that I had made the wrong decision. 'Mum and Dad would have come if you had asked them. They would have got on fine.'

'I hope I don't make a fool of myself,' I had said the previous evening, when Kwadzi and I had gone through the itinerary for a final time. It wasn't just the church ceremony I was worried about. There was the part that came after, when the guests would congregate in a large hall and both of us would have to dance our way through them to the sounds of rumba music. I had initially thought that a few token steps would have been acceptable, but when I was instructed to start dancing lessons several months before the actual event I grew increasingly nervous as the big day approached.

'What happens if I trip over my feet? What happens if

everyone laughs at me?' Somewhat ungraciously I was glad that Brendan, my best man from Ireland who would also have to perform, had looked worse than me at rehearsals. If nothing else his own faltering steps would divert people's attention from my own. He looked nervous as we sat in church and while the pastor proceeded with his lengthy sermon I could see him shuffling his feet in anticipation of what would come later.

For the first time in several hours I had time to speak to Kwadzi when we sat in the car that would take us to ZANU PF Headquarters. It had a hall that could be rented out for wedding parties if space was limited in other locations. She could see I was anxious. 'So what if you make a fool of yourself? It's all good natured and everyone appreciates someone who doesn't mind being laughed at. In any case,' she concluded, as we pulled up outside the hall where the music blared out in anticipation of our arrival, 'the crowd will be watching Brendan. So just relax.'

I lost track of time between stumbling out of the car and ending up at the top table. When I glanced at my watch I realised we had taken about half an hour to dance our way across a space that would normally have taken us only a few minutes to walk. As Kwadzi had said, the laughter and amusement was all good natured. As we twirled around we were greeted with appreciative applause and whistles of encouragement. Grown bold by the reception Brendan began to try out some moves that were not part of the routine we had practiced. He seemed disappointed when we finally sat down, claiming he could have continued for considerably longer.

Of the people that came up to greet us, Sekuru was the most emotional, almost in tears as he embraced me and telling me how pleased he was that I had not disappointed the crowd with the steps he had taught me. I could remember no dancing lessons where he had ever participated.

Despite it being a 'dry' wedding, in deference to Kwadzi's father who was a church minister, he had managed to find some alcohol and had imbibed a fair amount by the time he reached us. He gave a speech about how relieved he was that I had now found the right woman, announcing to the table that he had been worried about me from the first day we had met. I was almost thirty and had no children. As far as he could see I had no girlfriends either. 'I've lived with white men before and I can see that they can do without sex for years,' he declared. As Kwadzi collapsed, giggling beside me, he told anyone who would listen that without sex every night he would fall seriously ill.

At one of the tables, fussed over by a group of solicitous relatives, was Kwadzi's maternal grandmother. She had travelled from the communal area of Murewa where she lived, to attend the wedding. Her failing health and her dislike of Harare, which she considered to be too noisy, dirty and crowded, made her presence all the more significant. For me she was one of the most important members of the family, for the simple reason that Kwadzi set great store by her opinion. She had told me once that if her grandmother didn't approve of our relationship then we had little chance of progressing further.

My first trip to meet her, therefore, had assumed something of the nature of an inspection. I was nervous throughout the two hour drive it took from Harare to reach her village. 'Is there something I should do? How should I behave?'

'Don't pretend to be anyone different than who you are,' Kwadzi had told me. 'She sees through people and their charades. If she likes you, she'll say so. If she doesn't, she'll make that very clear too.'

A visit to a grandmother to introduce a boyfriend was not a casual event in Shona culture and would only take place a considerable period of time after a relationship had started. So it was well over a year after we met that we had travelled to Murewa together.

I had been introduced to Kwadzi through work, after I had requested an audience with officials in the Ministry of Education to discuss the placement of a speech therapist we had recruited from the UK. The head of School Psychological Services had introduced me to her deputy and told me that this was the person in her department I would have to liaise with. Then she had left us alone. For the next hour I stumbled through my questions and found various excuses to prolong the discussion, long after what we needed to get through had been completed.

'I think I've met someone,' I confided to Sekuru that same evening.

'Who is she?'

'Her name is Kwadzi and she works for the Ministry of Education. That's all I really know about her.'

'Maybe she's married? Maybe she has a boyfriend? Perhaps she's an Ndebele. These women are known to beat up their husbands.'

'Well what I do know is that she is witty, attractive and intelligent. The rest I can find out later.'

The following day I phoned the department again. 'Is it a Miss or Mrs. Nyanungo I should speak to?' I asked the receptionist. 'I don't want to cause offence by using the wrong title.'

'Oh, that's a Miss,' she replied, and I fancied I heard an amused giggle before she put me through to her boss's line.

I had made up a story about some extra paperwork that we required to process the placement of our volunteer. 'I'll need your signature, I'm afraid. Would now be a good time to come over?'

When I entered her office a short while later the receptionist asked me to wait since 'Miss Nyanungo' was busy with someone else. She came out after some minutes with a young man on the end of her arm. He was smartly dressed, handsome and clearly at ease in her presence and from the way they interacted I guessed they were more than casual friends. Maybe Sekuru had been right after all.

'Can I introduce you to my brother?' she said, as I rose to greet her. 'His name is Washington, just like the capital of the United Sates.'

Our business was concluded in only a few short minutes, since that was all it took to sign the document I had fabricated. As she escorted me out of her office I knew that if I did not say something now it would be difficult to find another excuse later. The pretext I had given to meet her was a flimsy one and she had remarked that she would never have guessed that the bureaucracy in my own organisation was worse than her own.

'I'm fascinated by other cultures,' I said. 'It's one of the reasons I came to Africa. But Harare seems pretty impenetrable. I probably need someone to show me around.'

'Why don't you read the newspaper?' she said, echoing something I already knew. 'It has a section that lists everything that is happening in this city.'

Then as she was about to shake my hand to say goodbye, I managed to blurt out the invitation that I had rehearsed with Sekuru the previous evening, when he had told me that African women appreciated men who were direct and could speak their minds. 'Would you like to come out with me this weekend? We could go somewhere and listen to music.'

There was a momentary silence, punctuated by the coughing of the secretary in the background who had overheard everything I had said. I worried then that I had been culturally insensitive, despite Sekuru's advice. In Sudan such a request would have been met with a curt refusal and a probable end to any future meetings. First you had to speak to the parents. Then you invited the girl. Maybe that was how it was here too.

'Unfortunately I'm busy this weekend, so I'll have to decline your offer.'

Before I could turn tail she added that the following weekend she would be free. 'I'll show you a place where you can hear some authentic Zimbabwean music. I'll see you then, unless your organisation needs another signature.'

Over the next few months I became an expert on the contemporary music scene in Harare. Every weekend there was another band to see, or the same one playing in a different venue. Whether it was because of her popularity or because it was the same crowd we followed around the city, Kwadzi seemed to know everyone who was there. Even members of the various bands we heard would come up to greet her and on several occasions we were waved through at the entrance without having to pay.

'We all went to school together,' she replied, when I asked her how she knew all these people. 'Besides, it's a close society and many of our families are related in one way or another.'

Thomas Mapfumo was her favorite musician and judging by the crowds he attracted to his performances, that appreciation was widely shared. He had been imprisoned during the war at different times and according to Kwadzi it was his music and lyrics that had inspired many of the younger generation to fight for their independence. Kwadzi would occasionally translate for me the songs that he sang and one thing I remarked was that his criticism of corruption, incompetence and nepotism seemed directed at anyone who merited it. 'That's one reason why he is so popular,' she said. 'He's not in anyone's pocket.'

'But have you kissed her yet?' Sekuru asked, when I told him one weekend that we were going to another show.

Maybe I looked surprised, since he told me to lighten up. 'I've seen white girls on television. They kiss just like ours. That's one thing we share across our different cultures.'

Despite wanting to I was worried that such a blunt expression of my feelings towards her might end up putting her off our developing friendship. I knew that Kwadzi belonged to a religious family. Her father was a Methodist minister. Her mother was prominent in the church too. On some Sundays Kwadzi ran a scripture class for a group of children from the inner city of Harare. I remembered too her pronouncements against alcohol when I had drunk too much at one of the shows we had attended. She had told me that she didn't like men who made fools of themselves. There had been unanswered phone calls for some time before our weekend routines had finally resumed.

But Sekuru was adamant. 'All that friendship stuff is fine for a while, but women like to be kissed too. You've had enough time to get to know each other. She might get tired of waiting for you to make the first move, and find someone else.'

That evening I dropped her off at her home as usual, in the early hours of the morning after a long night listening to another band. As she moved to get out of the car I leant over and planted a kiss on her cheek. She looked surprised and turned abruptly towards me. 'You've blown it,' I thought. 'This time you've gone too far.'

But again I was wrong, unable to read the signals. 'Excuse me Chris, but I'm not your mother. If you want to kiss me, then do it properly.'

'First a kiss. Then it's the parents,' Sekuru had predicted, and sure enough a short while later I was invited round for Sunday lunch to meet her mother and father.

'So what does that mean?' I asked Sekuru, who had become my principal advisor on the issue.

'It's a big deal, that's what it means. No girl in Zimbabwe would ever invite you to meet her parents if things weren't getting serious. Make sure you greet them properly, act respectfully and for goodness sake don't kiss her again in front of them.'

I had been nervous and worried as that Sunday approached, constantly asking Kwadzi how I should behave. But she told me to relax, that her family was more laid back than others and less 'traditional' in dealing with visitors such as me.

This turned out to be true, since they were not at all preoccupied with the formalities and decorum Sekuru had prepared me for. Kwadzi had looked surprised when I had turned up in smart clothes and wearing the one tie in my wardrobe. 'Chris, it's not a job interview you've come for. We're just sharing some chicken and potatoes, that's all.'

While I engaged her father in a discussion about the history of the Methodist Church in Africa, Kwadzi, her mother and sisters disappeared to the kitchen to prepare dinner. The noise and laughter that came from their direction filtered through to where we were sitting. I had noticed before on my travels in Africa that women seemed to have much more fun on their own. The moment a man appeared in the place they were gathered, they would assume a more decorous persona, as if pretending the behaviour that was expected of them. But I knew that Kwadzi's family was different when her father got up and announced that we would join them. 'Seems as if they've found a subject that is more interesting than our own.'

At the dinner table when we were about to eat, Kwadzi's mother asked me to recite a prayer. We had never said prayers before meals in my own family. My father, who was a pronounced sceptic when it came to religious matters, had only ever taught us some irreverent lines. These were the only words that now came back to me but I wondered if 'holy, holy round the table, eat as much as you are able,' would be met with quite the same spirit of humour that had greeted them at home. There was a picture of 'the Last Supper' on the wall behind me, another one of angels ascending to heaven above the kitchen door, and several other biblical illustrations scattered throughout the house. This was a family clearly attached to their church.

But I also remembered Kwadzi's previous advice to be myself. 'My family don't like pretence and neither do I.' So taking a deep breath I recited my lines, worried even as I did so that perhaps I had gone too far.

I needn't have worried. After a moment's silence Kwadzi's father burst into laughter and slapped me on the back. 'Good for you,' he said, as his daughter gave me a gentle kick under the table. 'We like someone with a sense of humour. That's how we are in this family.'

'My grandmother is more formal than my parents,' Kwadzi had told me, a few days before we made our trip to Murewa. 'You'll have to learn how to greet her in the correct fashion.'

According to Sekuru that meant placing a knee on the ground, clapping my hands together in a particular way and then going through a round of greetings that had to be recited in a precise and formalised sequence. He was a stern teacher. 'No, not like that. Your fingers have to touch together like this when you are clapping. You're not at a Thomas Mapfumo concert applauding his music.'

All of which made me even more nervous than when I had first met Kwadzi's parents, and increasingly apprehensive the closer we got to Murewa. After the town and on a track to where her grandmother lived there were surprised stares and shouts of astonishment from the children we passed. 'You're probably the first Murungu to have come this way for some time,' Kwadzi said, 'so don't get upset if all the neighbours come round to have a look at you too.'

Kwadzi's grandmother was an imposing figure. She held court among her chickens, cats, dogs, nieces and nephews on a large straw mat spread out in the front yard of her property. The house itself had seen better days but I could see how grand it must have once been, standing out even now from the more humble dwellings of the village around it.

Kwadzi's grandfather, who had died a number of years previously, had been a prominent local businessman involved in the transport sector. Inside the front gate there were the rusting remains of a large truck, one of several he had owned during his heyday. Poor investments and the outbreak of war had affected his business, and of the fleet of vehicles he had once owned the shell of the Bedford was all that remained.

I stumbled through the greetings I had practiced while the rest of the family hovered in the background. Kwadzi's grandmother remained inscrutable and after I had finished, fixed me with a penetrating stare. Should I stay where I was? Should I stand up? I turned towards Kwadzi for guidance but she was pretending interest in something that one of her cousins was showing her. This moment was between me and the family member she most respected and she was not about to intervene on my behalf.

'You can call me Ambuya,' her grandmother finally said, motioning me to stand up.

'Now show me what you've brought for me.'

As I walked to the car to find the gift that Kwadzi had suggested we should buy, I wondered what the penalty might be if she didn't like it. Banishment seemed most likely, and an end to my relationship with her granddaughter. But thankfully she seemed appreciative of the box of live day-old chicks that we had purchased from a factory on the outskirts of Harare. Kwadzi had told me that her grandmother reared the best chickens in the district and that this box of fifty would soon be transformed into a handsome profit. Ambuya counted them one by one, inspecting each of them carefully to check their quality. A niece was summoned to shepherd them into a small enclosure, where they were fussed over by several hens and introduced to their new home.

We were to stay and eat lunch, Ambuya then announced, and pointed to a bird that was running around the yard. 'That's the best one I have,' she said, adding that she would personally cook it herself for our dinner. But before she could do so someone had to catch it, and from the way she looked at me I was left in little doubt as to who that 'someone' was.

For the next few minutes I chased the chicken around the yard, conscious of how my clumsy attempts had become the source of considerable amusement. The family had been joined by a group of curious neighbours who had stopped to see what all the commotion was about.

I refused the help of one of the onlookers. I felt that I was being scrutinised to see if I was worthy of Ambuya's favourite granddaughter and I could recognise that this little test was not about my proficiency in catching chickens but about my perseverance, sense of humour and willingness to indulge an old lady. Finally I managed to corner it against a wire fence. To applause from all the spectators I brought it squawking and fluttering to where Ambuya was sitting, who rewarded me with my first smile of the day and a nod of what I took to be approval.

'She likes you,' Kwadzi said, as we watched the prize bird of the household being prepared for the pot.

'How do you know?'

'She only cooks for people she likes. That's her way of telling everyone that you're now part of the family. Word will soon get around that Ambuya made you dinner.'

Visiting Kwadzi's grandmother became something of a regular routine thereafter. Thankfully there were no more tests but I was instructed to sit beside her while Kwadzi shared the latest gossip and scandals from Harare. On a couple of occasions Ambuya would drive back with us and I enjoyed her recounting the history of the area, and reminiscing about her own life in a part of the country that despite its proximity to the city seemed like a world apart.

On the outskirts of her village were a series of dramatic rocky hills, with large granite boulders perched on top of them as if they had been placed there by a deliberate hand. The local legend was that several giants had fought over the territory, and these boulders were the remains of the ammunition they had gathered to hurl at each other. Several of these places had a special significance within the culture of the district and could only be visited if the local chief gave his permission. There was a cave where spirit mediums from other parts of Zimbabwe would come to pray for rain. There was a stream where women who were infertile went to bathe, and again I was struck by how prevalent traditional beliefs still were in Shona society when Ambuya told us that visitors came in their thousands.

On one of our after dinner walks near her home, Kwadzi and I stumbled across an abandoned settlement, surrounded by barbed wire and sentry towers. Ambuya told us that during the war they were not allowed to stay in their homes. The authorities were worried that the local population was being converted to the nationalist cause at evening meetings conducted by the freedom fighters. During the day they were allowed to work in their fields but as soon as dusk approached they were escorted into these 'protected' villages and locked up for the night. If the intention was to win the hearts and minds of the local population, it backfired. Ambuya claimed that the practice of forced resettlement had pushed many of the villagers into supporting the very movement it was supposed to turn them against.

Occasionally I would volunteer to help clear the undergrowth that threatened to take over the ancestral graves a short distance from the family property. I knew from my visit to Sekuru's home that the Shona preferred to have their dead relatives buried beside them. This was in contrast to what happened in my own part of the world, where graveyards were hidden away at the edges of towns and villages, or concealed behind walls where they were out of sight and out of mind.

'They're there for both our sakes,' Sekuru had told me when I had asked him why deceased family members were buried close by. 'Our ancestors protect us, but in return we keep them company. They get lonely, just like people. And if they feel neglected they get angry too. That's when bad things happen to families. It's our grandparents reminding us that they have been forgotten.'

My interaction with her grandmother in particular made me feel closer to a culture that until I had met Kwadzi seemed impenetrable and distant. I had constantly felt like an outsider looking in. This was different than in other parts of the continent where I had not encountered such reserve, an unwillingness to open up in front of strangers.

I realised that race was a factor. The way that whites had behaved in their interaction with the indigenous population of this country had left a legacy of mistrust that was difficult to break through. This was never openly stated nor aggressively presented. Shona people were polite, courteous and friendly. But unlike Sudan and Algeria where I had felt more at home, here there was a barrier beyond which you never passed. 'This is as much of ourselves as we are prepared to share with you,' was the statement that seemed to define my previous interaction with Zimbabwean friends and colleagues, 'Further than that you are not permitted.' Apart from Sekuru's, I had never been invited into any of their homes.

I was not so naïve as to think that these barriers would disappear, just because I had acquired an African girlfriend. Kwadzi, who was always blunt and forthright, had reminded me of that on several occasions, not in an unfriendly or disparaging way, but as something that she wanted me to be aware of even as our relationship deepened. She had admonished me once when I had remarked that wealth and class more than race and ethnicity now defined the parameters of discrimination in her country.

'Unless you had my skin colour you could never understand the depth of how much that defined us. Sure, that's not a reason for us to be bigoted in return, to replicate the patterns of behaviour we suffered. But don't expect that people here will readily open their doors to you as a white person and share their lives with you as if you are a long lost friend. We did that once and woke up the next day to find ourselves strangers in our own country.'

I had met Kwadzi's relatives. I had been accepted by her grandmother. We spent our weekends together and we had even gone to Scotland where I had introduced her to my parents. I had been nervous about that meeting wondering how they would react, but things had turned out fine and there was none of the awkward silences I had feared beforehand.

'So there's only marriage that's left,' Sekuru had said, several months later when he had asked me what my intentions were about our future together.

'We're fine as we are at the moment,' I had replied

somewhat defensively. I added that I needed more time to figure things out, since such a decision would be the biggest of my life and not one that I could ever take lightly. 'Besides, Kwadzi has never said anything about marriage either. I'm sure she's happy with how things are.'

Sekuru snorted. 'Here in Zimbabwe the man proposes. No woman would ever raise the subject herself. That's not done, but that doesn't mean to say she isn't thinking about it.'

Truth to tell Sekuru wasn't informing me of anything I didn't already know. If I couldn't provide a more stable, legally recognised relationship with Kwadzi I knew that sooner or later what we had together would not be enough. Welcomed as I had been by her family too, I knew that there were limits to their acceptance of me until I became a 'mukwasha, a formal son-in-law with all the obligations, duties and entitlements that that would mean.

What held me back were not the issues my father had raised about cultural differences and racial prejudice in whatever society we might end up in. My reasons were more selfish than that, but no less valid.

One was about my freedom and independence, my lack of commitments that meant I could up and leave whenever I wanted. Another was about Kwadzi's unwillingness to accommodate my nomadic orientation. She was the oldest daughter in her family, the one that her siblings looked up to and in many ways depended upon. She was deeply attached to her family and on one occasion, when I had asked her whether she had ever thought of living in another country, she had said that she would be lost without them, that a life outside Zimbabwe was not an option. Part of me knew that the sacrifices in terms of life style and options would therefore be mine, that in later years a feeling of having given up too much might come back to haunt me.

It was not long after my chat with Sekuru that Kwadzi had to visit another part of the country for several weeks. I had been anticipating some time on my own: a weekend reading my books; a break from Thomas Mapfumo; perhaps a drive to a part of the country I had never seen before. But as the days without seeing her dragged on I was prompted to think about what it would be like if this became a permanent state of affairs. I imagined no more visits to Murewa to see Ambuya, no more planning our weekends together, and no more evenings in each other's company. I realised the emptiness that would mean in my life and though I guessed that such a space would eventually be filled by other people and other places I knew there would be regret too at having missed out on happiness. That was not a future I wanted to contemplate.

'I'm not sure how things are done here,' I said, when I picked Kwadzi up shortly after she had returned. We were sitting in a parking lot in the city centre eating the sandwiches I had purchased for lunch. 'I also know it's not the most romantic of locations, but I've thought about it for some time and I've decided to ask you to marry me.'

There was the same silence as when I had asked her out on our first date and I had that same feeling of trepidation that she would say no. But in the slightly bemused, practical manner I was now familiar with she nodded her head and said that she thought marriage would be a good idea too. 'But don't ask me to change my name. No one can pronounce McIvor in our culture so I'd prefer to stick with what I've got. That's my only condition.'

Apart from being unable to pronounce my name I also knew that in her culture marriage was not a simple agreement between two people while the rest of the family remained passive bystanders. They would have to be brought into the decision too There would be negotiations about *roora*, the price paid by a prospective husband to the bride's family for the privilege of taking away their daughter. Even Kwadzi was not entirely sure of what all this would entail and said that she would have to consult an elderly aunt in order to find out what we had to do next.

She returned with a small notebook filled with instructions. 'Whatever happened to a simple yes or no?' I asked, as we went through the details of what had to be done. I had known there would be a process but not one as extensive and demanding as this.

Not for the first time Kwadzi reminded me that in important matters like getting married no one was regarded as an individual, a person with a life outside their family. 'The rituals surrounding births, marriages and deaths are what hold my society together. Conforming to these traditions, even for a modern woman like me, is not negotiable. You also need to remember that this is your passport into my family, and by family I don't just mean a small group of parents, brothers and sisters. It's the wider family that has to accept you, and while they will show you considerable latitude because you are an outsider, they will still expect you to show respect for how things are done among us.'

The first thing we had to do was find a go-between, a kind of good will ambassador who could negotiate on my behalf with Kwadzi's parents as to my suitability for their daughter. Since I had no relatives of my own in the country, one would have to be found.

Kwadzi's aunt had suggested a distant cousin whom she thought had the right credentials. He knew her family but was not so close that his impartiality in representing my interests would be compromised. A few weeks later we were on the road to Rushinga, a district in the far north of the country where he had last been heard from. We had his name, some vague directions to his village and that was all.

'If nothing else we'll see another part of Zimbabwe,' I had said, convinced we would not find him.

'He lives over there,' someone we had stopped on the road had said, when we asked him if he knew the person we were looking for. He pointed to a cluster of huts. There was a thread of smoke emerging from one of them, indicating that someone was at home.

When we greeted him I imagined that Kwadzi's cousin must be wondering what on earth we were doing visiting him in Rushinga. He had last seen Kwadzi several years ago. They had never been close. But here she was with a Murungu beside her, asking him about various members of the family she had lost touch with. If he was confused as to why we were there, however, he was too polite to say so. Both of them exchanged pleasantries for some time, never touching upon the reason for our visit.

It was only after we had drunk the tea his wife had prepared for us that he fell silent, a cue I assumed for explanations to begin. Kwadzi told him about our relationship, about the fact that we wanted to get married. But I had no one in the country that could represent me at discussions with her family, and of course a direct intercession on my own behalf was not permitted under the rules that surrounded such negotiations. 'Is this something you can do for us,' she asked, as I nodded my head to express my conviction that he was the right man for the job.

He seemed flattered that we had asked him. Kwadzi had explained that the role of a 'Munyai' was much respected within the society, since it was only responsible, upright and reputable individuals who were ever asked to discharge such a role. But his words were more reserved than his expression. 'Let me discuss this with my wife in private. The children will show you around the village. You'll have my answer by the time you get back.'

'Don't worry, he'll agree,' Kwadzi said as we walked around. 'But it's considered bad manners to look too eager. You're supposed to take some time to consider whether you're up to it.'

A short while later we were discussing with him the practicalities of setting up meetings with the family and the times that would be most convenient. He had work to do in Harare the following month and we agreed to meet then. He would need to know something about my own family, my background, my job and my prospects, since these things would feature in what he would say on my behalf.

As he began to detail the information he would need, it dawned on me for perhaps the first time that Kwadzi's family could always say no. Maybe they were not convinced that I was the right person for her after all. Though I had always encountered a friendly welcome whenever I had visited them, that did not necessarily mean that her parents would accept me as their daughter's husband. As Kwadzi had said, there were good reasons for Africans to be suspicious of white men. At the same time, was a job as an itinerant aid worker enough to convince them that I could provide Kwadzi with a secure financial future? I had a renewable contract but there was no guarantee from one year to the next that my organisation would sign it.

I must have looked worried. While Kwadzi spoke to his wife, her cousin placed a hand on my shoulder. 'I can see you're concerned. But the family would never have let your relationship get this far if they weren't prepared to accept you. Remember too that no one wants to upset Kwadzi either. That is one woman who always has her own way.'

Despite these reassurances I found myself several months later sitting nervously in my car outside the family home while my fate was decided somewhere inside it. Kwadzi had disappeared as soon as I arrived, telling me that she would not be expected to interact with me again until the negotiations were over. So it was left to her sisters to come out every so often to check that I was okay and to give me an update on how things were proceeding. They were not beyond teasing me either.

'You'll need to offer more cows,' one of them replied when I asked her what was happening. 'Your ambassador seems to forget that you're marrying royalty'

'Whatever it takes,' I had said to Kwadzi's cousin when we had previously discussed what I was able to afford. But what would happen if they wanted all my savings? I had heard about young couples struggling for years to pay off the *roora* that had been agreed as part of their marriage. Perhaps I would be in debt for the rest of my life.

Several hours later I was summoned inside. What could have taken them so long? If I was so acceptable, shouldn't the decision have been over in a matter of minutes? I didn't like the serious faces in front of me either. Apart from the immediate family and Kwadzi's cousin, her maternal uncle was there too. Normally relaxed and jovial he was much more solemn now as he pointed to a chair where I was to sit down and hear their verdict.

Kwadzi was the oldest daughter, he said. That was an important position in their culture since she was the one her parents most relied on and who had the responsibility of looking after her brothers and sisters. Within the wider family Kwadzi was also special. I must have known that she had almost died as child, when a lamp exploded in front of her leaving her badly burnt. It was the prayers of her relatives that had pulled her through and now everyone, himself included, felt protective towards her.

'So it's no easy matter giving her away. We need to be sure that the person she ends up with will care for, look after and keep her happy. But we have listened to the representations on your behalf and have also taken account of Kwadzi's wishes in this matter. Based on what they have told us, and on what we know about you already, we have agreed to hand Kwadzi over to your family.'

There were some conditions I would have to agree to, however, and he asked Kwadzi's cousin to take me into another room to discuss with me what they had come up with. The list was not long. There was a suit, a walking stick and a hat for Kwadzi's father. There were several cows for her mother. Material would have to be procured for the wedding so that Kwadzi's bridesmaids would be appropriately dressed. The strangest item was an umbrella for an uncle, which for some reason had to be purchased in London. It all looked reasonable and affordable and not at all what I had feared while sitting in my car speculating about an impoverished future. 'I agree to everything,' I said, as soon as he concluded. 'Are you sure that's all.'

It turned out that there was one more thing I would have to accept as a condition for our marriage. 'This is something that Kwadzi insists on,' her uncle said, when we returned to the room to communicate my agreement.

I wondered what it could be; a special gift for someone; the type of ring I would have to buy; an assurance that if we lived away from her family enough provision would be made for her to visit them regularly. 'Whatever it is I'm sure it's fine. Everything else you have asked me for has been entirely reasonable.'

'Well maybe this demand is one that might prove more difficult,' he said, maintaining his stiff, formal manner. 'Kwadzi has no intention of dancing at her wedding with someone who can't keep up. You'd better start lessons right away.'

14

Looking Back

'I don't care how many people your organization has fed or how long you have been working in our country. As far as I'm concerned every bit of maize you distribute is a criticism of my Government. It's like saying that we can't look after our own people, that we are incapable of managing our own affairs. I'm closing you down.'

I sat with my mouth open in the same office, in the same Ministry, in which we had been congratulated ten years previously for our response to a drought that had affected the western part of Zimbabwe. Although I was now working for another charity, the aid we had delivered then was little different to the aid we were delivering now, but somehow it had become subversive, an affront to the Government, something that lessened the hold of the authorities on the population.

'The statistics on sanitary improvement are not interpreted by the natives as progress in the fight against illness, but as further proof of the oppressors hold on the country.'

These words had been written by the author Franz Fanon forty years previously. In the same way, our food deliveries were now perceived by some of Zimbabwe's leaders not as a benevolent gesture or an expression of solidarity but as a means of undermining them in the eyes of their people. The official I was speaking to accused me of being an agent of neo-colonialism, part of a plot to return the country to a state of dependency.

My first thought as I walked out of that office to inform my staff that our programme was indefinitely suspended was that something terrible had happened in the intervening period to have led to this state of affairs. When I left Zimbabwe in 1993 to take up a post in another part of Africa, the country had seemed much the same as when I had first arrived. Sure, there had been challenges and difficulties. Failed policies and outside interference had been less than helpful, but Zimbabwe still manifested the spirit of openness and optimism that had impressed me throughout the seven years I lived there. A sense of hope for the future, and the determination of people to see their new country succeed, made it an exception in a continent increasingly known for its corruption, abuses of power and civil conflicts. 'Zimbabwe – The Hope for Africa,' was the title of a UN report of the 1980s. Much of the literature I had read during that period was written in a similar vein.

Less than a decade later, however, and not long after I had returned, Zimbabwe was in economic free fall. It had the highest inflation rate in the world. The health statistics were now showing an increase in maternal and child deaths. Life expectancy was going down rather than up. Instead of the weather being responsible for food shortages, it was the collapse of agriculture that accounted for the queues of hungry people we were feeding in parts of the country that had previously produced a surplus. I recalled the positive comments and appreciation that had greeted aid programmes in the 1980s, when international charities were seen as partners in a common struggle to tackle poverty. Now we had become part of a third column to destabilize the Government, and our efforts were greeted in some circles with suspicion and mistrust.

The more I pondered the more I came to the conclusion that what was happening now was the consequence of a longer past, of issues that the country had inherited and failed to deal with. I knew that political change had taken place in the few years I had been away and that there was a new party challenging for control, but that by itself could not entirely explain what was happening. The common assessment of the 1980s and 90s as a kind of honeymoon period in Zimbabwe's history would have to be rethought. Hadn't Sekuru's nephew told me, during our walk through the communal area where he lived, that people were getting impatient, that there was 'an explosion' waiting to happen? That conversation had taken place in 1985. It was now 2002.

He had been mainly referring to the ownership of land. People, he said, had gone to war and made sacrifices to address that issue, but over 4,000 commercial farmers, predominantly white, continued to own the most fertile and productive parts of the country. The bulk of the rural population did their best in overcrowded and often unproductive areas but the sight of nearby commercial farmland lying idle and underutilized was a source of frustration.

So was the Government's lethargy in addressing the issue. It was common knowledge that that when resettlement had taken place it had been done in a haphazard, inefficient and tokenistic manner. I had witnessed that for myself while visiting several cooperatives which had been given land that the government had purchased from commercial farmers. With inadequate inputs, limited training, few services and no credit many of these schemes had collapsed. The people I spoke to had reverted to what they knew best, subsistence farming for their own survival. The failure of such programmes created something of an excuse to maintain the status quo and do little about the problem that was simmering beneath the surface. Neither Government, nor commercial farmers, nor international donors who had pledged (in

1980) substantial financial support for land reform, had really done enough to defuse the explosive situation.

My familiarity with the commercial farming sector had deepened beyond my reading and a few conversations with local friends and colleagues. Almost a year before I left I had been asked by my organization to write a book on the plight of the million or so workers who formed Zimbabwe's commercial farmworker labour force. Some of our activities had brought us into contact with that community and I had written back to my head office about the poverty and marginalization that afflicted them. Largely ignored by Government who said they were the responsiblity of their employers, frequently exploited by farm owners who said that social welfare was the state's responsibility, bypassed by most aid agencies who did not want to intervene in such a politically sensitive area, commercial farmworkers had the worst health, education, shelter, water and nutrition statistics in the country.

Over a period of several months I toured a large number of farms in the northern parts of Zimbabwe. What I saw cautioned me not to make blanket judgments. In Dendere Farm, near the town of Centenary, I was invited to stay overnight with the farmer and his family before touring the property the following day. I had free rein to speak to any of the workers in private, and if I spotted anything in terms of their living conditions which I thought could be improved I was welcome to share my observations.

The compound where the labourers lived had recently been rebuilt. The brick houses had running water and electricity. The farmer had constructed a health clinic and staffed it with one nurse. His wife supervised a primary school of over three hundred children. The owner's philosophy was simple. 'A happy labour force is a productive one. If I look after them I know I will get better work in return. I tell my fellow farm owners that they should see welfare not as an expense but as an investment.'

Neither that argument, nor his example, had convinced his neighbours to follow suit. Some of the other compounds I visited were among the worst settlements I had seen during my time in the country. The labourers complained about their living conditions and were often employed in hazardous work, including spraying of crops with pesticides and other chemicals without being given proper protective clothing. A doctor at Bindura hospital told me that many children in commercial farms had serious respiratory ailments, because of the dust they breathed in as babies when their mothers sorted tobacco in large barns with no ventilation.

'They get the minimum wage,' one owner declared when I asked him why he had spent so little on looking after the farmworkers who made his enterprise so profitable. 'Besides, you don't know these people like I do. Give them too much and they will only demand more.'

One of the issues that most shocked me was what happened to workers when they were too old to continue in the farms where some had been employed for decades. Because the legislation was weak on this issue and so much depended on the whims of the employer, very few labourers received any compensation or remuneration to cushion them in their old age. They were simply given a final salary and told they had a few days to vacate their houses for the family that would replace them. What made it worse was that, frequently, they had no homes of their own to return to. A large part of the farmworker population was comprised of migrants from Malawi and Mozambique who, unlike their local counterparts, had no entitlement to land in Zimbabwe's communal areas and, because they had been away from their countries of origin for so long, had nothing to go back to either.

In the impoverished district of Muzarabani in the far north of Zimbabwe I visited a community that was almost entirely comprised of former farmworkers. I spoke to Luis Dimango who had arrived from Mozambique in the 1950s. He now lived in a mud hut on the edge of the Zambezi River, where he was dependent on the charity of his neighbours. After thirty years on a farm near the town of Banket he had been dismissed when he began to lose his eyesight, a consequence of the chemicals he had to spray for much of his working life. Two months extra salary and a week to vacate his home was not much of a reward for many years of service.

When I asked him why he had not returned to Mozambique, where he still had family, he looked surprised as if the answer was obvious. 'I have no money. How could I return in these rags? I am too ashamed to go back. People would say that my life has been wasted.'

Land that could have been better shared. Labourers that could have been treated more fairly. An extreme divide between rich and poor that could have been addressed more equitably. An accommodation between the races that fell short of genuine reconciliation. As I thought of Zimbabwe's contemporary problems it seemed to me that lack of foresight and prudence had come back to haunt the country. That did not mean to say that Zimbabwe in the 80s and 90s had no positive things about it. The UN report was not entirely wrong in claiming it had something to offer the rest of the continent, but the collapse that was now taking place provoked the reflection that this period had also offered a space to resolve long standing economic, racial and political issues. This opportunity had not been taken, and although these tensions were now being exploited by the beleaguered Robert Mugabe government to justify its hold on power, the fact remained that such ammunition should not have been left lying around.

'History will tell if we have all done enough,' Mabel said to me as we discussed Zimbabwe's future in 1989. We were sitting in the Vumba Mountains sipping tea and discussing the war in Mozambique next door, both convinced that the kind of turmoil that was taking place there could never occur in calm, safe and placid Zimbabwe. Maybe history had made that judgement sooner than we had expected. Land invasions had by now erupted in commercial farms. Killings and beatings were taking place, and a country that once aroused envy and admiration in the region now prompted little more than pity. Zimbabwe had been given two decades of peace and stability to sort itself out but had not been wise enough in preparing for its future.